GRADUATES:
THE SOCIOLOGY OF AN ELITE

GRADUATES: THE SOCIOLOGY OF AN ELITE

R. K. Kelsall, Anne Poole
and Annette Kuhn

Department of Sociological Studies, Sheffield University

METHUEN & CO LTD

First published 1972
by Methuen & Co Ltd
11 New Fetter Lane London EC4P 4EE
© *1972 R. K. Kelsall, Anne Poole and Annette Kuhn*
Printed in Great Britain
by Richard Clay (The Chaucer Press) Ltd
Bungay, Suffolk
SBN 416 66050 9

Distributed in the USA
by HARPER & ROW PUBLISHERS, INC.
BARNES & NOBLE IMPORT DIVISION

CONTENTS

ACKNOWLEDGEMENTS

In our first publication, *Six Years After*, we were able to express our gratitude to some of the people who had at one time or another assisted us, especially the eight thousand graduates who by completing questionnaires made our work possible. Here we should like, first of all, to thank Miss Margaret Osers who helped, on the research side, to unravel some of the masses of data as they first appeared from the computer, and Miss Beryl Ibbotson who, as secretary to the unit, has for the past few years been an invaluable member of the team.

We are also indebted for a great deal of help and advice to the administrators of the cooperating universities, especially Vice-Chancellors, Registrars, Appointments Secretaries and their staffs.

We should like also to extend our thanks to those whose expert knowledge we have sought from time to time, and would like to mention in particular Dr D. J. Evans, Mrs Rosemary Ross and Mrs Judy Lay for their valuable contributions on the computing side. We also welcome this opportunity to thank Dr Robert and Dr Rhona Rapoport who, on many occasions over the last few years, have generously given their help and advice, particularly as regards women graduates. Mr Geoffrey Hawthorn, too, has offered many constructive suggestions for the preparation of the chapter on marriages and families. We should also like to thank our colleague, Dr Michael Poole, for his support and encouragement during the six years of the Research Unit's existence and we are particularly grateful for his help in the preparation of the present book. Thanks are also due to Miss Moya Davies for her assistance in compiling the index.

Finally the three of us must record our gratitude to the Social Science Research Council for the generous grant which has enabled us, after the operational analyses of our material financed by the Department of Education and Science, to undertake sociological studies of the type included in the present volume. We hope to publish more results and discussions arising from other parts of the graduate survey in the near future, and are grateful to the Scottish Council for Research in Education for agreeing to finance important further work relating specifically to those who graduated from Scottish universities.

R. K. Kelsall
Department of Sociological Studies   Anne Poole
Sheffield University   Annette Kuhn
May 1971

INTRODUCTION

The major national survey which forms the basis of the present volume owed its origin to the initiative of the Statistics Committee of the Secretaries of University Appointments Boards. That committee had done pioneer work in producing data on the first employment of graduates of British universities, an exercise resulting in an annual official publication on this subject ever since 1963. In order to throw light on the careers of graduates after a lapse of time substantially longer than a single year, the Department of Education and Science agreed to finance two independent national investigations, one relating to those who had embarked on higher degrees and the other (the present one) concerned with those who had successfully completed first degrees, whether or not they subsequently studied for higher degrees and other postgraduate qualifications as well.

It was decided to send questionnaires to a very large national sample consisting of every woman and every other man (except those whose permanent address was overseas and who subsequently returned overseas) who had successfully completed an internal first degree in 1960 in faculties other than medicine, dentistry and veterinary science at any university in Great Britain other than Bristol and a few of the smaller London colleges. Information was sought on what had happened to them in the six-year postgraduate period up to 1 October 1966. At the end of fifteen months, contact had been successfully achieved with, and completed questionnaires duly received from, some four-fifths of the sample, and it was established that the non-respondents did not differ from the respondents in respect of any known basic characteristics (e.g. sex, university group, subject group, degree class) sufficiently to introduce bias when using the respondents' answers as a reflection of the position in the whole sample. The women who responded numbered 3582, and the 4702 men respondents have, in our analyses, been 'grossed up' to 9404 to put the material relating to the two sexes on the same footing and to eliminate the confusing element of the different sampling fraction in the two cases.

One of the most difficult early decisions to be taken concerned the content of the questionnaire, for though it was clear that fairly full information on education and career patterns in the six years or so since graduation must in any case be sought, opinions differed widely as to the nature and amount of other data that could reasonably be asked for without too great a risk of prejudicing the chances of a satisfactory response rate. Undue caution would have meant losing unique opportunities of examining interrelationships between important social, educational and demographic variables in a type of elite population never previously studied at first hand and not likely (if only because of the enormous difficulty and expense of doing so) to be contacted again. In the event we decided to build around the hard core of strictly educational and career issues a range of other questions designed to illuminate, at least in a preliminary way, many important areas of sociological interest, and it is this decision that has made the production of the present study possible.

Some idea of the volume of material resulting from this large-scale national survey may be gathered when it is mentioned that the coded data necessitated the use of nine 80-column Hollerith cards for each respondent. Analysis and discussion of such a vast store of invaluable information will inevitably have to be spread over several years, but it may be useful to indicate at this point what it has been possible to do so far.

The three of us collaborated in producing a first report on the survey late in 1970 under the title *Six Years After*,[1] and readers are referred to that study for full details on such basic matters as the content of the questionnaire, the university institutions taking part, and the precise definition of categories used in the analysis of the postgraduate education and career data. The text and 104 tables in that report clear the ground, as it were, for what now follows and what will follow in the future. Straightforward breakdowns of the sample (both respondents and non-respondents) are provided by sex, by faculty and subject, by class of degree and by university group. Some of the basic characteristics of the respondents are given – age, whether and if so when they married, what children they had and when, and their social class of origin as measured by the occupation of the father at the time the respondent entered university. A great deal of attention is naturally given to the educational history of respondents subsequent to taking the first degree. Had they, whilst undergraduates, and for what reasons, considered or not considered further study or training after graduation and, if they had done so, of what type? In this event, had they actually embarked on any full-time or part-time postgraduate study or training and, if so, of what type, with what purpose and with what result? Similarly full treatment is given to the employment history of respondents since originally graduating. What was their initial distribution according both to their sectors of employment and their functions, how was this distribution related to their other basic characteristics (sex, subject, degree class, university group and postgraduate qualifications), and how did it change over the period covered by the survey? The whole question of change and stability from first to 1966 employment is studied, and the various manpower flows and counterflows and their possible explanations and implications are examined. Analysis is made of the limited information on income resulting from the survey. Preliminary discussion takes place on the nature and implications of the career plans of respondents on entering university, before finals, and on graduating, and of the relation between these and their actual careers. A separate chapter is devoted to the extent of, and reasons given for, being employed overseas, and another takes a first look at the basic data relating to women respondents.

Having cleared the ground in this way, we had next to consider which areas to open up in our second book (the present study), and we decided to concentrate attention on a number of interrelated issues of particular interest to sociologists. The first of these was social mobility, and a brief introduction to the contribution Annette Kuhn has made to this subject in Chapter 1 may be appropriate.

Many of us are not entirely satisfied by an approach which assumes a society characterized by social strata arranged in a national prestige hierarchy, of which most people are supposed to have a broadly similar picture, and in which a certain amount of movement upwards and downwards takes place both intergenerationally and intragenerationally; movement associated on the one hand with factors pertaining to the individual such as intellectual ability, formal education, achievement motivation and marriage, and on the other hand with societal factors such as less-than-replacement fertility in the upper strata, changing demands for different types of work skill, and so on. Nevertheless, however unsatisfactory such a model may be in various respects, if we are interested in trying to establish even in a rough way how open a given 'open' society really is, we may have to settle for at least a preliminary approach of this kind. This, at all events, was broadly how the question posed itself to David Glass and his associates when they made their large-scale pioneer attempt at the direct measurement of the changing extent and nature of social mobility in Britain by interviewing a ten thousand sample of the adult population in 1949.[2] We may usefully remind ourselves of the advantages and the limitations of that survey. The major advantage was, of course, being able to obtain mainly factual data direct from a sample representing the whole of the adult population of that time, and not merely a section of it. Coupled with this was the dynamic aspect of the enquiry arising from the fact that, as the whole adult age-range was covered, the experience of the oldest and the youngest age groups could be compared and light could therefore be thrown on the changing extent of social mobility. A major limitation was, of course, the relatively small numbers in the statistical cells relating to those with, say, a university education or in high-status occupations. Most of the analyses in the first published symposium were in practice confined to male respondents, which at once halved the size of the sample, and for many purposes the top two Hall/Jones categories (professional and managerial) had to be amalgamated in order to provide statistically viable numbers of cases at this end of the social scale. Viewed from today's standpoint, a second limitation arises from the fact that those who were adult in 1949 had been unable themselves to benefit from the reforms of the 1944 Education Act. The picture that could be presented was, therefore, of the degree of openness of our society prior to the coming into operation of that legislation.

In respect of both these limitations, the data resulting from our graduate survey form a very useful supplement to the Glass social mobility enquiry. For though we can say nothing new about the population at large, the number of our graduate respondents is sufficient, even when the sexes are separately analysed, to enable viable statistical cells of, say, graduate men with working-class fathers, to be closely compared with others in respect of many of the basic variables relevant to social mobility studies. And although our respondents are so much of an age that we cannot compare the experience of a younger with that of an older group, since their education has taken place entirely in the post-1944 Act era the mobility or lack of it exhibited by their experience is highly relevant to assessing the impact of that educational milestone. Moreover, as Annette Kuhn shows, the intelligent use of demographic and sociological material does enable us to say, with some degree of confidence, how typical or otherwise of the working class as a whole or particular segments of it our upwardly mobile graduates in fact were.

We asked our respondents a good deal about their aspirations at different points within the time span of their undergraduate lives; and though some preliminary attention is given to this aspect of the survey in *Six Years After*, a much fuller and more sophisticated analysis of our material is undertaken by Anne Poole in Chapter 2 of the present study. We perhaps tend too readily to assume that the main social class and family influences on the educational progress of children are concentrated on the pre-school and school periods of their lives, and that by the time a few of the socially disadvantaged have somehow overcome their handicaps and secured a university place, these influences are a spent force. In *The Chosen Few*, for example, Furneaux tells us that 'occupational-group membership acts as a very important determinant of academic history throughout the stages of education up to that of entry to sixth forms'.[3] However true this may be if we interpret the term 'academic history' very narrowly, Anne Poole uses the material from our graduate survey to show how both aspirations, and also fields of employment actually entered, vary according to type of social and family origin. This confirms the evidence of a previous enquiry, when the answers to a question on 'occupation in mind' of those admitted to British universities in October 1955 showed a strong social origin bias when sex, faculty and university group were held constant.[4]

In Chapter 7 of *Six Years After* some aspects of the marriage and family building data resulting from our graduate survey are touched upon, but only to an extent calculated to whet the appetite for more. In the third chapter of the present study Annette Kuhn undertakes a thorough reanalysis of our material in this area, and compares her findings with other available demographic data. She brings out some very interesting contrasts by faculty, by sex and by social origin which are likely to form the basis for argument and discussion among specialists in this field for a long time to come.

In the final chapter Anne Poole closely examines the role of the highly educated woman in contemporary society and the many anomalies and disturbing features that emerge when the relevant information furnished by our own women respondents is scrutinized. The ongoing research of Robert and Rhona Rapoport in this area is, of course, of outstanding importance. We are particularly glad to have been able to help them even in a small way by giving access to a subsample of our graduates who were willing to cooperate. This has also been of direct benefit to us in that, for this subsample, much additional material has therefore become available, relating in this case to an eight-year instead of a six-year period since first graduation.[5]

Throughout our work we have constantly been made aware of the value of being able to draw upon such a large national sample for our data, by contrast with the difficulties inevitably faced by those who have perforce to be content with small and often unrepresentative samples as sources for their material. Our aim has therefore been to make the fullest possible use of the unique opportunity provided by the mass of stored information at our disposal, and the present book represents a further important step in the process of making generally available our findings regarding this elite group – the graduates of British universities.

NOTES

1. R. K. Kelsall *et al.*, *Six Years After* (Sheffield University, Department of Sociological Studies, Higher Education Research Unit, 1970).
2. D. V. Glass (ed.), *Social Mobility in Britain* (London, Routledge, 1954).
3. W. D. Furneaux, *The Chosen Few* (London, Oxford University Press, 1961) 70.
4. R. K. Kelsall, *Applications for Admission to Universities*, (London, Association of Universities of the British Commonwealth, 1957), Chapter 6.
5. For further details of the methods used in our survey, see R. K. Kelsall *et al.*, 'The questionnaire in a sociological research project', *British Journal of Sociology*, **23** (1972). In press.

Chapter One

RECRUITMENT OF AN ELITE

The social composition of groups which wield power or influence in society, the extent to which social statuses are passed on from generation to generation, and the means by which people may change their ascribed statuses, are all important questions, the answers to which – if there are answers to be found – must reveal a great deal not only about the system of stratification in a society, but also about that society's very nature, how it operates, changes and continues to exist.

A detailed enquiry into the social backgrounds of the men and women who graduated from our universities in a particular year could provide, for British society, some far-reaching answers to these important questions, and in this chapter we intend to show how socially exclusive an elite group can be, how rarely the son of a labourer can find his way into university – and what sets him apart from the vast majority of labourers' sons who (as sociologists have shown again and again) have little enough chance even of receiving a selective secondary education. We also open the investigation, taken up substantively and in detail in Chapter 2, of the way in which people's social backgrounds continue to exert an influence in various respects well into their adult lives. In the present chapter, however, the data dealt with pertain immediately to the study of social mobility, and are therefore presented and discussed from an appropriate viewpoint.

Social mobility, which is commonly held to be a feature inherent in class societies, can be defined simply as the social movement of groups or individuals within a stratification system. This, of course, begs a definition of stratification, and in view of the lack of consensus among sociologists on this subject it is perhaps hardly surprising that, faced with the confusion which any thought about its fundamental nature seems inevitably to engender, many have sought to avoid the essentially unanswerable by retreating into the comfortable hidey-hole of operationalism. Perhaps this is the only way out as far as empirical sociology is concerned, and indeed this book does not set out to deal in any great depth with social stratification *per se*. However, perhaps some attempt should be made to clarify what we mean in this and the following chapters by terms like 'social class' and 'social status'.

It has been a longstanding tradition in sociology to look at people's social positions as it were from the outside. People are differentiated by what they are seen to have or not to have in the way of money, power, land, education and so on, and this principle extends to various definable subjective attributes such as values, attitudes and interests. However, the number of, and in particular the nature of the relationship between, the classes so defined have been more frequently the subject of dissensus than have the criteria by which people are differentiated, as the term 'class' itself suggests: the word simply means a group or aggregate which differs in some way from other groups, and as such gives no indication as to the nature of the relationship between classes or indeed if there is any relationship between them at all. 'Status' is a term sometimes used interchangeably with 'class', but the concept of a status group suggests some kind of hierarchy – a status is *in relation to* some other status. It is significant that when people's social positions are not looked at from outside by the sociologist, that is when the 'subjectivist' approach is used, and people are asked to assign themselves to social classes and/or explain what they mean by class or status,[1] it becomes obvious that laymen also

B

see the social positions of themselves and others as something which is essentially externally defined and objective.

The empirically fallacious distinction between 'subjectivist' and 'objectivist' approaches to social stratification only serves to divert attention away from the fundamental question of the relationship between class or status groups, or in other words, how the stratification system works. Weber's three-dimensional stratification model (class, status and power), which relates primarily to the attributes of people in different social positions, also suggests the operation of power and prestige factors in the relationships between different social groups. The economic and political attributes of classes and parties lend themselves to power relationships, while the status group attributes of honour and style of life are particularly, but not exclusively, expressed in prestige relationships. Stratification is multidimensional, then, both in the attributes of members of different social groups and in the social relations between these groups. Furthermore, these attributes and relationships are multi-bonded:[2] that is, political power, material wellbeing and high status are positively interrelated, although probably rarely in a completely one-to-one manner. The degree, however, to which this ideal type of complete intercorrelation between all the dimensions of stratification is approached will differ culturally and historically, this of course being an important indicator of the nature of a society's stratification system.

There is abundant empirical evidence to suggest that the various criteria by which people are socially evaluated by themselves, each other and researchers, reflecting (and shaping) as they do the nature and working of the stratification system, are themselves in varying degrees interrelated,[3] and a large part of the confusion about the fundamental nature of social stratification must be due to the number and complexity of these interrelationships. However, out of all this confusion one criterion in particular – occupation – emerges as a fulcrum around which, in industrial societies, other class, status and power attributes pivot. The importance of work (and hence of the absence of work[4]) as a criterion of stratification takes on particular significance, when, as in industrial societies, work roles are generally visibly separate from non-work roles. Because work is invariably necessary to subsistence, in societies in which rewards for work are in the form of money or goods the basis of a class system exists if rewards (and also working conditions) vary. If the chances of entering certain occupations depend on such factors as gentility of birth, education or accent, and if certain consumption patterns and general styles of life are associated with particular occupations, the institutionalization of a status system becomes possible. Similarly, if the incumbents of some occupations possess greater power or authority than others, support is given to the power dimension of stratification.

Occupation, then, is the main operational criterion by which people's social positions are judged, both by the sociologist and the layman. This is not only because a person's occupation or transparent lack of one is a visible and easily ascertainable attribute, but also because it is a significant attribute in all the dimensions of stratification, possesses connotations of both power and prestige relationships, and is centrally related to many other class, status and power attributes.[5]

When describing the social position achieved by the university graduates who took part in the present survey, we will often have cause to use the term 'elite', and it is perhaps appropriate now to discuss whether such a term is justified in this instance. An elite, essentially, is a social group of 'chosen' people, by implication a chosen few. On the grounds of this basic definition alone, we are unarguably justified in applying the term to our graduates, who indeed constitute a 'few' (something around 3 per cent of their age group),[6] and are also a 'chosen few' in that entry to university is the culmination of a process of formal selection which for some began as early as the day they first set foot in the infants' school at the age of five. Those educated in the independent sector, besides having had to jump the academic hurdles of Common Entrance and GCE, have by definition been 'selected' by virtue of having had parents rich enough or ambitious enough to pay for an education, something which only a tiny minority of parents are able or prepared to do.[7]

However, connotations other than the basic attribute of being a select minority have come to be associated with the concept of an elite. Referring back to the above discussion of social class, such connotations will embrace the *attributes* of a particular social group and its *relationships* with other social groups. As to the attributes of an elite, it is suggested that (again dividing stratification into its dimensions) such a group will be possessed of favourable class attributes, such as large incomes and ownership of capital, possibly in the form of inherited wealth. They will be accorded honour commensurate with a high-status life style manifest in the consumption of certain types of material goods and services such as education, and to the extent that an elite is a closed group, the privileges it enjoys by virtue of its status may become legally, as well as morally, sanctioned. Finally, an elite will wield power as a group; Weber defined this power as the ability to '(influence) a communal action, no matter what its content may be'.[8]

The mention of power as an attribute leads on to the consideration of this factor as one aspect of the relationship between elites and other social groups. The concept of an elite has very often been used synonymously with the concept of a 'ruling class', and indeed the possession and deployment of power on the part of elites must be considered the most important dimension of the relationship between them and other social groups. Power can be wielded in different sectors, such as industry, state bureaucracies and the military,[9] but is usually done so by different people so that few societies, especially stable ones, approach being totally monolithic. It is justifiable, therefore, to talk about pluralities of elites in many societies, not least our own. However, the statement that elites will be favourably placed as far as status attributes are concerned suggests that these groups also stand in a relationship of prestige to other social groups. Although prestige is not generally seen as being so necessary to the concept of an elite as is power, it is true that elite groups may expect and obtain deference on the part of members of other social groups.

How do our graduates measure up to these factors which are more specifically associated with elites? As regards their class attributes, it is true that even very early in their careers their incomes were higher than the national averages for men and women of all ages,[10] and we do know that this differential will probably increase as they grow older,[11] but we are in no position to say how they compare with the general population as to the ownership of capital and inherited wealth: probably, because of their social backgrounds and earning power, they are relatively well placed in these respects, but all the same we might expect most of them to be without substantial capital. We can assume, however, that these men and women enjoy high status in the community by virtue of their occupations and education. A lot of them earn enough to display relatively affluent patterns of consumption, if they wish to do so, and a substantial number will be entitled to status honour by virtue of their birth into high-status families and marriage to high-status partners. Very few of them though, especially at this early stage in their careers, are in a position to wield the amount of power usually associated with the concept of elites as ruling classes. They are not a ruling class, for only a handful of them are in occupations commonly considered to be the prerogative of such a class. In 1966, for example, out of 9404 men there were eighty-four administrative grade civil servants, six members of parliament, and 618 managers, the majority of whom were very probably in relatively low-grade posts. This suggests that our graduates are by no means a tightly knit ruling clique. Our findings do suggest, however, the existence of an 'elite within an elite' composed of men with certain attributes (see Chapter 2), and it is likely that if the recent past is any guide, many of these men will assume importance in the various corridors of power.[12] But for the majority of university graduates, entry into such a rarefied atmosphere is highly improbable. But even though they are not a ruling class, the power these graduates as a group hold by virtue of their occupations must be out of all proportion to their actual numbers in the population: teachers and other professional workers, civil and public servants, members of the clergy, and even research workers wield power – or perhaps influence is a better word – of different degree and kind. Furthermore, many of the positions they hold are ones of relative prestige in their own communities or places of work, where people may defer to them as experts, at least in their own areas of specialization.

On the whole, then, our graduates can be considered an elite in some ways but not in others. They do constitute a select few, a very small proportion of their age group, they do have relatively high incomes and, by definition, they have all received a long, advanced and expensive education. They have almost without exception been in high-status occupations since they graduated, and in addition many of them come from professional backgrounds, while most of the married have middle-class partners. Their occupations, too, indicate that as a group they have substantial influence in society and their expertise in various areas means that they are likely to be the objects of some deference. In spite of all this, it is clear that they are not a ruling class in the sense of a small elite group capable almost of face-to-face interaction, and also that any deference which comes their way is likely to do so in the workplace or in their immediate community rather than in society as a whole. Although they are possessed of many of the concrete attributes of elites, therefore, it does appear that the relational aspects of their coexistence with other social groups, which Bottomore for one by implication considers more important than the concrete attributes of elite position,[13] are probably of an upper middle class rather than of an exclusively elite character.

Essentially, the use of the term 'elite' to refer to graduates is not totally justified. Nominally, and for the sake of clarity in expression, though, it most probably is, for 'elite' is a good shorthand way of describing the relatively very favourable social position of university graduates: they are, so to speak, 'relatively elite'. For the sake of convenience, therefore, we shall continue to use the term within conceptual quotation marks to refer to our graduates. The actual quotation marks will be omitted for the sake of style, but it should be remembered that they are really there, and that we are by no means asserting that our respondents are in all senses of the word an elite.

Any discussion of social mobility, the subject of the present chapter, must by definition be in terms of some explicit theory or model of social stratification such as the one we have advanced above, and for this reason, if difficulties in the way of studying stratification arise as a consequence of the elusiveness of concepts like class and status, so of course must they occur when dealing with social mobility, a dynamic aspect of stratification. If stratification is multidimensional, then so is social mobility. If stratification dimensions are multibonded, so are those along which mobility occurs. If occupation is an adequate operational expression of social position on any stratification dimension and also of the dynamic aspects of that position – the possession or otherwise of power and/or prestige – then a change in occupational category is an adequate indication of social mobility. One warning here, though: occupation is likely to be more strongly related to *some* of the other indicators of social position for the non-mobile than for the mobile, because occupational movement is not always accompanied by simultaneous change in other attributes.[14]

In a non-revolutionary situation, mobility becomes possible (other things being equal) when there is change in the society's occupational structure and in the class distribution of available vacancies, and also when the variations in fertility between social classes mean that some groups are unable to replace themselves intergenerationally, and so must eventually accept recruits from other social groups.[15] Such a structural analysis of a society's mobility potential is, however, insufficient for the purposes of much sociological study, since net mobility due to these factors could conceal great or small gross mobility (or total amount of interchange between social classes), and gives no clues as to degree of mobility (or the relative accessibility of some social groups to socially mobile individuals of various origins). It therefore says nothing about the 'openness' of the society in question, and moreover gives no indication as to how and why some members of a social group experience mobility while others do not. Because of the nature of the occupational and demographic factors at present operating in industrial societies – whereby middle-status jobs in the service and consultancy sectors of industry are expanding in numbers at the expense of lower-status semi-skilled and unskilled manual jobs, while at the same time the relatively low fertility of middle- and high-status groups is creating further opportunities for net upward mobility from lower-status groups – it is likely that the amount of downward mobility in a society will be a good indicator of its openness, since this is more likely to be 'pure', or free from any 'demand' component, than is upward mobility.

Related to the openness of a society is its popular ideology about the stratification system and its fluidity, the possibility and desirability of social mobility, and the legitimate means whereby such mobility may be achieved. Any variations in mobility ideologies within society tend more or less to reflect the different opportunities available to, or seen to be available by, different social groups.[16] Elizabeth Bott's research, although very small-scale, is indicative of the general prominence of hierarchical stratification models in public consciousness – models which, unlike some dichotomous ones, by their very nature permit social mobility. As regards ideologies about social mobility in particular, Turner[17] suggests that the normatively upheld pattern of upward mobility in Britain tends to the sponsorship ideal type, whereby potential climbers are selected in a controlled way by elites or their agents and placed in a situation in which they can be 'resocialized' in order to be adequate members of their eventual class of arrival. The British education system, Turner says, celebrates this type of mobility ideology in those of its selective State schools and independent schools which provide places for boys and girls from working-class homes. The introduction to this country of comprehensive education on the face of it might suggest a shift towards the American 'contest-mobility' pattern, but recent research has shown in fact that our stratification system is probably rather resistant to such rapid change through education reform.[18] However, these developments in educational policy do serve to show that the sponsorship norm is an ideal type, towards which everyday knowledge about social mobility only tends: there is also public approval of types of mobility which circumvent the means institutionalized by the predominant normative pattern.[19]

The relationship between education and social mobility in

actual fact as well as in the public consciousness has already
been touched on, and in Britain today, as in many other industrial societies, education is a very important legitimate
avenue of social mobility (particularly of the intergenerational
type), as our own findings are not alone in showing.[20] However, there are certain other means by which individuals can
and do change their social positions, both intergenerationally
and intragenerationally – for instance adult education, acquiring one's own business, marriage – and the variety and types
of such avenues available for social mobility may give some
indication of the fluidity of a class structure. In some societies
there may be moral, normative or even legal constraints to the
use of some or all of the channels of mobility, while in others
the use of all channels may be strongly and positively evaluated,
as the 'American Dream' suggests. Between these two extremes
lie the many kinds of situation most likely to exist in fact, and
research has shown that even the American Dream itself no
longer measures up to reality. Popular evaluations of the
various means of achieving social mobility may or may not
alone constitute effective indicators of the true fluidity of a
class system, since they may be in immeasurable part *post facto*
rationalizations of the type of occupational and demographic
demand discussed above.[21]

The nature of such occupational and demographic demand
factors, as they operate in Britain today, would lead one to
expect the greatest expansion of mobility opportunity to be for
manual working-class (or professional middle-class[22]) people
entering the lower middle-class realm of white collar clerical
work. The data from the Family Census of 1946, as well as our
own findings, indicate a social class 'V-effect' in fertility: non-
professional salaried employees and non-manual wage earners
have fewer children than people either above or below them in
social status, while at the same time there has been continued
expansion in these particular occupational areas. This brings
us to the question of the university graduates who took part in
the present survey: virtually without exception, these men and
women were employed, or had at some time since their graduation been employed, in high-status professional and managerial

posts, rather than in the routine type of non-manual work in which there would be the most room for socially mobile individuals. On the basis of the demand factors, which assume total father–son inheritance of status, we might therefore expect our data to show rather limited sources of heterogeneity in the social origins of our graduates. But we have already pointed out the shortcomings of this kind of 'structural demand' approach, among which was the fact that it can give no indication as to the total amount of interchange between social classes: there may be a large degree of intergenerational mobility *out of* the elite groups, aside from demand factors, leaving vacancies for talented, ambitious or otherwise suitably qualified entrants of non-elite origin. The degree to which such recruitment occurs, together with the social background of any entrants, may tell us how open we can consider our class system to be.

The sociological interpretation of social phenomena is often better achieved by looking in detail at exceptional minorities than by making universally applicable generalizations to entire populations, and clearly the findings of this survey can in no way quantitatively indicate the overall extent and degree of social mobility in this country. But apart from the interest attaching to these findings in themselves it is possible, by looking at patterns of social inflow and marriage in a cohort of university graduates and by examining the backgrounds and careers of the socially mobile and stable among them, to contribute significantly to an understanding of the nature and operation of social stratification and social mobility in Britain today.

Patterns of social mobility

With the aim of presenting new findings on a subject which has never before in this country been examined in such great detail, findings which, it is hoped, will contribute to a sociological understanding of stratification and mobility in Britain, it is proposed firstly to deal with general patterns of social mobility and stability among the men and women who graduated in 1960 from British universities. This involves an investigation of their social origins for two generations back, and of any observable patterns of social inflow into this elite group, and also an examination of their marriage and family building patterns as far as possible in relation to their social backgrounds.[23]

That university graduates are predominantly from middle-class homes is well known, and the social origins of our respondents were in fact reported in our earlier publication:[24] but since these data have an important bearing on the present discussion, they are reproduced once again (Table 1), and can be seen to be broadly in line with other findings on the topic. The data presented to the Robbins Committee, which relate to undergraduates in 1961 and 1962, show that 71 per cent of them were from non-manual homes, while 25 per cent were from manual working-class homes, and a similar difference in social origin between men and women as that shown in our own data is also indicated. Of young people admitted to universities in 1955, 74 per cent of the men and 81 per cent of the women were of non-manual social origin, while 26 per cent of the men and 19 per cent of the women were of manual origin.[25] Both these pieces of evidence suggest that the majority of those in the present survey who gave no information about their fathers' jobs were very probably from non-manual rather than from manual homes: in other words, the proportion of graduates of middle-class origin is very probably underestimated here, which will lead to an *overestimate* of the amount of social mobility into this group of graduates.[26]

Our findings on social mobility are clarified by the use of the index of association, a statistical artefact based on various hypotheses of perfect mobility.[27] By reason of the method by which the index is calculated, a situation of perfect mobility is represented by an index of one, and the greater the value of the index above this, the lesser does the actual situation approximate to the ideal type. By applying this index to data collected in various previous studies of social mobility, the relatively high degree of intergenerational association of status in elite groups is readily observed (Table 2). The highest incidences of status inheritance are recorded for high-status, mostly professional, groups; and although the social class groupings used in these studies are diverse, the statement that status inheritance is highest among elites can be advanced with confidence, since it is in line with other findings on social mobility in many industrialized societies.[28] The fact that there are high rates of intergenerational association of status in elite groups does not necessarily mean that these groups are difficult to enter, since changes in the occupational structure may mean that there is expansion in the number of positions available which are classified as elite, apart from the fact that a little intergenerational downward mobility from elite groups is invariably observed. Nevertheless, Fox and Miller have shown that mobility into elite strata is much more difficult than entry into any other class, regardless of class of origin, especially in Great Britain.

It is likely, therefore, that in a group of university graduates, the vast majority of whom assume positions of very high status, there will be a large proportion of sons and daughters who have 'inherited' their fathers' statuses, or in other words, many of them will have remained intergenerationally socially stable. It is also likely that the sources of any social heterogeneity in such a group will be very limited. The data already presented in Table 1 are in support of the first hypothesis, since it has been shown that half of our graduates had fathers in the top two social classes, which represented in 1961 only one-quarter of the population.[29] That the sources of heterogeneity in social origins within this group of graduates are very limited is further indicated in Table 3, which shows the contributions made, through intergenerational mobility, of men and women from routine non-manual and skilled, semi-skilled and unskilled manual backgrounds to the composition of an elite stratum (that is, university graduates).[30]

In this group of graduates, almost all the social heterogeneity is due to the upward mobility of sons and daughters of skilled manual and routine non-manual workers, the semi-skilled and unskilled components being negligible. An appreciable proportion of the non-elite fathers could indeed be called middle class, since they were engaged in routine non-manual occupations when their children entered university. Leaving aside, then, all middle-class fathers, the inflow from the manual working class only totals 30 per cent for men and 23 per cent for women, and the greater part of this inflow is accounted for by the sons and daughters of skilled manual workers, who perhaps unexpectedly form a larger proportion of the graduates than do children of routine white collar workers.

Looking at the question from a different standpoint, the index of association may be used to give some indication of the relative chances of men and women born into different social classes of graduating from university and thence of taking up high-status positions in society. The perfect mobility hypothesis in this case is that the distribution of fathers of people in this elite group would correspond to the class distribution of the population as a whole if there were random association between the statuses of fathers and children. Table 4 gives some indication of what we should expect if this were the case, and compares these expectations with the actual situation.

This shows most forcibly that children of middle-class origin had much greater opportunity than children of working-class origin to graduate from university. Men and women with fathers in the professional class were in a particularly favourable position in this respect, since they had about four times the chance of the remaining middle-class children of obtaining a university degree: it is patently clear that '. . . the son of an elite father had the best opportunity to become an elite himself'.[31] It is interesting in the light of the data presented in Table 3 to find that people of skilled working-class origin had in fact *less* opportunity than those from lower middle-class homes to graduate, despite the fact that they constitute a larger proportion of our graduates. This is simply because the skilled manual class forms a much larger proportion of the population as a whole, and so on the hypothesis of perfect mobility, a correspondingly larger component of sons and daughters of such fathers would be expected in this population of graduates.

On the question of the average *degree* of mobility, it has commonly been observed that the majority of social mobility is short range,[32] that is, between neighbouring social classes. Centers, for instance, having found that 69 per cent of the sons of fathers in skilled manual occupations had undergone social mobility (the father–son association in this category was low, showing an index of 1·1), demonstrated that, of these mobile sons, more than half had moved into the two neighbouring categories.[33] Centers calculated from his findings that the average degree of mobility over two generations was only 0·35 of a grade or social class upwards, the most mobile groups being those at the extreme ends of the scale, and the least mobile being the sons of white collar workers. Mobility from the semi-skilled and unskilled working class into elite groups was therefore negligible, a situation which echoes the low propensity of people of these origins to enter university. Figures such as 2·3 per cent and 1·5 per cent of sons of semi-skilled fathers experiencing upward mobility into the professional category [34] are typical indicators of the rarity of long distance social mobility.

We have already seen that those among our graduates who did undergo intergenerational social mobility were likely to have moved over relatively short distances, being for the most part of lower middle-class or of skilled working-class origin, while only a few had been sharply mobile from the unskilled and semi-skilled working class. However, this observation can be expressed more exactly by calculating the average number of classes through which graduates had moved, if they did move, and it transpires here that mobility of both sexes is on average in an upward direction, but that men were mobile over a longer average social distance (1·06 classes) than women (0·50 classes).

Although social mobility was therefore on balance in an upward direction, the fact still remains that intergenerational association of status is a most compelling feature of this group of graduates. Exceptions to this rule in the main consist of sons and daughters of routine non-manual and skilled manual workers, while children of semi-skilled and unskilled manual workers were very few and far between.

Our graduates were all born before the outbreak of World War II, and the careers of many of their fathers may well have been affected by the war and by the Depression of the 1930s.

The data which we collected relating to the occupations of this group of fathers permit an analysis to be made of their career mobility over the twenty years or so which elapsed between the birth of their children and the entry of these children to university in the late 1950s: this should reveal whether the fathers themselves were a particularly successful group of men. We can, however, only measure fairly sharp movement *between* classes at two points in time, and so any changes in a father's status *within* a social class, or any ups and downs in his career in the interval between the two points in time, must go unrecorded. For these reasons, together with the fact that a few fathers would have retired from work and so suffered a loss of status by the time their sons and daughters went up to university, the extent of their career success may be somewhat underestimated in our findings, and this should be borne in mind when looking at them.

Table 5 shows that of fathers originally in each social class (except the Forces) the majority were still in that same class when our graduates entered university. The most stable groups were the professions, the intermediate non-manual and the skilled manual workers, 72, 79 and 69 per cent of whom respectively had remained in the same social class over the period, a finding which, incidentally, bears out the hypothesis that career stability is in part a function of the amount of training one has had for one's job.[35] In contrast to this, intragenerational mobility in the routine non-manual and in the semi-skilled and unskilled manual classes was relatively high, and the fathers who had moved out of these groups during their working lives had, for the most part, undergone *upward* mobility. A third of those originally in routine non-manual occupations had moved into the intermediate category, while skilled work accounted for a substantial proportion of those who had earlier been doing other types of manual jobs: moreover, some 14 per cent of those originally in semi-skilled work had moved into intermediate non-manual occupations, some of them perhaps as a result of the emergency teacher training facilities available after the war for mature students.

This group of fathers had, as a whole, been upwardly mobile

during their careers. The average distance over which fathers whose social class was known on both occasions (No. = 10687) had been mobile was 0·15 of a category upwards, and this figure takes into account the very large group of fathers (No. = 8069) who had remained stable. It is difficult to make any confident inferences from this about the occupational success of this group of fathers as compared with that of the male population of their age group as a whole. We should, however, expect the average degree of mobility here to be smaller, other things being equal, than in the population as a whole, since, as we have already seen, this was a 'topheavy' group of men, concentrated in the higher-status non-manual classes – and it is known that average mobility tends to be in a downward direction from higher-status positions and in an upward direction from lower statuses.[36] This is, of course, partially an artefact of the two-ended status hierarchy scales in common use in stratification and mobility research, and is in line with our own findings (see Table 6). The only overall data on intragenerational mobility among fathers of men *and* women with which our own findings can be compared, are those produced in Svalastoga's Danish mobility study of 1954,[37] which reported that 'the mean sex-weighted increase of social status from age 30 to age 60 in the paternal generation is 0·13', which compares with our own 0·15, a figure slightly larger than Svalastoga's, when, other things being equal, we should have expected it to be smaller. Although we cannot come to any firm conclusions on such slim evidence, this perhaps suggests that the fathers of our graduates were a relatively successful group of men in their own careers.

The overall figures for intragenerational status increase conceal wide class variations and our findings show a negative class gradient in the mean status change of the respondents' fathers, with the exception of skilled manual workers, who experienced a lesser degree of intragenerational mobility than did the routine non-manual workers, evidence perhaps of the difficulty of crossing the invisible manual/non-manual line intragenerationally.[38] In spite of the overall greater degree of upward mobility of the manual as compared with the non-manual fathers, there is little evidence here of widespread long-range mobility. No fathers had been mobile over as many as five categories in either direction, and only nineteen had moved up (and even fewer – seven – had moved down) four categories over the period. Indeed, as Table 5 shows, most of the career mobility recorded was either one class up (1157 fathers) or one class down (613 fathers).

As regards the social class of the respondents' paternal grandfathers, we find that the majority of this generation of men had been in non-manual work of various grades, which, at a time when even clerical posts were at a premium, undeniably places them in the middle class. 1818 of the women's and 4308 of the men's grandfathers are known to have been middle class, proportions of respectively 64 per cent and 61 per cent of all the grandfathers whose social classes are known. These figures are in line with our findings on the social class of the graduates' fathers, as regards both size and difference according to respondents' sex. Our graduates, and especially the women among them, are in all ways a middle-class group of people.

It is of interest, however, from the point of view of social mobility research, to trace the patterns of social mobility over three generations when the third arrives in an elite group, and to relate any such patterns with earlier findings on the subject. Svalastoga's data[39] show that the most common three-generation mobility patterns in his group of Danish sons (that is, the third generation) were:

(*a*) Stability over three generations.
(*b*) Grandfather–father descent with father–son ascent.
(*c*) Grandfather–father ascent with father–son descent.

In other words, where intergenerational movement occurs, 'social mobility from grandfather to father is negatively related to social mobility from father to son'. The British social mobility study reported similar findings, adding that it was only in the three situations outlined above that observed values were greater than those which would be expected in conditions of perfect mobility.[40] Knowing this, and with the premiss (because the non-manual class is not subdivided) that our

C

graduates could only be intergenerationally either stable or upwardly mobile, we should expect that the intergenerationally stable will have had middle-class grandparents, as will the mobile, and their fathers are therefore likely to have undergone downward mobility. Social ascent over the three generations will have occurred relatively rarely. Using a hypothesis of perfect mobility, we wish therefore to find out 'whether inter-generation changes were greater or smaller than would have been expected if the final results of changes . . . in the two successive generations remained fixed in the society, but if, at the same time, there were equal chances to "ascend" or "descend" or to remain fixed in status'.[41] To this end, the ratios of observed to expected values have been calculated as in Table 7, which relates to male graduates only. As predicted above, stability over the three generations and the descent/ascent pattern were both observed more frequently than would be expected on this hypothesis of perfect mobility, the ratios being respectively 1·08 and 3·49: also more common than anticipated was the ascent/stability pattern (1·16), something which was not in fact observed in the other studies referred to, and there-fore apparently peculiar to this particular group of men. Ascent over the three generations was, as predicted, less common than expected, as was grandfather–father stability with father–son ascent. Table 8 presents comparable data for women graduates: these exhibit similar underlying patterns, though the descent/ascent pattern shows an even greater ratio of observed to expected values for women than for men, suggesting that where women have been upwardly socially mobile by means of higher education, which they are less likely than men to be, this tends more often to be the end step in a three-generation pattern involving a father who had undergone downward mobility, rather than any of the other possibilities.

This brings us to the specific question of the social mobility of women. In the past it has been customary to sidestep this issue by studying social mobility only among men, or, where women *are* discussed, to talk of social mobility through marriage rather than through their own educational or occupational achieve-ments. Presumably this has been the case because, in a society in which women are expected to retire from work at marriage or first childbirth, their role tends to be seen primarily as that of wife and mother and only secondarily as that of wage-earner. In addition to this, there is the undeniable fact that women occupy a different range of occupations from men, rendering somewhat difficult any comparison between the occupationally-based social classes of fathers and daughters in the normal course of events.

However, the women with whom we are concerned here can be assigned relatively easily to a social class group by virtue of their university education and possession of degrees. Furthermore, nearly all of them are, or have been at some time since their graduation, in high-status occupations classified either as professional or intermediate non-manual. For these reasons, we are in a position legitimately to compare them with the men among our graduates as to various aspects of their social origins and mobility. We have already done this to a certain extent, but it may be useful to bring all our findings together.

First of all, in common with other investigators, we find that women graduates were more likely than men to have come from middle-class backgrounds, which means, of course, that women were less likely than men to have been socially mobile. The figures for the degree of mobility bear this out, for while the men had moved on average through something more than one social class intergenerationally, the women had moved up only half a category. Moreover, the women were rather more likely than the men to have had middle-class grandfathers. It is clear from this that women graduates as a group are even more thoroughly middle class than their male counterparts, an observation highlighted by the fact that out of the 3582 women who took part in the survey, only *eighteen* came from unskilled working-class homes. These sex differences very probably stem from variations in attitude towards education for men and for women. For men, education can fairly obviously be seen to have an overt instrumental function as far as future careers are concerned. For women, however, it is often considered to be superfluous from this point of view and other attitudes come to the fore, such as the 'finishing' function, which is very much a characteristic of the education of upper middle-class girls, hence the heavy predominance of women of these origins among university graduates. There are other institutions of further education in which differences in the social origins of men and women students are even more marked – for instance, art colleges and colleges of education – and these are perhaps more obviously performing some kind of finishing function for girls from high-status homes.

It is commonly considered that marriage is one of the main avenues of social mobility – especially for a woman, who in societies in which principal economic roles are taken by men generally assumes her husband's status on marriage, having previously enjoyed or suffered that of her father. Berent's findings for the British mobility study[42] bear this out, for it was discovered that men were more likely to marry 'below' themselves in both educational and occupational status than were women. Such heterogamy, or indeed heterogamy of any kind, was not the rule however, for 45 per cent of husbands and wives were from the same social class of origin, and in as many as 72 per cent of the marriages the standard of education of husbands and wives was similar. It appears, then, that although the incidences of both social and educational homogamy were significant, it was education which was the more salient factor here. Class background and education are, of course, by no means unrelated, as our own findings among many others[43] indicate, and Berent in fact found that in upwards of 83 per cent of marriages there was agreement on one or both of these counts.

Because of differences in the relative availability for marriage of men and of women graduates, a tendency for men graduates to marry 'down' educationally is bound to be observed, even ignoring the fact that this would be likely to happen in any case, and in fact nearly eight in ten of the husbands of married women graduates, but only about a third of the wives of men graduates, had been to a university (Table 52). Although this proviso does not of course apply where social class as opposed to educational level is concerned, it is nevertheless plain that women graduates were very much more likely than men to be socially as well as educationally homogamous: just over 90 per cent of the husbands of women respondents were, like the women themselves, in the 'top' two social classes, while only 61 per cent of the men graduates had partners of similar adult social status (Table 51). Very few graduates of either sex, however, had married manual workers, despite the fact that about one in five of them were themselves from working-class homes; although any residual gradient according to social origin operating in this connection may be brought to light by analysing in terms of perfect mobility the association between respondents' fathers' classes and those of their spouses, where random association between the two variables equals 1 (Table 9). There is evidently no clear association here, except where both partners are or were in the manual working class. Otherwise the indices are all very close to unity, especially in the case of the women, an observation which signifies little or no relationship between the two variables.

It is clear, therefore, that those of our graduates who had married by October 1966 had chosen as their partners people similar to themselves in educational level and achieved social status rather than in social background. This is even more true of the women than of the men (of whom one-third had wives of lower middle-class status), while very few graduates of either sex had married manual working-class people. Although there was agreement between the partner's social class and the respondent's social origin in some 40 per cent of marriages (Table 10), this figure is little more than would be expected under conditions of perfect mobility. All these findings make it plain that the decisive factors in the choice of marriage partners by these graduates were in fact their education and, in consequence, their achieved social class.

On the question of the relationship between social class and mobility and the timing of marriage, demographic evidence is rather sparse, but such that there is shows that in Britain there is a positive social class gradient in average age at marriage and also that during this century there has been a decline in the age at marriage in all social classes. The social gradient operates both where the classes of the fathers of the bride and groom, and also when those of the bridegrooms themselves,[44] are considered (the two, of course, are not unrelated, as we have shown), which naturally introduces complications if, as has happened here, some of the bridegrooms have been intergenerationally socially mobile; for in such cases, while the respondents are of high social status (and on the evidence quoted above we should expect them to marry later than their lower-status contemporaries), their fathers are of lower status, a factor associated with earlier marriage on the part of their sons. The variables thus pull in opposing directions, the outcome of the conflict being that both factors exert some effect on age at marriage. Grebenik and Rowntree found that non-manual husbands do marry later than manual husbands, and also that non-manual husbands with manual fathers marry earlier than intergenerationally stable non-manual husbands. Evidence produced by Mukherjee also lends some support to this finding where there has been social mobility through marriage.[45] We are thus led to predict that although our graduates will probably have married relatively late for people of their generation, there may be a gradient in age at marriage according to their social origins.

Our data unfortunately do not allow us to give the average *ages* at which our respondents entered the matrimonial state, but instead we know at what stage in relation to their university careers they had married: for example, before or during their course, on graduation, or *x* years after first graduating. This is no great drawback, for there were in general no large differences in respondents' ages, and for the majority (97 per cent) of them, higher education entailed postponement of marriage anyway, and so differences in year of marriage rather than average age at marriage will be discussed here, with the understanding that any differences in the former will entail a corresponding difference in the latter for the majority of respondents. It is clear that at the time of the survey our graduates were somewhat less likely to be married than people of their age in general (Table 48), this being some evidence for the continued existence of a social class gradient in age at marriage, for as we have shown above, our respondents were a high-status group as regards both social background and adult social class. As to the relationship between age at marriage and social mobility, care must be taken to make allowance for a very important factor here, namely postgraduate study, for just as we have seen that their first degree course at university delayed marriage for most of our graduates, further study or training also has this effect, especially for women.[46] Making control, then, for this variable, data relating time of marriage to class of origin are presented in Table 11. The 'c' column in each box shows social class gradients in the expected direction for men – that is, the lower the status of his father, the less likely was it for the graduate son to be unmarried at the time of the survey: but in the case of the women, the gradients are in *the opposite direction*. The 'a' and 'b' columns, on the other hand, show gradients in the predicted direction for women with non-manual and skilled manual fathers[47] who were married by 1 October 1966: in other words, graduate women of humbler social origins show a lesser propensity to marry, but if they *do* marry, they tend to do so earlier than those of higher-status origin. This may point to the existence among socially mobile women of a subgroup which has overcome the many obstacles in the way of their attainment of a higher education by particularly strong academic and occupational drive. Women, particularly working-class women, have a much smaller chance of entering university than men, which suggests that the women of working-class origin among our graduates would have needed stronger motivation in order to achieve what they have done than would their male counterparts. This would explain any discrepancy in marriage patterns between men and women, and the data relating to the very few sons of unskilled workers and daughters of semi-skilled and unskilled workers lend further support to the proposition that the more difficult it is for a man or woman to enter university, the more ambitious or highly motivated he or she will need to be to overcome the difficulties. Such ambition is associated with the deferment-of-gratification pattern which may become manifest in a propensity to postpone marriage or to remain unmarried.

Higher education and the working class

It was suggested above that a structural analysis of net mobility as resulting from demand factors can only give a partial picture of social mobility in a society, for not only will such a picture conceal the gross amount of interchange between social groups, but it also ignores the important question of *differential mobility*, or why some members of a group are upwardly or downwardly mobile, while the rest (usually the majority) remain inter-generationally stable. We have already examined and discussed the patterns of mobility and stability among our graduates, and having made these analyses of the inflow of people into this elite group, the question of differential mobility, and in relation to this, any differences between those graduates who have been intergenerationally mobile and those who have not, may be examined. That is to say, we shall try to isolate the causes of individual mobility, although of course 'causality can never be proved beyond doubt, no matter what the nature of one's empirical evidence'.[48]

We are assisted in this aim by the fact that our graduates are alike in that virtually all of them have high-status occupational roles and most of them middle-class marriage partners and that, as we demonstrated earlier, in the attainment of these attributes, their university education has been the most salient factor, although background is still an extremely important determinant of the chances of actually obtaining such an education. We can suggest then, on the basis of the findings already discussed, that social background is an indirect deter-minant of graduates' present positions, while their education is a direct determinant. The accuracy of this statement is demon-strated when we consider those among our graduates who have been intergenerationally socially mobile: along status dimen-sions they do not ostensibly differ to any appreciable extent from the intergenerationally stable (although there does seem to be some regression, a question to which we shall return later). The socially mobile graduates have, by virtue of their attainment of professional positions, more or less successfully used the standard avenue of mobility – education.

If, however, the social mobility undergone by graduates of non-elite origin, in particular by those from working-class homes, is in fact of the pure sponsorship type, there would remain no significant social differences at all between mobile and stable graduates, a proposition which can readily be investigated, since all the data required to do so lie within the scope of the present survey. As regards isolating the causes of differential mobility, a first step is to compare certain social characteristics of graduates who have been upwardly mobile with those of stable members of their class of origin. Any consistent social differences which emerge may plausibly contribute to an explanation as to why these men and women in particular should have been intergenerationally mobile. Because such people have undergone an appreciable degree of mobility and because potentially causal factors might thus emerge more clearly, the discussion concerning socially mobile graduates is restricted to those of manual working-class origin only.

It has been estimated that probably less than two in every hundred of the boys and girls who were born in the late 1930s of working-class parents entered university.[49] For such young people, going to university represents a significant degree of social mobility, and the obvious questions which arise are: how and why are they different from the other 98 per cent or so of their class contemporaries?, and what is the reason for their differential mobility?

When considering the question of differential mobility, we inevitably encounter some uncertainty regarding some of the characteristics which set socially mobile individuals apart from their social background, in that many of these factors might equally well be causes or effects of mobility. To isolate causal factors, a first step should be to consider their temporal sequence. Characteristics operative before individuals achieve an appreciable degree of social mobility by entering university are obviously better qualified to be considered as causal factors than are characteristics not so fixed in time. If the upwardly mobile working-class men and women among our graduates differ from stable members of their class of origin in various ways, we may be able to establish these as direct or indirect causes of their mobility by means of *ex post facto* explanations in terms of established sociological knowledge.

Empirically, it appears fairly easy to isolate characteristics antecedent to social mobility by studying groups of people likely to experience mobility, but who are not yet actually mobile, although this method does involve the risk of potential inaccuracy in that some of these people may not in fact eventually undergo mobility. The alternative method of asking individuals who have experienced social mobility about their past is subject in some areas of investigation to more subtle errors arising from poor recall, rationalization and hindsight on the part of respondents. Much American research has used the former method, the procedure usually being to survey working-class high school pupils whose potential mobility is seen to be expressed in a desire to attend college. In this survey, we are, of course, restricted to the latter method, the disadvantages of which are probably attenuated in this instance by the fact that we sought very little attitudinal data, our questions being limited, for the most part, to requests for rather detailed factual information.

One immutable factor which is by its very nature bound to antedate mobility is the size of a mobile individual's family of origin: there is general agreement that upwardly socially mobile people come from families with a smaller number of children than the average for their social class as a whole. Jackson and Marsden commented on this characteristic of some men and women of working-class origin who went to grammar school in Huddersfield and obtained 'A' level GCEs, as did Scott in his examination of the family backgrounds of teachers, while Svalastoga comments with regard to his Danish mobility data that 'males from sibling groups of size five and above have smaller chances of social ascent and greater chances of social descent, social origin constant'.[50] Related to this, of course, is the wellknown finding that the measured intelligence of children is negatively related with family size in all social classes,[51] which means that even if intelligence is only partially correlated with social mobility,[52] those who experience such mobility will tend to be from families smaller than the norm for their class of origin.

Our own findings (see Table 12) show a class relationship of the expected order: the average family of origin sizes of graduates of non-manual and manual background are in fact the same – 2·24 – while for the population as a whole we observe the familiar class differential. Our figures, it should be remembered, constitute an overestimate since they are not restricted to live births only to graduates' mothers, including as they do adoptees and stepchildren. Incidentally, it is interesting to note here that when class differences in family size are examined in more detail, the 'V-effect' first observed in the 1946 Family Census still obtains for this generation of graduates' parents (Table 13), despite the fact that our working-class parents obviously had fewer children than the average for their social class.

There are various sociological factors associated with upward social mobility which may in themselves be related to the demographic variable of family size. One such factor is the existence of status discrepancies within the families of origin of upwardly mobile people. If, as is often the case, the father's occupation is the sole criterion by which a family's social position is empirically judged, status discrepancies will arise if the husband has received an education incommensurate with his occupational level, or if his wife differs from him as to her educational or occupational level, or both. Such discrepancy may also arise if a parent has undergone intergenerational mobility and retains contact with, and perhaps the values of, the group of origin.

There are several American 'pre-mobility' studies whose results have some bearing on this question, highlighting, for instance, the link between college aspirations on the part of working-class high school students and their mothers' education and work,[53] and 'the bread-winner's education (being) high relative to his occupation and . . . the education of the mother (exceeding) that of the father'.[54] Jackson and Marsden's findings,[55] although unfortunately based on a very small sample, do indicate that these American findings may also be applicable to British society. We might therefore expect that the families of the mobile men and women among our graduates will show some typically middle-class characteristics, such as education of a parent beyond the elementary school leaving age of fourteen, or the existence of a middle-class grandparent. We asked our respondents about the type of school last attended by each of their parents, the age parents left school, and whether either parent had had any further education, part time or full time. Respondents were also asked to classify the main occupation of their fathers' fathers according to one of three categories.

Tables 14 to 17 do indeed show certain non-working-class characteristics in the families of graduates of manual working-class origin. About three in ten of both fathers and mothers of these people had had more than an elementary education, usually having been to a grammar school or its equivalent, and in addition a very small number had been to independent schools. Moreover, up to a quarter of all these parents had left school after the age of fourteen, which until 1944 was the terminal education age of the vast majority of State school children. It seems that mothers were slightly better off than fathers in both these respects, which suggests that at least a few of these women had married 'down'. In around a quarter of the working-class families, too, one or both parents had undergone some form of further education, either full time or part time. It appears, then, that among graduates from families in which fathers were manual workers, there was a noticeable amount of discrepancy between this manual occupational status and the educational levels of one or both parents. As to the question of status discrepancies between graduates' fathers and grandfathers, we find that 26 per cent of the fathers' fathers had had non-manual occupations, a figure which is in fact about four times greater than would be expected on the hypothesis of perfect mobility (Tables 7 and 8). The degree of concentration of these non-working-class characteristics within the families of the upwardly mobile is an important issue, and further investigation reveals that such attributes were fairly evenly distributed among these families, with albeit a slight tendency for the characteristics designated here as 'middle class' to be concentrated together. For instance, families of mobile graduates with middle-class grandfathers and a parent (or parents) whose education continued beyond school were twice as likely to have been middle class also on the remaining four dimensions (35 per cent) than to have possessed no other middle-class attributes at all (18 per cent).

Our findings also indicate that the educational levels of the brothers and sisters of upwardly mobile graduates were frequently higher than one would normally expect in working-class families. The fact that 17 per cent of graduates from working-class backgrounds had siblings who had also been to university, and that 10 per cent and 8 per cent of them had respectively younger and older siblings who were college-trained teachers, suggests that in about a quarter of the families of origin of the mobile graduates in which there was more than one child, at least two children – the respondent and a sibling or siblings – had attained a level of education which would ensure their upward mobility beyond doubt.[56] Thus status discrepancies of various kinds obviously occurred to a substantial extent within these families, and here our observations are in line with the earlier findings mentioned above.

Another sociological factor relevant to the question of differential mobility is the fact that those working-class parents whose children do undergo upward social mobility tend to have high status within the working class. Various data relating to the social origins of British university students show that about four in five of students from working-class homes had fathers of skilled manual status. This tendency also obtains at the level of selection for secondary education,[57] and in American educational 'self-selection' too,[58] and our data are in agreement here: when they entered university, respectively 19 and 14 per cent of the fathers of men and women graduates were in skilled manual occupations, while only 7 and 5 per cent of their fathers were in semi-skilled or unskilled manual jobs at that time. The incidence of downward career mobility on the part of fathers who were in manual work when their children went to university is not very large (Table 5), contrary perhaps to expectation. If the fathers of upwardly mobile graduates are 'sunken middle class', this tends to be for other reasons than their personal career failure. Indeed, we saw earlier that the graduates' fathers, especially those in manual work when respondents were born, were probably a rather successful group of men as far as upward career mobility is concerned.

The unmistakable existence of various middle-class attributes in the families of upwardly mobile graduates suggests some reasons why these young people in particular should have achieved mobility through higher education, particularly when we remember how remote university seems to most working-class people. After all, even universal primary education is historically very recent, and to this day selective schools and streams in the State sector which prepare pupils for higher education often remain relatively impervious to the infiltration of working-class children. The comparatively small average numbers of children, and the status discrepancies, in the families from which the upwardly mobile come, together with their high status within the working class, are all interrelated factors operating to one and the same end. Parents with only one or two children are more likely to be in a sufficiently favourable financial position to envisage higher or further education for their children than are parents of a larger family. Again, since family size is negatively related to social status within the working class, those who occupy high-status positions within this class (skilled workers) will tend to have fewer children than, say, unskilled workers. This nexus of family size, economic and status factors may moreover be associated with a set of values arising from contact on the part of the upwardly mobile respondents and their parents with typically middle-class attitudes towards the usefulness and desirability of education,[59] resulting perhaps from education of one or both parents in excess of the working-class norm for their generation, or from their downward mobility from the grandparents' generation. The fact that the families of graduates of working-class origin tend to differ in certain ways from those of working-class people in general and to differ in the direction of greater 'middle class-ness', can be seen as an indirect cause of differential mobility. A more direct cause is likely to be the outcome of the interdependent operation of all these factors in terms of family values – the acceptance of higher education as both desirable and within reach.[60]

The value aspect of the causal model is difficult to test in a questionnaire survey, especially when it is someone else's attitudes – in this case those of the respondent's parents – which are the object of enquiry. However, parents' attitudes to education in general, and to that of their children in particular, are usually seen to be manifest in the degree of encouragement to succeed at school given by them to their children, and linked with this, their ambitions for their children. A positive association between attitudes of parents and attitudes and actions of children as regards higher education seems to obtain regardless of other factors, particularly social class, which themselves determine values.[61] Such encouragement or pressure, if it is a direct cause of upward mobility on the part of graduates of working-class origin, is likely to have been exerted by most of their parents, while we should suppose that in general working-class parents are less likely to encourage their children to go to university than are middle-class parents, even when their children attend the same type of secondary school. This supposition is both theoretically plausible and empirically verifiable: for a working-class child, entry into a selective secondary school is usually sufficient on its own to ensure upward social mobility, while for middle-class children such an education alone can often at best only secure intergenerational stability.[62] Clearly, even if *relative* aspirations are equal in all social classes,[63] desire on the part of parents for their children to obtain higher education will be directly related to social class level. In order to test the prediction that the parents of the upwardly mobile men and women among our graduates had been instrumental in the encouragement of their sons and daughters to go to university, we can examine the answers given to an open question asking for details of any person considered by the respondent as having had a major influence on his or her education and career; and the replies to another question we asked, this time about the attitudes parents of respondents had to their children's ambitions to go to university, may also prove helpful here.

It is evident from both Table 18 and Table 19 that the parents of graduates from working-class homes played an important part in encouraging their sons and daughters to go to university, and indeed were seen by a substantial proportion of the upwardly mobile graduates as major influences in their lives. It is interesting to note that mothers were slightly keener than fathers for their children to obtain a higher education, an observation which may well reflect the existence of some status discrepancies of the sort discussed earlier within the families of upwardly mobile graduates.

Related to the role of parents in encouraging young people to utilize their chances of upward mobility is the influence of 'significant others' outside the family. It has been suggested [64] that upwardly mobile working-class people make more use of extra-familial encouragement than do their middle-class counterparts, although the evidence is not altogether conclusive. [65] There is general agreement, however, that parents, peers and adults outside the family may, and often do, exert some influence on the educational and occupational aspirations of upwardly mobile people, the source of dissensus being the relative importance of the different groups. [66] We have seen in Table 18 that among those graduates of working-class origin who admitted to having been influenced in their career and education by one particular person, upwards of four in ten mentioned school teachers in particular, and men in fact were more likely to have been influenced by teachers than by either or both of their parents. In apparent contradiction with some of the American evidence, friends were very rarely seen as having exerted a major influence in our graduates' lives. It is probable, however, that the attitudes and actions of friends, particularly school friends, did serve to shape and reinforce the aspirations of many of the upwardly mobile graduates, even if such people were seldom perceived as exerting any *major* influence. When we compare these findings with those relating to the non-mobile graduates, we can immediately see substantial differences (Table 20). Graduates with high-status non-manual fathers were much more likely to have been strongly influenced in their lives by a parent, or both parents, and less likely to have been influenced by people outside the family, such as school teachers and friends, than were graduates from working-class homes: this contrast is particularly noticeable among the men, and these findings strongly support the hypothesis that upwardly mobile people are often encouraged in their aspirations by significant others outside the family. Interestingly enough, upwardly mobile graduates were less likely than the non-mobile to be able (or willing) to recall any one particular person who exerted a major influence on their education and careers – there is a small but consistent social class gradient here.

The fact that the mobile were less likely than the stable respondents to name one or both parents as having had the greatest influence in their lives may on the face of it appear to contradict what was said earlier about the importance of pressure and encouragement on the part of the parents of upwardly mobile graduates: but clearly, it matters little how keen a parent is for his child to go to university if he is ignorant of the mechanisms of the application for and securing of a university place. Working-class parents, who are unlikely ever to have had any direct contact with higher education, are less likely to be able to offer practical guidance to their children than are middle-class parents, many of whom will have been to university themselves, or have had informal contact with people who have done so. This explains the particular significance to respondents of working-class origin of the influence of school teachers, for it is the teacher who explains how to go about getting a university place and who recommends what to study and which university to choose. Such a person gives indispensable guidance when parents and other family members can offer no practical advice. For instance, a man whose father was a road sweeper wrote, when asked about the major influences in his life: 'I was in a backward children's class after leaving hospital at the age of ten. The teacher had to persuade the head to allow me to sit the 11-plus'; and a woman whose father was a Town Hall caretaker and who entered university

D

when she was 24, said she had been influenced in her education and career by 'evening class tutors, mainly W.E.A.'. But it was very much more common for graduates from working-class homes to have been helped and influenced by teachers at the maintained grammar schools which nearly all of them had attended. In short, then, parents can give the moral support which helps a young person in deciding whether or not to stay on at school until the sixth form and then to apply for a university place, but they may be unable to offer any concrete assistance in getting him there, and this is where the school teacher's experience becomes vital. To the extent that parents are in this position, guidance from anyone outside the immediate family becomes indispensable to the student.

The differences here between men and women graduates of all social backgrounds perhaps merit some comment. The relative representation of the sexes in institutions of higher education suggests that it is still rather difficult, for whatever reason, for women to obtain university places. In girls' schools, the staff are less likely to exert pressure on the pupils to apply for university entrance – colleges of education, for instance, are seen as a viable and obviously acceptable alternative for the further (or 'finishing') education of young women. This means that if a girl is to go to university, support must often come more exclusively from outside the school, most often in the form of encouragement from parents, and the general perception of the woman's adult role as primarily home-centred probably means that girls will often need relatively strong encouragement or motivation in order to decide to go to a university at all.

It is plain that there are various factors in the backgrounds of graduates of manual working-class origin which set them apart from the working class as a whole – family status discrepancies, middle-class grandparents, very few or no brothers and sisters, high status of fathers within the working class – and we have argued that these attributes can be viewed as interrelated but independent indirect causes of differential mobility.[67] These factors all operate in the same direction and link with a nexus of values, in particular values about education, subscribed to by parents or other relatives of the upwardly mobile graduates, and very probably also by the graduates themselves. These values, manifest in working-class parents' enthusiasm about their sons and daughters going to university are, it is suggested, the direct cause of differential mobility. This suggestion may be placed within the framework of reference group theory, whereby young people of working-class background who are destined for upward mobility come into contact at home with 'middle-class' behaviour patterns and values and thus may undergo some degree of anticipatory socialization.[68] This process may be reinforced (rather than initiated) [69] by the selective State secondary schools which such people attend, so that teachers become an important source of guidance to pupils with family-supported mobility aspirations.

We have shown so far that people who undergo intergenerational social mobility, and in particular mobility from the manual working class via higher education into the professional middle class, are in various ways atypical of their class of origin. In order to test whether university education has acted totally effectively as a channel of mobility for these people, some comparisons may be made between the mobile and the stable among our graduates. To the degree that in Britain social mobility approaches the 'sponsorship' ideal type, we should expect the standard educational mobility channels – selective secondary school plus higher education – to operate in such a way that upwardly mobile people are in no way different from the intergenerationally stable (or, for that matter, the downwardly mobile) within their class of arrival.

Beginning once more by examining demographic factors, we turn to the examination of various events *postdating* the mobility process, in particular the marriage and family building patterns of the graduates themselves. Evidence on whether these patterns are related to social origin appears inconclusive: Perrucci, for instance, found that although postponement of marriage was general among her engineering and science graduate respondents, there was no consistent relationship between social origin and the interval between graduation and marriage: postponement of marriage due to continued exposure to higher education seemed to override any other differences within the group.[70] This is roughly in line with our own findings, for it is clear that higher education, both under-graduate and postgraduate, was the most important factor determining when our graduates got married (see Chapter 3). Allowing for the universal delaying effect of full-time study, we found a certain degree of regression to the normal class gradient in age at marriage for men – that is, the lower the father's status, the sooner after graduation the son married – but in the case of the women the gradient was neither clear nor consistent. Explanations for this inconsistency as well as for the various discrepancies in the men's gradients have already been offered, and so will not be repeated here: it only remains to state once more the paramount importance, to graduates of all social origins, of their exposure to higher education as a determinant of the timing of their marriages.

The timing of the birth of the first child is, not unexpectedly, also subject to postponement due to continued full-time study (Table 54), and it is clear when control is made for this factor that upwardly mobile graduates again did not differ in any consistent way in this respect from those who had not been mobile, and moreover that there was little or no relationship between social background and size of family of procreation, the picture at this stage being one of substantial similarity between graduates of all social origins (Tables 57 and 58). Therefore no obvious and consistent differences in marriage and family building behaviour are apparent between socially mobile and stable graduates, which suggests that if these demographic variables are any guide, upwardly mobile graduates would indeed seem to be fairly extensively integrated into their class of arrival.

Along several sociological dimensions, however, there are certainly some discrepancies to be observed between graduates of different social origins. For instance, they differ in the way in which they have made use of the system of higher education – the direct means by which, socially mobile or not, all the graduates have achieved their present social position. Any observed differences in the use of this avenue may well be related to variations in motives for going to university, a question which is discussed separately. Differential use of the higher education system as a means of achieving high status will show itself in differences in subjects read at university by men and women of various social origins, for present evidence suggests that science, and especially technology, tend to appeal more than arts and social sciences to students of working-class origin. Surveys of the social composition of Polytechnics, Universities of Technology and the former CATs may be relevant here, since these institutions were set up in order to expand higher education in science and technology and also to broaden the social base of recruitment into occupations related to these subjects. Engineering courses in these institutions are apparently more heavily subscribed than pure science courses by young people of manual working-class origin, while both attract greater proportions of working-class students than do either arts or social science courses.[71] It seems that students from working-class homes tend to find higher education in 'practical' and vocationally oriented subjects such as engineering, more culturally acceptable than a 'liberal education', which after all, can be, and often is, seen as a luxury, a form of conspicuous consumption.

Parents of upwardly mobile university students as well as the students themselves must for various reasons find university education more acceptable than do parents of CAT or Polytechnic students, but it is still likely that both parents and students will tend to prefer technology and, by association, science courses, not only because these are seen to be related to future work, but also because they are likely to lie within the occupational experience of many manual working-class fathers, especially those with industrial skills. This argument applies in particular to men, but it can also be extended in more general terms to women from working-class homes, with whom arts rather than technology courses are popular, since arts subjects are seen to be a fit female vocational preparation for teaching, a profession which is known to attract the upwardly mobile.[72] National evidence presented to the Robbins Committee regarding the social origins of university students indicates that, relative to their proportion in the student body as a whole, men from working-class homes were over-represented in science and technology faculties, and that women of manual origin were slightly over-represented in arts and science faculties.[73] Our own data (see Table 21) are broadly in line with these findings, particularly as regards the tendency of mobile men to read pure science and of mobile women to read arts: the social sciences were very clearly most popular among non-mobile graduates of both sexes.

The relationship between social origin and academic achievement is by no means clear, and it should be remembered that any findings on the subject may be biased by this tendency for upwardly mobile students to be over-represented in certain faculties, since proportionately more good degrees (firsts and upper seconds) are awarded in science and technology than in other subjects.[74] Because evidence from a number of studies ostensibly indicates that there is no consistent relationship of any kind between social background and degree class,[75] it has been suggested by R. R. Dale that the social composition of the various types of universities may be an important consideration here: that is, to the extent that working-class students find it difficult to enter a particular university, an *inverse* relationship between social class and class of degree will tend to emerge,[76] so that the levels of social 'exclusiveness' of different kinds of universities, as well as subjects read, need to be taken into consideration.

Clearly, by far the most exclusive universities as far as men and women from working-class homes are concerned are Oxford and Cambridge, while the University of Wales is relatively very 'open' in this respect (Table 22). These two extreme cases stand out visibly from the rest, particularly where women are concerned, which means that on the basis of Dale's theory we should predict that among Oxbridge graduates, upwardly mobile men and women will have obtained better degrees than the intergenerationally stable, while this will not be the case among graduates of the University of Wales. In addition, we may perhaps discover a gradient in class-related academic performance according to the 'exclusiveness' of the remaining university groups. Taking the two extreme cases only, Table 23 shows that the expected relationship clearly emerges in the case of graduates in pure and applied science, where at Oxford and Cambridge upwardly mobile graduates are more likely than the non-mobile to have been awarded good degrees, while at the University of Wales the obverse would appear to be the case. However, among graduates in the humanities no relationship of any sort clearly emerges between social origin and degree class. When these data are examined in more detail, taking all the university groups into consideration, there is no consistent positive association between the level of 'social exclusiveness' of the different types of university and the degree performance of their upwardly mobile graduates, other than in the limiting cases already mentioned, and it is only among male technologists and perhaps female scientists that there are gradients of the kind which might have been expected on the basis of Dale's theory. We are forced to conclude, then, that our data only partially substantiate the theory relating bias against working-class students with relatively good academic performance on the part of such students: the relationship clearly operates at the extreme ends of the 'open-exclusive' scale, but here only for graduates in pure and applied science.

The explanation for this is perhaps to be found in the essential differences between the sciences and the humanities as disciplines. An important, if not an indispensable, prerequisite of success in the humanities is the ability to control and manipulate words and the concepts which find their expression in words. To the outstanding scientist, on the other hand, articulateness in these terms is perhaps not essential, for any abstract concepts which he uses are unlikely to have to be expressed verbally. Put thus in simplified (perhaps oversimplified) terms, the relevance here of the social aspects of language learning and use in its relationship to thought processes [77] becomes immediately obvious. It may well be the case that working-class students in arts and social science faculties suffer some residual disadvantage as compared with their middle-class contemporaries in terms of proficiency in dealing with abstract ideas and their verbal expression, and this will show

up in their academic performance. The scientist or the tech-
nologist from a working-class home, however, suffers no such
disadvantage, since excellence in his subject does not necessarily
require verbal and conceptual proficiency of this kind.

It was suggested above that any differences between the
socially mobile and the stable in the use of higher education as
a means of achieving high status may well be the outcome of
differences in motives for going to university. Relevant here is
Hyman's findings that working-class people value security and
economic gain more than do middle-class people,[78] which is
not necessarily to say that the middle class does not value
economic gain and security at all, but that perhaps they are
in a position to take these things for granted in their lives and
to divert their aspirations to more altruistic objectives such as
intellectual development. Class-related values are in general
probably fairly realistic in terms of the situations in which
members of the different social groups find themselves, and
therefore, to the extent that the British working class is on
average less occupationally and financially secure than the
British middle class,[79] these American findings are also applicable to British society. On the basis of this, it would be expected
that the upwardly mobile among our graduates would stress
instrumental motives for going to university more frequently
than the non-mobile, who might be more inclined to take
material desiderata for granted and to stress, say, desire to learn
more about a subject, desire to meet people, or other expressive
motives. The data used to test this hypothesis are the replies to
an open question asking graduates why they felt keen (if in fact
they did so) about going to university: the answers given fell
into various attitude clusters, of which not all could be con-
fidently classified as either 'instrumental' or 'expressive', and
so for the purpose of the present analysis, we have taken into
consideration only those replies which could be so classified.

Table 24 shows that upwardly mobile graduates were, as
anticipated, somewhat more likely to give as reasons for their
desire to go to university considerations of an instrumental
nature and were less likely to stress expressive considerations
than were the non-mobile. Although, as we have seen, gradu-

ates with fathers in manual occupations exhibit various characteristics of a middle-class type in their backgrounds, this finding is clear evidence of the residual salience of social origin as a predictor of the values of the socially mobile.[80]

We have seen so far that graduates of various social backgrounds do not differ very much as regards demographic attributes such as marriage and family building, since exposure to higher education rather than social origin has been the principal influence on these particular aspects of their lives. But when motives for going to university and the utilization of this institutionalized channel for the achievement of high status are considered, certain differences do arise between the upwardly mobile and the intergenerationally stable. Thus it might reasonably be expected that some differences between the two groups obtain after their university careers are over, particularly in the world of work.

Although upwardly mobile people are, almost by definition, more 'ambitious' in terms of social distance than intergenerationally stable people in a single class of arrival, there is evidence to suggest that they are not so much so in terms of goals fixed in a prestige hierarchy, and indeed our own findings, as we shall see in the next chapter, show most forcibly that this is the case with our graduates. We shall observe that although it is undoubtedly true that all, or nearly all, the graduates had made, in relation to the total range of occupations available in society, high-status career choices (not a very surprising finding in the light of common-sense knowledge), there are noticeable differences between stable and mobile graduates in choices of occupations, differences which are not unexpectedly carried over into their actual careers, so that some regression of achieved to ascribed statuses clearly emerges. Thus, although our graduates are clearly a very high status group as a whole, Table 25 shows that within this high-status universe there is a consistent and definite positive relationship between social origin and adult social class. The single minor exception to this – the case of women in routine non-manual work – is accounted for by the greater tendency on the part of women of higher social origins to take up secretarial types of employment, while upwardly mobile women are particularly likely to become school teachers.

On the face of it, then, the mobile and the stable graduates would appear to be more or less indistinguishable, having merged into a homogeneous high-status group. Nevertheless they do in fact differ in certain ways, and the respects in which they do so – motives for going to university, activities at university, and subsequent careers – are socially most significant, indicating as they do that important class differences and variations in life chances still exist even after people of diverse social backgrounds have attended similar types of secondary schools and have had similar experiences of higher education. Although their education has clearly been a direct determinant of their achieved status for graduates of all backgrounds, the indirect effects of social origin are still visibly in operation here.

Stratification and mobility in Britain

A great deal about the class system in this country can be inferred from these findings about the social backgrounds of university graduates and the patterns of social stability and interchange which have culminated in their arrival in a small but important social stratum. First of all, we have confirmed earlier findings about the relative exclusiveness of elite groups in Britain to entrants of non-elite origin. That is to say, the degree of intergenerational status inheritance in these groups, if our respondents are any guide, is extremely high, while the chances of entry for people of manual working-class origin are particularly low, and even, for certain sections of the working class, negligible: sharp upward mobility is something which occurs extremely rarely. It seems that any flexibility in the education system resulting from the 1944 Education Act has operated to the advantage of the lower middle class rather than the working class, an observation which we are not the first to make. Our evidence points furthermore to the existence of a massive component within elite groups of people whose families have enjoyed very high status for at least three generations. We have also been able to examine the much neglected question of social mobility on the part of women by means other than marriage, and have seen that women in elite groups are of higher status origin than men, and that, by corollary, elites are even more closed to women than they are to men of non-elite backgrounds.

It appears moreover that where there *is* social heterogeneity among entrants into an elite group, there are social characteristics which predispose certain types of people to enter the group intergenerationally, for instance fathers who have themselves been intergenerationally downwardly mobile and/or who have achieved upward intragenerational mobility through success in their own worklives. These characteristics link with certain other factors in the backgrounds of graduates of working-class origin which form components of an essentially middle-class life style, and combine with a set of values about education which are very much akin to those typical of the middle class, and it is very probable that it is in fact these values which have directly caused the differential mobility of the men and women concerned.

In spite of any diversity in their social origins, there is no doubt that graduates form a homogeneous group in relation to the rest of society, for they constitute only a tiny proportion of their age group, they are all, of course, graduates, they all are or have been in high-status occupations, and as a group they exhibit similar marriage and family building patterns. We have said earlier that total social homogeneity among graduates, regardless of their social origin, would be observable if social mobility in Britain approached the 'sponsorship' ideal type. But when we look at our graduates more closely, we find certain important differences within the group, which are related in a uniform way with social background and which therefore lead to the unavoidable conclusion that higher education in Britain is not a totally effective channel of upward social mobility, even for those observably exceptional individuals from working-class homes who do manage to enter and graduate from universities. Whether or not this should be the case is of course a matter for value judgment, but it should be understood that, contrary to popular and perhaps academic supposition, it is not so.

On the whole, therefore, the picture presented by our findings is of a stratification system which remains very much closed at its top end, despite the fact that some social heterogeneity is required here by virtue of both occupational and demographic demand factors. Clearly, there is some mobility into this group, as our findings show, but such mobility as there is arises from extremely restricted social sources, and perhaps represents little, if anything, more than the *net* mobility required by demand factors: in other words, very little social interchange is going on at this end of the social scale. Since it was suggested earlier that the degree of social interchange is a better indicator of the fluidity of a stratification system than is the net mobility rate, which largely represents the outcome of occupational and demographic demand factors, we are obliged to conclude that, whatever may be happening in other areas of the class system, in Britain there is still very little room at the top for people of humble social origins.

NOTES

1. For examples of this approach, see R. Centers, *The Psychology of Social Classes* (Princeton, University Press, 1949); E. Bott, 'Class as a reference group', *Human Relations*, vol. 7 (1954) 259–85; M. Kahan *et al.*, 'On the analytical division of social class', *British Journal of Sociology*, vol. 17 (1966) 122–32.

2. This is T. H. Marshall's term, used in Chapter 5 of *Sociology at the Crossroads* (London, Heinemann, 1963).

3. R. Centers, *The Psychology of Social Classes*, 216–17.

4. People who have no work roles (e.g. women, children, the 'leisure class', the unemployed) take on the social evaluation given to their means of support (husband, father, inherited wealth, State benefits).

5. That there exists general consensus in society as to the evaluation of occupations and the social position of their incumbents is demonstrated, for instance, in D. V. Glass (ed.), *Social Mobility in Britain* (London, Routledge, 1954) 34.

6. Committee on Higher Education, *Higher Education* (London, H.M.S.O., 1963) Appendix Two (A), 4, Table 3.

7. Ian Weinberg points out that the 84 schools which he includes in the public school system educate 'not more than 1 per cent of the age group': *The English Public Schools: the Sociology of Elite Education* (New York, Atherton Press, 1967) xiii, and Chapter 7. 'Independent efficient' schools, a larger group, account for $2\frac{1}{2}$ per cent of 17-year-olds: see A. Little and J. Westergaard, 'The trend of class differentials in educational opportunity in England and Wales', *British Journal of Sociology*, vol. 15 (1964) 301–16.

8. H. H. Gerth and C. W. Mills, *From Max Weber* (London, Routledge, 1948) 194.

9. T. B. Bottomore, *Elites and Society* (London, Watts, 1964). See also C. Kerr *et al.*, *Industrialism and Industrial Man* (London, Heinemann, 1962) Chapter 3.

10. In October 1960, manual workers in certain industries earned average gross weekly wages of £14 10s. 8d. (men) and £7 8s. 4d. (women), while in October 1959, administrative, technical and clerical employees earned £22 13s. 8d. (men) and £9 17s. 7d. (women) (*Ministry of Labour Annual Report* 1960, 68–9). This compares with average weekly incomes of our graduates in their *first jobs* after graduation of £25 9s. 3d. (men) and £18 15s. 0d. (women, with some postgraduate qualification).

11. M. Abrams, 'Rewards of education', *New Society*, 9 July 1964, 26; 'Graduates "rewarded for earlier sacrifice" ', *Guardian*, 5 January 1970. See, on the other hand, T. Husen, 'Status pays better than schooling', *Times Educational Supplement*, 26 December 1969, 4.

12. M. Abrams, 'British elite attitudes and the European Common Market', *Public Opinion Quarterly*, vol. 29 (1965) 240; R. K. Kelsall, *Higher Civil Servants . . .* (London, Routledge, 1955) Chapters 6 and 7; I. Weinberg, *English Public Schools*, 6 and Chapter 6.

13. By reason of his including among elites trade union leaders and revolutionaries (T. B. Bottomore, *Elites and Society*). G. D. H. Cole, in *Studies in Class Structure* (London, Routledge, 1955) 124–8, also talks about 'working-class elites'.

14. For example, the relational aspect of social position, a status attribute, is perhaps less susceptible to change than certain material aspects. This is one of the reasons for the social and psychological discomfort experienced by some socially mobile people. The term 'relational' is used by J. H. Goldthorpe and D. Lockwood, 'Affluence and the British class structure', *Sociological Review*, vol. 11 (1963) 133–63.

15. D. Lockwood, 'Social mobility', in A. T. Welford *et al.* (eds.), *Society: Problems and Methods of Study* (London, Routledge, 1962) 509–20; S. M. Lipset and R. Bendix, *Social Mobility in Industrial Society* (Berkeley, University of California Press, 1959) 57–60; K. Svalastoga, *Prestige, Class and Mobility* (London, Heinemann, 1959), 356–61.

16. For evidence of this, see E. Bott, 'Class as a reference group', *op cit.*; D. F. Swift, 'Social class, mobility-ideology and 11-plus success', *British Journal of Sociology*, vol. 18 (1967) 165–86; J. Ford, *Social Class and the Comprehensive School* (London, Routledge, 1970), Chapter 6; D. Lockwood, 'Sources of variation in working-class images of society', *Sociological Review*, vol. 14 (1966) 249–67.

17. R. H. Turner, 'Sponsored and contest mobility in the school system', *American Sociological Review*, vol. 25 (1960) 855–67.

18. J. Ford, *Social Class and the Comprehensive School*.

19. R. H. Turner, 'Acceptance of irregular mobility in Britain and the United States', *Sociometry*, vol. 29 (1966) 334–52; D. V. Glass (ed.), *Social Mobility in Britain*, Chapter 3.

20. *Ibid.*, Chapter 10; K. Svalastoga, *Prestige, Class and Mobility*, 364; and S. M. Lipset and R. Bendix, *Social Mobility in Industrial Society*, 189–91.

21. R. M. Marsh, 'Values, demand and social mobility', *American Sociological Review*, vol. 28 (1963) 565–75.

22. This in fact is less likely on grounds of demand, because there has also been some expansion in professional types of occupations, while there has been an actual reduction in the amount of manual work available.

23. Data on these topics have been compiled from replies to several questions in the schedule, and the Appendix contains an explanation of the various methods used here.

24. R. K. Kelsall *et al.*, *Six Years After* (Sheffield University, Department of Sociological Studies, Higher Education Research Unit, 1970) 15. Unless otherwise stated, throughout this chapter the social classes of fathers are based on their occupations at the time respondents entered university.

25. Committee on Higher Education, *Higher Education*, Appendix Two (B), 4, Table 5; also R. K. Kelsall, *Applications for Admission to Universities* (London, Association of Universities of the British Commonwealth, 1957), Table 15.

26. This may be partially offset by the tendency to upgrade fathers' occupations (K. Svalastoga, *Prestige, Class and Mobility*, 340), the net result of which would be an underestimate of the amount of mobility. However, the detailed nature of the information sought in this context would inhibit any tendency to upgrade.

27. See D. V. Glass (ed.), *Social Mobility in Britain*, 189. An explanation of the method used to calculate the index of association is contained in the Appendix.

28. See, for example, the data quoted by T. Fox and S. M. Miller, 'Intra-country variations: occupational stratification and mobility', in R. Bendix and S. M. Lipset (eds.), *Class, Status and Power* (Glencoe, Free Press, 1953) 574–81; and K. Svalastoga, *Prestige, Class and Mobility*, 348.

29. General Register Office, *Census 1961* (*England and Wales*) (London, H.M.S.O., 1966).

30. Cf. T. Fox and S. M. Miller, 'Intra-country variations', *op cit.*, 577, Table 4.

31. *Ibid.*, 579.

32. For example, by D. V. Glass, *Social Mobility in Britain*; K. Svalastoga, *Prestige, Class and Mobility*; and R. Centers, *The Psychology of Social Classes*.

33. R. Centers, 'Occupational mobility of urban occupational strata', *American Sociological Review*, vol. 13 (1948) 197–203.

34. E. F. Jackson and H. J. Crockett, 'Occupational mobility in the United States', *American Sociological Review*, vol. 29 (1964) 5–15.

35. S. M. Lipset and F. T. Malm, 'First jobs and career patterns', *American Journal of Economics and Sociology*, vol. 14 (1955) 247–61.

36. See, for instance, D. V. Glass (ed.), *Social Mobility in Britain*, 184–5; and R. Centers, 'Occupational mobility of urban occupational strata', *op. cit.* These data refer to intergenerational mobility.

37. K. Svalastoga, *Prestige, Class and Mobility*, 314–15.

38. That the non-manual/manual dichotomy has, apart from its analytical convenience, some sociological significance has been remarked upon by M. Kahan *et al.*, 'On the analytical division of social class', *op. cit.*; S. M. Lipset and R. Bendix, *Social Mobility in Industrial Society*, 165–9; and T. Husen, *Talent, Opportunity and Career* (Stockholm, Almqvist and Wiksell, 1969) Chapter 6.

39. K. Svalastoga, *Prestige, Class and Mobility*, 342–4.

40. D. V. Glass (ed.), *Social Mobility in Britain*, 285–6.

41. *Ibid.*, 285.

42. *Ibid.*, Chapter 12.

43. See, for instance, J. W. B. Douglas, *The Home and the School* (London, MacGibbon and Kee, 1964); J. Floud *et al.*, *Social Class and Educational Opportunity* (Melbourne, Heinemann, 1956); D. V. Glass (ed.), *Social Mobility in Britain*, Chapter 5; A. Little and J. Westergaard, 'The trend of class differentials in educational opportunity in England and Wales', *op. cit.*; G. Kalton, *The Public Schools* (London, Longmans, 1966); Central Advisory Council for Education (England), *Fifteen to Eighteen* (London, H.M.S.O., 1959).

44. E. Grebenik and G. Rowntree, 'Factors associated with the age at marriage in Great Britain', *Proceedings of the Royal Society (B)*, vol. 159 (1963) 178–98.

45. In D. V. Glass (ed.), *Social Mobility in Britain*, 342. Comparison here is between status levels of bridegrooms' fathers and fathers-in-law.

46. Of men, 29 per cent of those who obtained some type of postgraduate qualification and 25 per cent of those who did not were still unmarried in 1966. The corresponding figures for women are 33 per cent and 18 per cent. See Chapter 3 for more detailed discussion.

47. Ignoring for the moment women with semi-skilled and unskilled fathers, who are very few indeed, so that too much reliability should not be placed on the percentages in the last two rows of the table.

48. H. M. Blalock, *Causal Inferences in Non-experimental Research* (Chapel Hill, University of North Carolina Press, 1961) 3.

49. See M. Craft (ed.), *Family, Class and Education: a Reader* (London, Longmans, 1970) 37, Table 2.2.

50. B. Jackson and D. Marsden, *Education and the Working Class* (London, Routledge, 1962); W. Scott, 'Fertility and social mobility among teachers', *Population Studies*, vol. 11 (1958) 251–61; K. Svalastoga, *Prestige, Class and Mobility*, 404.

51. J. W. B. Douglas, *The Home and the School*, 94–5.

52. C. A. Anderson *et al.*, 'Intelligence and occupational mobility', *Journal of Political Economy*, vol. 60 (1952) 218–39.

53. I. Krauss, 'Sources of educational aspirations among working class youth', *American Sociological Review*, vol. 29 (1964) 867–79.

54. R. H. Turner, 'Some family determinants of ambition', *Sociology and Social Research*, vol. 46 (1962) 397–411. See also R. A. Ellis and W. C. Lane, 'Structural supports for upward mobility', *American Sociological Review*, vol. 28 (1963) 743–56.

55. In *Education and the Working Class*, Chapter 3.

56. Jean Floud makes a similar point in a preliminary report of the Nuffield enquiry into the recruitment of teachers, *Enquiry into the Social Characteristics of the Teaching Profession* (London University, Institute of Education, Unpublished, 1957) 5. It should also be mentioned that something approaching four in ten of the *non-mobile* graduates who took part in the present survey had a sibling or siblings who had been to a university.

57. D. V. Glass (ed.), *Social Mobility in Britain*, 142.

58. I. Krauss, 'Sources of educational aspirations among working class youth', *op. cit.*; E. Cohen, 'Parental factors in educational mobility', *Sociology of Education*, vol. 38 (1964–5) 404–25.

59. For empirical evidence on class-related values, see, for instance, H. H. Hyman, 'The value systems of different classes', in R. Bendix and S. M. Lipset (eds.), *Class, Status and Power*, 426–42; M. L. Kohn, 'Social class and parental values', *American Journal of Sociology*, vol. 64 (1959) 337–51; J. Klein, *Samples from English Cultures* (London, Routledge, 1965), vol. 2; R. Centers, *The Psychology of Social Classes*.

60. See H. M. Blalock, *Causal Inferences in Non-experimental Research*, 18–19. No causal model can ever be perfect, especially in the social sciences, because of the necessary simplification of the real situation by the elimination of some variables. We are unable to estimate the contribution of other variables in this situation, because our data do not permit this. See note 67 below.

61. D. J. Bordua, 'Educational aspirations and parental stress on college', *Social Forces*, vol. 38 (1960) 262–9; R. L. Simpson, 'Parental influence, anticipatory socialization and social mobility', *American Sociological Review*, vol. 27 (1962) 517–22; W. H. Sewell and V. P. Shah, 'Social class, parental encouragement and educational aspirations', *American*

Journal of Sociology, vol. 73 (1968) 559–72; F. Musgrove, 'University freshmen and their parents' attitudes', *Educational Research*, vol. 10 (1967) 78–80.

62. For evidence see, for instance, D. V. Glass (ed.), *Social Mobility in Britain*, 172; and D. F. Swift, 'Social class, mobility-ideology and 11-plus success', *op. cit.* This argument also operates in the case of comprehensive secondary education, since most comprehensive schools have 'grammar streams' – see C. Benn and B. Simon, *Half Way There: Report on the British Comprehensive School Reform* (London, McGraw-Hill, 1970) 379.

63. For a useful exploration of this idea, see S. Keller and M. Zavalloni, 'Ambition and social class: a respecification', *Social Forces*, vol. 43 (1965) 58–70; and also F. G. Caro and C. T. Pihlblad, 'Aspirations and expectations', *Sociology and Social Research*, vol. 49 (1965) 465–75.

64. By R. A. Ellis and W. C. Lane, 'Structural supports for upward mobility', *op. cit.*; and by E. L. McDill and J. Coleman, 'Family and peer influences on college plans of high school students', *Sociology of Education*, vol. 38 (1965) 112–16.

65. See F. Musgrove, 'University freshmen and their parents' attitudes', *op. cit.*

66. R. L. Simpson ('Parental influence, anticipatory socialization and social mobility', *op. cit.*) found that potentially upwardly mobile boys had received pressure from both parents and peers, but that parental pressure had been the more salient.

67. There are other variables associated with differential mobility, in particular achievement motivation and the ability to defer gratification, which do not fall within the scope of the present study, offering as they do an explanation on a social psychological level. See the work of David McClelland, and also B. Stacey, 'Some psychological aspects of intergeneration occupational mobility', *British Journal of Social and Clinical Psychology*, vol. 4 (1965) 275–86; H. J. Crockett, 'The achievement motive and differential occupational mobility in the United States', *American Sociological Review*, vol. 27 (1962) 191–204; G. H. Elder, 'Achievement motivation and intelligence in occupational mobility', *Sociometry*, vol. 31 (1968) 327–54, for fuller treatment of these topics.

68. For a discussion of this concept and of reference group theory in general, see R. K. Merton and A. S. Kitt, 'Contributions to the theory of reference group behaviour', in R. K. Merton and P. F. Lazarsfeld (eds.), *Continuities in Social Research* (Glencoe, Free Press, 1950).

69. That this is the case is demonstrated by a great deal of evidence, including the following: B. Jackson and D. Marsden, *Education and the Working Class*; J. W. B. Douglas *et al.*, *All Our Future: a Longitudinal Study of Secondary Education* (London, Davies, 1968); Central Advisory Council for Education, *Fifteen to Eighteen*. Virtually all selective State

E

schools are day schools, and the situation might be different if this were not the case: see I. Weinberg, *The English Public Schools*, 8–9, on boarding schools as 'total institutions'.

70. C. C. Perrucci, 'Social origins, mobility patterns and fertility', *American Sociological Review*, vol. 32 (1967) 615–25.

71. G. Payne and J. Bird, 'The newest universities – 2: what are their students like?', *New Society*, 23 October 1969, 641–3; C. T. Sandford *et al.*, 'Class influences in higher education', *British Journal of Educational Psychology*, vol. 35 (1965) 183–94; F. Musgrove, 'Social class and levels of aspiration in a technological university', *Sociological Review*, vol. 15 (1967) 311–22.

72. J. Floud and W. Scott, 'Recruitment to teaching in England and Wales', in A. H. Halsey *et al.* (eds.), *Education, Economy and Society* (Glencoe, Free Press, 1961) 527–44.

73. Committee on Higher Education, *Higher Education*, Appendix Two (B), 428; see also R. K. Kelsall, *Applications for Admission to Universities*, 9, and Table 14.

74. See R. K. Kelsall *et al.*, *Six Years After*, 10; Committee on Higher Education, *Higher Education*, Appendix Two (A), 144; and B. McAlhone, 'Degrees of scandal', *Guardian*, 19 March 1971.

75. F. Brockington and Z. Stein, 'Admission, achievement and social class', *Universities Quarterly*, vol. 18 (1963) 52–73; J. G. H. Newfield, 'Some factors related to the academic performance of British university students', in P. Halmos (ed.), *Sociological Studies in British University Education* (Keele, University Press, 1963) 117–30; R. R. Dale, 'Reflections on the influence of social class on student performance at the university', in *ibid.*, 131–40.

76. *Ibid.*, 136.

77. Basil Bernstein's work in this field is well known. See, for instance, 'Some sociological determinants of perception', *British Journal of Sociology*, vol. 9 (1958) 158–74.

78. H. H. Hyman, 'The value systems of different classes', *op. cit.*

79. Manual workers are more subject to redundancies due to market fluctuations than are non-manual workers. Also, much non-manual work is salaried, which means that an employee must be given one month's (or perhaps even three month's) notice if his services are no longer required, while manual workers are usually hired on a weekly, or even hourly, basis. Furthermore, non-manual workers are often the beneficiaries of special pension and/or superannuation schemes.

80. This is in line with Hyman's findings ('The value systems of different classes', *op. cit.*). Of relevance to this question is the fact that our evidence shows that although nearly all parents, regardless of their social class, were keen for their children to go to university, there still remained a slight class difference on this account, in the direction expected on the basis of the hypothesis.

Chapter Two

GRADUATE MEN AND WORK

The attitudes of men graduates towards work and their actual experience of employment in the years immediately following graduation are the central concern of this chapter, in which we are able to demonstrate, in the main, that a university degree is a key to entry to a wide variety of professional, managerial or executive positions.[1] For while only an insignificant number of 1960 graduates were able not to work at all and thereby form a leisured intelligentsia, few again abandoned the advantages of a high-status occupation in favour of unskilled manual work. Doubtless the knowledge that a university education offers occupational rewards such as these exerts a strong pressure on successive generations of students to embark on and stay the course of a first degree.[2] At the same time, moreover, they are attracted by these forms of employment because they offer the stability and orderliness of occupational life which are characteristic of a career.[3] Of course, this is at present the prerogative of the relatively few and is seen in some measure as a return for the long period of formal training during which the student's skills and aptitudes are developed, often with little specifically vocational reference.[4]

Indeed, the links between undergraduate study and employment are by no means direct. Clearly a student in an arts faculty, for example, acquires few skills specific to any career, with the possible exception of teaching. In fact the link between university education and employment depends largely on the assumption that a general intellectual and cultural heritage, which it is believed is transmitted in a degree course, is in some ways applicable to most occupational fields.[5]

Yet we have found that divisions based on family background have generally been more salient than any specifically academic criteria to our graduates' lives. It comes as no surprise, therefore, that the same social divisions were found to be pertinent to the link between university study and postgraduate experiences at work. For the most part, graduates' assessment and experience of work owed more to their social origins than to their intellectual performance. Of further significance, as we hope to show, was the fact that the universities were relatively ineffective in mitigating these effects of social background during the process of higher education itself.

By way of illustrating these themes, our attention focuses on our graduates not simply as units of production but as people, looking first at their occupational aspirations at the time they entered university. These aspirations are then contrasted with their plans for work on graduation. And finally the graduates' actual employment patterns are discussed in conjunction with their assessment of their working conditions six years after graduation.

Aspirations of graduates on entry to university

Among other things, our graduates were asked to recall the particular occupations they had in mind on entry to university, and it is on the basis of these recollections that our analysis of employment aspirations begins. A cautionary note is in order at the outset, however. The graduates were questioned only at one particular point in time (that is six years after graduation) and therefore their responses could have been somewhat inaccurate recollections of an earlier period in their lives. More seriously, too, it is of course possible that their recollections were merely rationalizations of recent courses of action with regard to employment. This is in some ways unlikely since, as we shall see, it was possible to show certain changes in our graduates' aspirations over time. And, indeed, any potential weaknesses of this kind are, in our view, more than compensated by the value of our findings in illustrating the clear relationship between family background and graduates' ambitions.

Almost half of our male graduates in fact had no particular career in mind on entering university (Table 26). This is scarcely surprising since, as we know, young people frequently delay making a firm commitment to a job as long as possible. To be sure, they may take steps which have unintended and in some ways irreversible consequences, such as excluding themselves from certain types of employment by subject specialization, but in fact few decisions are of this nature because only a limited number of courses of study at a university are vocational. [6]

It was nevertheless possible to show some link between subject and career choice for those men who had some form of occupation in mind during the early stages of their university life. Table 27 shows clearly that on the whole those people who studied arts subjects had a particular preference for school teaching; social scientists in contrast were far more likely to opt for some other form of professional employment, while scientists and technologists were spread more evenly over the range of careers, though they showed a special preference for non-university research, design, development or production.

But the subject of degree was not the only nor the most significant factor associated with career choice. It was evident, for example, that both type of school and university attended were of importance in this context though, as we shall see, these in their turn were associated with the underlying influence of family background and can, of course, be considered as indices of social class. Our interschool comparison (Table 28) quite clearly shows a significant difference in attitude between men who had attended fee paying schools and the rest of the male graduate body. Whereas those who had been educated in the private sector aspired particularly to administrative, professional (other than teaching) and miscellaneous types of work, the State-educated placed an emphasis on teaching (in both

schools and universities) or research, design or production outside universities.

These same tendencies were noticeable when we went on to
examine our graduates' aspirations in relation to the type of
university they attended. There was no question, first of all, that
universities varied considerably in terms of social exclusiveness
measured, that is, by the proportion of graduates from particular social backgrounds in each university setting (Table 22).
Not surprisingly, Oxford and Cambridge were the most
socially exclusive (only 13 per cent of their male graduates having had manual working fathers), but there were also marked
variations between other university groupings. Just under a
quarter of men graduating from London (24 per cent) and
Scottish universities (24 per cent) had manual working backgrounds compared with Smaller Civic (30 per cent), Larger
Civic (35 per cent) and Welsh universities (43 per cent).

Now social exclusiveness was by and large positively related
to the proportion of graduates aspiring to the more prestigious [7]
professions, management and university teaching rather than
school teaching or research and development – though in the
latter instance particularly the trends were not entirely consistent. Table 29 shows the considerable disinclination of
Oxbridge graduates to think in terms of a teaching career, and
this is particularly marked if we bear in mind the large number
of these graduates who were studying for arts degrees. By way of
contrast, graduates of the University of Wales and of universities in the Smaller Civic group were especially likely to aspire
to a teaching career. Again, while research, design and production appealed to between 26 and 33 per cent of men who
opted for particular careers in most university settings, only 12
per cent of Oxbridge graduates were attracted by this form of
employment.

Although, as we shall see, our graduates' aspirations for work
were shaped particularly by their family backgrounds, there was
nevertheless some evidence to suggest that these tendencies were
strengthened by the type of university they attended, for there
were certain variations observable between universities in the
propensity of graduates *from the same background* to opt for certain

kinds of career (see Table 30). Thus, considering first the graduates from professional backgrounds, proportionately more of those who had thought in terms of a particular career and who attended Oxbridge and Scottish universities, preferred the traditional professions, compared with their colleagues (with the same social backgrounds) in other universities. Again, graduates at Oxbridge from these relatively privileged homes were particularly unlikely to opt for research, design and production work. Moreover, although the trends were by no means entirely consistent, graduates from manual working backgrounds attending Welsh and Smaller Civic universities were particularly attracted by school teaching, again in comparison with their counterparts from identical class backgrounds in other university settings.

But overall the differences in aspirations were, as we have hinted, in large measure related to social class factors as measured by father's occupation. Clearly the attitudes of those who, say, attended independent schools and who took degrees at Oxford or Cambridge owed a certain amount to the social composition of these institutions (Table 31). But, significantly, family background differences were evident within each university grouping. In consequence, among the graduate body as a whole it was possible to trace clear differences between the aspirations of those from more privileged home circumstances and their colleagues whose social circumstances were less advantageous. Consistent with our earlier findings, those from higher-status backgrounds showed a preference for administrative positions and particularly for the older professions, such as law and accountancy, while graduates from working-class backgrounds were far more likely to be attracted by teaching (see Table 30). Again, graduates from higher-status homes were relatively more likely than others to have some clear conception of their future careers at the beginning of their university lives.

Thus, if we consider in turn some of the main types of graduate employment and bear in mind that upwards of 40 per cent of our sample had no clear career in mind on entering university, it was noticeable that the professional services section appealed most to those of more privileged birth. Indeed, one-third of all graduates whose fathers had professional occupations and who had a career in mind at this time aspired to this form of employment, while at the other end of the scale, only 13 per cent of their colleagues from manual working homes thought in terms of a career in the professions. There was, to be sure, little difference in the aspirations of working-class graduates and those whose fathers had some routine grade of non-manual work, but the overall influence of social class on aspirations to a professional career is unmistakable.

The same trends were observable in the administrative or managerial sector, though in this instance the influence of social origin was somewhat less marked. Nevertheless, graduates from professional backgrounds were more likely to choose a career in administrative or managerial employment (14 per cent) than were those from working-class homes (9 per cent).

The two chief forms of employment which appealed most to working-class graduates were research, development and production, and teaching: in both these instances there was an inverse relationship between social class and preference for these careers. Taking first research, development and production, about one-third (32 per cent) of all working-class graduates who had thought in terms of a given career opted for this type of work compared with 22 per cent of those from professional backgrounds. Nevertheless, there were important variations between particular university groupings which are worth mentioning. Disinclination for this type of work was particularly marked among graduates from all types of background at Oxbridge, while in certain other universities the class gradient was exactly in reverse of the general trend; this was true of London, Smaller Civic and Welsh universities (Table 30).

In view of these inconsistencies, it is worth pointing to certain other factors which complicate the influence of father's occupation on the choice of a career in research, design and production work. First, the category contains quite a wide variety of functions, not all of which may be equally attractive to graduates of different classes. Secondly, the faculty composition of different university groups is of importance here, since universities with particularly strong arts faculties (see Table 32) are unlikely to have a large proportion of graduates aspiring to careers to which many pure and applied scientists are drawn. And finally, the lack of affection for these careers among many graduates from professional backgrounds was most marked in the older, and to some extent more exclusive, universities (such as Oxbridge and Scottish). Thus the influence of social class, in this particular instance, should be qualified by reference to a number of other factors.

But this argument does not apply to those graduates who opted for a career in teaching. In all university groupings, graduates from working-class backgrounds were far more likely to think in terms of a career in teaching than were their counterparts from middle-class homes, the proportions overall being 28 per cent and 10 per cent respectively. Moreover, the less exclusive the university group (as measured by the proportion of working-class graduates in each setting) the greater these tendencies appeared to be. Thus in Welsh universities, for example, 43 per cent of graduates from working-class backgrounds with a particular career in mind opted for school teaching compared with only 9 per cent of graduates whose fathers worked in a professional capacity.

On the basis of the above data, therefore, we are able to find considerable support for the argument that graduates' aspirations are formed particularly by their families of origin. This in turn casts doubt on the relevance of academic criteria in graduate deployment and also leads one to question the view that choice of occupation is a rational process in the specific sense of matching a career with one's particular capacities and abilities. Rather the possibilities of rational choice are clearly confined within the bounds of experience and knowledge, these being limited in turn by social background factors only marginally related to personal aptitudes and ability. Thus although we would not quarrel with the view that choice is a rational and conscious act of deciding from a range of known alternatives,[8] we would place emphasis on the social factors which restrict these 'known alternatives' – factors, indeed, which are determinants of choice in the negative sense of severely limiting the range of possibilities for those with less privileged home circumstances. And, in a sense, restrictions on choice are also placed on the graduates from higher-status backgrounds who are probably unlikely to consider, say, a career in teaching, whatever their aptitudes in this direction.

These arguments, of course, have theoretical implications. Recent studies in the sociology of knowledge,[9] for example, have pointed to the importance of social class as a location point for 'social images' and views of the world, since social classes clearly limit and indeed *pattern* the child's learning environment by determining in large measure his exposure to various aspects of culture.

> Members of different social classes by virtue of enjoying or suffering different conditions of life, come to see the world differently and to develop different conceptions of social reality, different aspirations and hopes and fears, different conceptions of the desirable.[10]

The end result, then, of a learning environment dominated and to a large extent determined by social class, is that members of different classes have very different images of the world and, more specifically, divergent conceptions of the possible and even desirable in so far as work is concerned. In this sense too, a dominant perspective on life acquired in a given learning environment 'runs ahead of experience, defines and guides it',[11] thereby acting as a basic reference point when new situations have to be interpreted and understood.

Knowledge, then, is in large measure grounded in experience, which is in turn very much the product of social class situations. In view of this it is of course scarcely surprising that studies of children at all stages of the educational process have demonstrated the link between social class background and performance in the education system.[12] Nevertheless, in a not insignificant number of cases, the social environment of those whose objective position is working class (as measured, say, by father's occupation) are in certain other respects distinct from other members of their class. Turner has suggested that 'when a child's ambitions are atypical for his class background, it is reasonable to suppose that the convergence among the components of his class position has been incomplete'.[13] Thus, although there were two and a half thousand men from working-class homes in our sample, they clearly differed in a number of important social respects from intergenerationally stable working-class children and their families.

We have of course discussed a number of these points of variation in the previous chapter, but in respect of the effects of social class on job aspirations some further comments are in order here. Now it appears first of all that working-class parents of successful children for one reason or another have, compared with working-class parents of less successful children, a relatively clear picture of middle-class life and have even internalized some of its attendant norms. Whatever may be the reason for this, the process of absorbing the images of middle-class life forms a basis for the educational success of their children. More generally, Halsey has usefully summed up the differences between the educationally successful working-class child and others from the same background; 'the educationally successful working-class child tends to come from a family which in its atmosphere and its psychology, if not in its material circumstances, is atypical of its class and aspirant in its social status',[14] a home in which a mixture of 'frustration, drive and ambition (was) such as to impel even the modestly gifted child through all the difficulties of primary and grammar school into the "middle class" invitations (sic) of college, university and the professional career'.[15] Thus although it remains generally true that 'the children who do the best work, are easiest to control and stimulate, make the best prefects, finish school with the best qualifications and references and get into the best jobs tend to come from the middle class',[16] graduates from working-class backgrounds by no means differ in all respects from successful children from middle-class homes.

And yet the process of assimilation into middle-class life is presumably never absolute. Rather for the 'successful' working-class child – successful, that is, in terms of educational performance compared with peers from his same class origins – there is presumably a delicate process of balancing aspects of two distinct cultures. It is possible, therefore, to conceive of the successful working-class child as occupying some form of intermediary position between the working and middle classes, being neither entirely typical of his class of origin nor yet again absorbing fully the perspectives and values of the middle class.

This, then, helps to account for our data on job aspirations. To begin with, as teenagers our successful working-class graduates almost certainly differed, in terms of aspirations, from young people in the working class as a whole. And in support of this there have been important studies in this area which are worth mentioning. One wellknown American study,[17] for instance, showed that working-class parents whose sons were *not* aspiring to a college education (the 'common man' group) expected that their sons would follow in their own footsteps as far as occupations were concerned and, indeed, that they would be fortunate if they even acquired a regular job. Moreover, they were in some ways 'fatalistic' about the possibilities of advancement, commenting that 'this was life' and so 'why think about it?'[18] In contrast, parents from similar social backgrounds whose sons wanted to go to college believed in 'getting ahead', were more sensitive to the existence of social hierarchies and 'thought more about the subject (of jobs) than those who were satisfied with their jobs'. Furthermore, they saw education as the key to social mobility and, indeed, used the middle class as their basic reference group. And yet there are good grounds for believing that the aspirations of parents of more successful and potentially more successful working-class children are in turn 'limited' in comparison with those of middle-class parents. Thus Swift has shown that working-class parents of educationally successful children, while hoping that their children would obtain non-manual jobs, clearly were considering careers which were modest by comparison with the hopes of middle-class parents. Further, they consistently underestimated the professional opportunities open to their children, thinking rather in terms of careers such as draughtsman, personal secretary or librarian – choices which were low on the list of middle-class parents' aspirations.[19]

In view of this, it is scarcely surprising that our graduates from manual working backgrounds had different expectations from their academic equals from more privileged homes, emphasizing careers such as teaching rather than the older professions. Previous explanations for such variations have generally been of two kinds: the first emphasizes the objectively scarce opportunities for working-class children, the second points to certain limitations in terms of their ambitions. Knupfer has been an important exponent of the first view.[20] He concludes that working-class people expect relatively little in terms of occupational reward in order 'to make life tolerable' in the face of the possible frustration at their lack of advancement, for while the majority of occupations in most industrial societies are manual, even if perfect mobility obtained the bulk of working-class children would take up manual occupations. In this sense, then, the somewhat 'fatalistic' interpretation of so many working-class parents, *vis-à-vis* their children's opportunities, is in some measure a rational and reasonable response to the genuine limitations on advancement inherent in the nature of the occupational structure. And presumably even among the most ambitious working-class parents this consciousness of scarce opportunities exerts some influence, leading them to encourage their children in the search for what are again, by middle-class standards, careers of a somewhat limited type.

We would in no way wish to quarrel with the main tenets of his argument but it clearly applies rather more particularly to the less successful working-class child than to our graduate sample as a whole. Turning then to the second argument, we may ask whether the view that working-class graduates have limited aspirations has any greater explanatory value? There is no question, first of all, that there have been many who have subscribed to this viewpoint:[21] Rosen, for instance, has argued that

while it is *probably true* that the notion that success is desirable and possible is widespread in our society, the implementary values have long been more *associated with the culture of the middle than of the lower class*. Middle class children are more likely to be taught not only to believe in success, but also to be more willing to take those steps that make achievement possible: in short, to embrace the achievement value system which states that given the willingness to work hard, plan and make proper sacrifices, an individual should be able to manipulate his environment so as to ensure eventual success.[22] (Italics ours.)

This is a case which has been echoed by many others interested in the relation between occupation and ambition. Hyman found that the working class placed relatively little emphasis on traditional success goals and less on the achievement of goals which would in turn be instrumental for success, compared with the middle classes. Davis, in support, has argued that a child's internalization of working-class values inhibits his social and economic betterment and that the culture of the lower classes obstructs the educational development of the children. This view is also held by Bendix and Lipset who have argued

that the cumulation of disadvantages at the bottom of the social scale is in large part the result of a lack of interest in educational and occupational achievement. In a country which is second to none in its concern with mobility and personal attainment it is clearly insufficient to attribute this lack of interest solely to environment.[23]

Mills, too, argues that the middle class is relatively more concerned with mobility: for them, he suggests, success has been 'an engaging image, a driving motive, and a way of life'.[24] And finally, as recently as 1968 Butler has asserted that levels of aspiration 'seem to be differentially distributed among children from high and low class families'.[25]

All in all, then, an imposing number of writers have argued that middle-class children are brought up in an environment conducive to the development of ambition and success and, furthermore, that this is in sharp contrast to the experience of working-class children. And yet, so far as our successful working-class graduates are concerned, is this explanation entirely satisfactory? To begin with, the concept of ambition is surely relative: it begs the question 'ambition with regard to what?' Now, in a sense, the ambitions of our middle-class graduates were little more than fairly realistic assessments of the possibilities open to them; possibilities which, incidentally, were actualities as far as their own parents were concerned. They were by no means striving for careers which were rare in their social background. By way of contrast, the working-class graduates were surely extremely ambitious, bearing in mind their manual backgrounds, even if, as we have seen, they were in turn limited by comparison with middle-class conceptions.

In general, then, we are by no means convinced by the view that our middle-class graduates were brought up in environments which placed greater emphasis on ambition than our successful working-class graduates. As Keller and Zavalloni have argued, the rank of a success goal varies according to the social distance of the observer from it.[26] And on this measure it was the graduate from a manual home who was more ambitious than any other. Indeed it is doubtful whether the concept of ambition is of any great value in this context. Once again, we would rather interpret graduates' aspirations in relation to the social environments which produce different knowledge and, by inference, different perceptions of the desirable in so far as jobs are concerned, since the 'pure' types of working- and middle-class environments undoubtedly produce different perceptions and valuations of the world. To be sure, a number of working-class children who are successful in middle-class terms do absorb certain aspects of a different culture and thus, as we have argued, occupy, particularly during these early periods of their lives, some form of intermediary position between the working and middle classes – often delicately balancing the contradictory elements of the two cultures. And though they obviously differ in terms of their attitudes towards work from their colleagues of the same class who have not benefited from higher education, it is scarcely surprising that they did not fully share the same conceptions of the desirable as their academic equals from higher status homes who, *by virtue of their class position*, are able to set their sights on what are, in working-class terms, even more distant horizons. But certainly we would not wish to infer from this that the upwardly mobile graduates in our sample were any less ambitious than the rest: again, as measured in terms of the social distance of a person from a particular goal, the steps that working-class graduates were expecting to take in their careers were obviously very considerable.

Changes in graduates' aspirations during their undergraduate years

That social class had such an important bearing on the job aspirations our graduates recalled having on entry to university may cause little surprise to many readers. It may be regretted that in a country which relies so much on its effective use of human talent there is not some greater consonance between job aspirations and the specific aptitudes of its people, but in view of our theoretical understanding of the nature of social classes and the way these profoundly affect 'knowledge' of the world, our findings could not be considered to be totally unexpected. This does not imply, of course, that changes could not be made which might at least modify these underlying influences, such as more effective careers information in universities as well as more guidance in schools, but anyone wishing for more root-and-branch reforms would have to begin to think in terms of tackling certain aspects of the underlying class structure itself.

As we have seen, one of the most important ways in which class attitudes are conveyed is through the family system. Thus, on the face of it, there were strong *a priori* grounds for assuming that as this influence presumably waned over the undergraduate years, so we might have expected some complementary reduction in the influence of social class on orientations to work. Indeed, we might have anticipated that a two-way interchange of ideas during undergraduate life would broaden the horizons of students from both working- and middle-class backgrounds: not only would the former gain increased knowledge and understanding of certain hitherto 'taboo' professions, but at the same time others from higher-status backgrounds might come to look more favourably on such careers as teaching if they considered themselves to have a particular aptitude in that direction. In effect, then, we might have conceived of a substantial diminution in the influence of social class in the 'melting pot' of university life during which students, mingling with others from various backgrounds in halls of residence, 'digs' or flats, and during many formal and informal social events, broaden their horizons and re-examine their past beliefs.[27]

As we shall see this hypothesis was not, in the event, confirmed. Indeed, there was little noticeable change in the aspirations of graduates from working-class backgrounds, and the overall influence of class on attitudes towards work was still very marked at the time of graduation. This is not of course to argue that the influence of the graduates' parents had not declined over these years, but it is to assert, and indeed to demonstrate, that where this influence declined it must have been substantially replaced by other social agencies (and especially by students' peers) which, on balance, tended to reinforce rather than to modify social class factors.

The 1960 graduates were asked to state what occupation (if any) they had in mind at the time of graduation. Now it may be recalled that upwards of 40 per cent of our sample had no particular occupation in mind on *entering university*, but by the time of *graduation* this proportion was merely 14 per cent (Table 26). These findings, incidentally, correspond quite closely to those of earlier studies. Third-year undergraduates contacted by the Robbins Committee had almost exactly similar commitments, and although Morton-Williams found only 10 per cent of students admitting no occupational preference in their final year at university, this figure is by no means inordinately different from our own.[28]

That graduates were more likely to have a firm career commitment at the end of their undergraduate lives compared with an earlier period comes as no great surprise, although the absolute number who were still undecided on graduation was undoubtedly quite considerable. Clearly, however, the nearer the time of actually having to earn a living the more likely it is that young people will come to a firm decision about their future employment.

F

This process of developing concrete and realistic career choices has been formally expressed before by Ginzberg and his associates, who included undergraduates in a study of the development of occupational interests among young people aged from eleven to twenty-four.[29] On the basis of their investigations they suggest that occupational choice may be envisaged as a chain of decisions during which an individual becomes 'increasingly aware of what he likes and what he dislikes, of what he does well and what he does poorly; the values which are meaningful to him and the considerations which are unimportant'.[30] This process includes three main stages – fantasy, tentative and realistic – each stage being largely irreversible. Realistic choices are, in the view of Ginzberg and his colleagues, normally made in adulthood; they are largely consequent upon prior experience necessary to make a satisfactory 'occupational choice'.

Up to a point, this model can be usefully employed in order to understand the overall changes in our graduates' career commitments. During the early stages of university life it appears likely that their choices were somewhat tentative but became more realistic as a result of experience gained in social intercourse at university and, indeed, during the educational process itself. The undergraduate years almost certainly at least provided the time (if not, as we shall see, the social environment) to work out their aptitudes and interests and become more aware of the opportunities open to them. This contrasts, incidentally, with young men who start work at fifteen or sixteen, at which time their development along the path to a 'realistic' choice is incomplete.

And yet although the Ginzberg model may help to make the process of occupational choice more intelligible, it would appear to underestimate the more subtle social class influences which, as we have seen, tend to limit the horizons of men with different social backgrounds. It is doubtful, then, whether even the more fortunate young men who are able to delay their choice of career and hence maximize the time available to develop a 'realistic' preference, have really been able to weigh up the merits of even quite a small number of potential careers before making a final, and perhaps irreversible, decision. This becomes apparent as we now turn our attention to the specific careers our graduates had in mind at the end of their undergraduate lives, and contrast these with their earlier aspirations.

Taking the men graduates as a whole, at the time of entering university approximately equal proportions had thought in terms of school teaching, research, development or production, and the professions. On graduating it was apparent that interest in both the professions and research, development and production had diminished, while there had been correspondingly more interest in administrative or managerial work, and a particular growth in the proportions wanting to take up a teaching or research post in a university (Table 26). These findings again correspond closely to those of previous British studies and reflect remarkably consistent work orientations among graduates in this country during the late 1950s and early 1960s.[31]

Although no employment sector actually suffered a *loss* of popularity, owing to the much higher proportion of graduates who had a firm career commitment at the end of their university course than at the beginning, Table 33 shows clearly that by far the greatest percentage growth was evident in the preference for teaching or research in the universities.[32] School teaching, in contrast, both attracted and lost potential recruits, as did research, design or production work outside universities, whose net gain was the lowest of all the main occupational groups.

On the basis of these data, therefore, we would regard job horizons as having been extended in only a limited way during the period of undergraduate study. To be sure, the possibility of an academic career became a major attraction and was, indeed, the one occupational category towards which graduates' attitudes changed substantially over time; but if anything, this was at the expense of a wide range of non-university careers some of whose popularity clearly diminished – a state of affairs which is presumably of some concern to those who would like to see talented graduates more evenly spread among different types of employment.

Moving on, then, to an explanation of some of these trends and of the patterns of aspirations generally demonstrated by graduates at the end of their university careers, we would again place particular emphasis on the influence of social class. But a word of caution is in order at this point. We would not wish to spoil what we consider to be an important case by overstatement, nor do we intend to convey the impression that there were no intervening variables which affected the main patterns of career choice. It is relevant, therefore, to direct our attention first at some of those factors which had no obvious relationship with social class.

Both subject and class of degree were outstanding examples of purely educational factors which had a major impact on career choice. In general, arts graduates were particularly attracted by teaching, social scientists by the other professions, and technologists by research, design or production in a non-university setting. Pure scientists' aspirations were more evenly spread between university work, school teaching or research, design or production (Table 34). Thus, except for the considerable growth in interest among pure scientists for an academic career, the relation of subject to career aspirations had persisted throughout the period of undergraduate study. Early subject specialization would appear, then, to limit the occupational horizons of young people in such a manner as to be by no means mitigated or even substantially modified during undergraduate life itself.

Class of degree, too, had an important bearing on career choice, though again its effect might cause some alarm to those seeking a more even spread of talent throughout the occupational system. Unquestionably the most educationally competent graduates (as measured by degree class) had been especially attracted by the prospect of a university post. Indeed, approximately half of all those with first-class honours degrees were thinking along these lines, as were more than a third of those who had gained an upper second (Table 35). There was a substantial difference between this educational 'elite' and the rest of the graduate body; those with undivided or lower seconds were likely to want to take up school teaching and the remainder to be spread fairly evenly between teaching, research, design or production, administration or the 'other' professions. Now although there was some evidence that research and development attracted graduates of varying measured ability, we have to bear in mind that these careers became relatively less attractive to graduates as a whole during their three years of undergraduate study. Moreover, there was no question that in terms of preferences the professions, and perhaps most serious of all, management, appealed particularly to the academically less well-qualified man. Of course there may be no real link between intellectual skills *per se* and, say, managerial quality, though the assumption of such an association is, as was noted at the beginning of the chapter, the main reason why the general intellectual skills transmitted in the universities are esteemed so highly.[33] It is thus clear that key posts in the industrial sector are for one reason or another distinctly unattractive to those who have shown themselves most able to absorb an intellectual heritage.

Having examined certain factors associated with career choice which had no obvious relationship with social class, we turn now to an outline of influences on job aspirations which were more closely connected with the latter. There was no question that the propensity of graduates within the same speciality and degree class range to think in terms of one kind of work rather than another, was dependent particularly on a number of indices of social class (Tables 36 and 37). This becomes clear if we examine in turn the effect of both secondary school type and social origin on our graduates' career plans at the end of their university course.

Now graduates from independent schools were particularly attracted on graduation by careers in the professions or management. This was in sharp contrast with those from local authority schools whose main preferences were, in descending order, teaching, research, design or production work outside a university, and a university career itself (Table 38). Clearly there appears to have been no major change in the patterns of occupational preference as a result of experiences at university. If we consider the main occupational categories in turn, there was first of all an almost identical association between type of school and interest in a teaching career at the beginning as at the end of the undergraduate period (see Tables 28 and 38). As we have previously noted, the prospect of a career in the universities became increasingly popular towards the end and therefore it was scarcely surprising that men from all kinds of school shared in this development. And yet even a university post appealed more to those with an LEA school background than to those who had been to an independent school: a tendency which was if anything slightly more marked on graduation.

But on balance, it was clear that as measured by type of secondary school attended, the influence of social class on aspiration in no way changed substantially between entry to university and graduation. To be sure, the graduates from higher-status homes came to show a lesser interest in the professions together with a fractional increase in preference for teaching, but the main observable change in their attitudes was confined to their growing preference for jobs in management which for them, alongside the professions, was still pre-eminent. By way of contrast the LEA graduates in no way lessened their interest in a school teaching career, which remained, along with research, design and production, the most common choice at the end of their course as it had been at the beginning, while the professions in particular became even less likely possibilities. Without doubt, then, the universities generally failed to provide a 'melting pot' environment so far as career aspirations were concerned. This is further illustrated by examining career preferences in relation to father's occupation: this shows that at the point of graduation, career choice owed as much to the effect of family circumstances as at the outset of higher education. Once again graduates from manual backgrounds showed a particular interest in school teaching or research, design and production. Furthermore, graduates from professional homes were highly unlikely to share these preferences, having a marked bent for the professions and administration. There were certain changes (see Tables 30 and 39) such as those described above in the patterns of aspirations but these, on balance, reflected changes in the attitudes of the graduate body as a whole and did not represent any substantial reduction in the influence of social class itself. The growing interest in a university career, for example, was evinced by graduates of all social classes. Indeed it could be that it was only in respect of the possibility of an academic career that the universities can be said to have widened the horizons of the men in this study; this was the only kind of employment, too, in which aspirations appeared to be largely unrelated to social origins, for graduates were almost equally likely to think in terms of a university career regardless of their family backgrounds.[34]

Comparing, then, the changes in aspirations of one and another group of graduates over time, it was apparent first of all that the universities had done relatively little to encourage the socially mobile graduate to reshuffle his ideas about future employment. They came, it is true, to show an interest in academic work and a declining concern for research, design or production outside a university, but these tendencies were out-weighed by their comparatively stable occupational aspirations; indeed the proportions of working-class graduates seeking careers in teaching, the professions and administration re-spectively were virtually identical at the beginning and end of their university days. In the same way, men whose fathers were professionals were also more attracted by a university career at the time of graduation, though in this instance at the expense of professional employment. The professions, however, still remained the single most significant choice for these men, while at the same time they increasingly opted for careers in manage-ment.

Before going on to attempt an explanation for the persistent effects of social class on this highly educated elite, we may pause to examine certain inter-university variations in career planning. These, in turn, have wider theoretical significance in so far as there are good *a priori* grounds for suggesting an association between changes in career planning and the social exclusive-ness of a given university setting. In particular, graduates with working-class backgrounds might more readily have absorb-ed middle-class evaluations of different kinds of work in a relatively exclusive setting in which they were able only to associate with men from other kinds of home. At the other extreme, in a less exclusive setting we might expect an intensification of the influence of their social background on graduates from working-class homes because these were reinforced by contacts with numerous others of a similar persuasion. Further, in the less exclusive settings we might even expect middle-class graduates to think more on the lines of, say, a teaching career if they had formed friendships with students from less privileged homes for whom this was an attractive possibility.

In the event, there was only very limited support for this argument, the trends being by no means wholly consistent (see Tables 30 and 39). Thus if we compare graduates of Oxbridge and Wales (which represent in turn the most and least socially exclusive university settings), it was apparent, first of all, that graduates from working-class backgrounds at Oxbridge had become particularly interested in management at the time of graduation. At the same time, however, their attitudes to professional employment became comparatively lukewarm and more of them actually opted for school teaching. Again, the evidence was inconclusive regarding the changes in aspirations among Oxbridge graduates from professional backgrounds, who might have been expected to become increasingly committed to the more prestigious careers. They did indeed, like their working-class peers, show a greater preference for management on graduation, but they also became more interested in school teaching: this, moreover, appeared to be at the expense of a career in the professions. So although there was some evidence to suggest that the attitudes of working-class graduates from Oxbridge became more akin to those of the middle class, whose preferences centred on higher-status careers, there were other tendencies which were not in accord with this 'social exclusivity thesis'.

Graduates from working-class backgrounds who attended the University of Wales did show marginally more concern for school teaching and relatively less interest in professional employment at the end of their first degree course. And yet it was for careers in research, development or production work outside a university (which, on balance, was looked upon favourably by working-class graduates) that interest diminished most among working-class graduates of Wales during the under-graduate period. In fact only the Welsh graduates from professional backgrounds demonstrated the full effects of the social exclusiveness thesis as outlined above, though their number was so small that even these data should be treated with some caution. Nevertheless these graduates did come to share in the patterns of aspiration more typical of the working-class students: they showed increasing commitment to school teaching and at the same time became less attracted both to management on the one hand and to professional employment on the other.

But all in all, the effects of higher education on our graduates' career aspirations were decidedly limited *whatever the university setting*. We found only slight and by no means entirely consistent support for the hypothesis that the social composition of univer-sities would have some part to play in the occupational aspira-tions of our sample at the time of graduation. Of far greater significance was the fact that the experience of a university education in no way mitigated underlying social class forces. One might reasonably ask why universities generally failed to provide a 'melting pot' environment where graduates were able to reshuffle their earlier career intentions and make their ultimate decisions after matching their aptitudes with the available opportunities in a more or less rational manner, and it is to this question that we now direct our attention.

We have already suggested that the direct influence of parents in the formulation of graduates' career plans may well decline as a consequence of the physical and often social separation between university and home life, a process generally far more marked at this time than in earlier periods of education, particularly among those who attended LEA schools. We have found, however, that social class factors were as pertinent in the choices of our graduate sample on graduating as on entry to university, and this suggests that certain other social pro-cesses were in operation which, on balance, tended to reinforce rather than to modify earlier parental influences. Joan Abbott has made one such attempt to demonstrate that a 'cultural gap' does in fact exist *within* the universities, as a consequence of social class divisions in the student body itself, which prevents the full assimilation and participation of students from working-class backgrounds into the activities of the middle-class student majority in any given university setting.[35] Basically, Abbott found that students appeared to feel class divisions were more blurred in universities but that they were present, nevertheless, operating in a latent manner but remaining a 'natural continuation' of the class divisions observable outside. This was particularly evident in friendship patterns and informal ties generally which tended to be, consciously or otherwise, formed along class lines. Thus undergraduates with given home circumstances tended to maintain close relationship with those from similar backgrounds, having little contact, except presumably in formal situations, with colleagues whose home environments were fundamentally different.[36]

Indeed in many ways the university environment offers considerable scope for the re-establishment of old class-based ties, particularly by undergraduates with working-class origins. In absolute terms, the number of such students in any given university is much greater than, say, the number in the sixth form of any grammar school, in which they might be subject to considerable pressure to take on middle-class norms. At university level there is scope for greater flexibility and tolerance of a wide variety of behaviour and attitudes and, at the same time, a fair-sized working-class minority in a comparatively large undergraduate body. Here, then, the socially mobile student from a working-class home has the opportunity of selecting friends whose attitudes and behaviour reflect those of his parents and friends at home.

Of course we would not wish to take this argument too far since, as we have noted, even graduates from manual working-class homes have absorbed some images and styles of life of the middle classes. But certainly their opportunities for establishing contacts with students similarly placed on the social border between these two classes were, if anything, considerably increased in the university context.

Now the same forces will presumably also push together students whose educational and social backgrounds were relatively privileged: those from, say, professional homes and independent schools would be just as likely as working-class students from State schools to prefer to establish patterns of friendship with those whose experiences and attitudes were broadly similar to their own. And, clearly, the net effect of these tendencies is, as we have seen, that the apparent influence of social background on job aspirations would appear in no way to diminish over the undergraduate period. Thus although the more conscious and direct effects of school and parents may decline in the university setting, they would appear to be reinforced in a more subtle way by the structure of informal contacts in the universities themselves.

The employment of graduates[37]

Social class factors can clearly operate in two distinct ways in so far as the employment of graduates is concerned. To begin with, as we have observed in some detail in the foregoing sections, family background, peer groups, school and university all play a part in shaping the 'level' and type of aspirations of particular graduates, effectively 'limiting' the horizons of those with less privileged circumstances while opening up the vision of 'highly prestigious' careers for the more fortunate. But there is another aspect to an analysis of graduate employment, that is, employers' perceptions of the capabilities of those who apply for openings in any given field.

Thus, in moving on to an examination of various aspects of graduates' careers we shall concentrate particularly on this second area and see that social class factors which, as we have already noted, profoundly shaped our graduates' aspirations, were once again by and large reinforced and indeed, in certain occupations, were clearly intensified during the process of selection itself. Moreover, these effects were most pronounced in the 'higher-status' fields of employment, with the result that certain professional occupations in particular were undoubtedly extremely socially exclusive.

These and other important findings will now be examined in relation to the actual employment of 1960 graduates six years after graduation, but once again a number of cautionary points are in order. First, we have no evidence to suggest, nor would we necessarily wish to imply, that there was any conscious bias on the part of employers against graduates from particular backgrounds. Rather, in so far as social class influences were discernible they were, we suggest, associated with subtle aspects of the socialization process as a result of which individuals reared in the same social circumstances come to speak the same 'class language'. Thus in the actual process of selection it seems likely that an applicant who by virtue of his upbringing shares many experiences and attitudes with his prospective employer would appear *to that employer* to be an attractive candidate. By the same token, it is clear that even those graduates from working-class backgrounds who decided, for one reason or another, to take up a particularly high-status career, would still find themselves up against a further hurdle when they actually came to compete with their more privileged contemporaries for places in these 'highly esteemed' fields of employment.

However, we would not only emphasize such elements as these in the selection of graduates for particular careers, but would also like to draw attention to other factors which complicate the arguments which follow. It will be recalled[38] that the graduate follow-up survey was instigated at the request of the Statistics Committee of the Secretaries of University Appointments Boards whose principal concern was to gather as much information as possible on the careers of graduates some years after graduation. In consequence, a very detailed record of employment was required in order to fulfil these more practical purposes of the investigation. At the same time, however, limitations of space prohibited the use of such detailed categories in the question concerned with occupational *aspirations*. As a result we were unable to make many direct comparisons between the aspirations of graduates and their eventual employment. But, on the positive side, as we shall see, the more detailed breakdown of actual employment did enable us to show that certain careers are extremely socially exclusive, which would have been impossible had we used a more general classification throughout.

It is worth mentioning, again, that we would not wish to overstate our main argument by implying that there were no other influences besides social class on our graduates' chances of embarking on specific careers. It is therefore appropriate to examine some of these influences before going on to observe the effect of social background *per se*.

Now taking the graduate body as a whole, advanced qualifications were undoubtedly an important key to many professional, managerial and executive positions. Almost all our graduates, indeed, obtained so-called middle-class occupations of this type: in fact, of the ten thousand men in this investigation, only two were actually engaged in manual work. Clearly, then, when we speak of the factors which influenced our graduates' chances of taking up particular occupations we are dealing with variations between work of a similar type, although not all careers were equally attractive to the most privileged, nor do they convey equal rewards in terms of power, privilege and remuneration. There was, however, a clear association between subject and class of degree and the employment of graduates as well as their aspirations. Thus a high class of degree was an essential prerequisite for a university career, while it came as no real surprise that arts graduates were unlikely to be working in industrial research but were particularly involved in teaching (see Tables 40 and 41). Scientists, by contrast, were more evenly spread between these sectors; and technologists, again not surprisingly, were highly likely to be in some form of industrial employment.

And yet it did appear that some forms of employment were relatively more 'open' than others, the 'more prestigious' fields being generally the most exclusive. Thus there seemed to be few barriers against entry to school teaching, for example, and as a result the vast majority of our sample who had thought in terms of such a career were able to achieve their ambitions. Again, those who sought employment in research, development or production work were generally fortunate in this regard, 65 per cent being engaged in posts such as these in 1966. University appointments, however, were much harder to obtain: only about half of the men who had wanted to work in a university setting were doing so six years after graduation. Moreover, many graduate men who had intended to take up other professional work failed to fulfil their ambitions; and among prospective managers the chances of success were even more limited, though in this instance, particularly, many of our graduates could well be successful later in their working lives.

Now the chances of obtaining work of a particular kind were undoubtedly dependent to a considerable degree on social background factors. To begin with, Table 42 shows the employment sector and type of work (in 1966) of graduates whose fathers were in upper non-manual, other grades of non-manual, or manual occupations at the time the respondents entered university. As expected, men with manual working fathers were particularly prone to be in the teaching profession while those from higher-status backgrounds were far more likely to be in commerce, private professional practice or managerial posts. Clearly these findings cause little surprise because, as we observed in our previous discussion, social background factors have a major influence on graduates' aspirations and, in consequence, a large number of men from working-class homes do not in fact compete with their contemporaries for employment outside education or industrial research.

On the other hand, we were able to make certain comparisons between the occupational plans of graduates and their achievements in most forms of employment six years after graduation, and these suggested that in the 'higher-status' sectors (the older professions and management) graduates from manual working backgrounds were actually *less successful competitors* than their colleagues from non-manual homes. Social class influences could not be solely attributed, then, to the large number of graduates who by the nature of their own aspirations excluded themselves from certain kinds of work. Thus whereas in Table 43 we see that the likelihood of graduates obtaining posts in school teaching or in the universities appeared to bear little relationship to social origins, graduates from working-class backgrounds who had thought in terms of a career in the other professions had something of the order of a 10 per cent poorer chance of realizing their ambitions than their colleagues from middle-class homes. And, in the administrative and managerial sector, their chances were even more slender by comparison with graduates from non-manual backgrounds though, oddly enough, those with the most privileged home circumstances appeared to compete somewhat less successfully than those whose fathers held intermediate or other grades of non-manual posts.

All in all, we were able to show that the influence of social origins on employment opportunities became even more marked when graduates actually came to seek specific careers. And whereas earlier on we observed certain class influences which substantially affected occupational choice, it was clear that social class played an important role in the achievement by graduates of their ambitions. On this occasion social class factors were reflected in the expectations of employers as regards a candidate's behaviour in interview and his suitability for a particular position. Again, we are not here intending to imply any conscious, calculative class bias on the part of employers; although clearly the long periods of training for certain professional qualifications together with, in one or two instances, an entry fee requirement, could have such an effect. But on the other hand entry into a university career, for example, also depends almost invariably on a substantial period of postgraduate training, yet in this instance, as we have noted, class factors would appear to have a negligible impact on the chances of graduates achieving their ambitions. The existence of a class differential in achievement of professional or managerial positions would appear to reflect the fact that graduates from upper-class homes had the advantage of understanding some of the 'cues' to social behaviour which would appeal to a prospective employer whose background was in many respects very similar to their own. Given a choice between two candidates with similar educational qualifications, then, an employer is likely to prefer the one whose attitudes are similar to his own and with whom, in consequence, social intercourse has been relatively easy.

Thus the net effect of social class on aspirations and the

achievement of ambitions as far as graduate employment is concerned was that certain kinds of work appeared to be extremely socially exclusive. Although in our sample as a whole, approximately one in four graduates came from working-class homes, very few of them came to hold positions in the legal profession, management or the administrative class of the Civil Service which were, by and large, filled by men whose families belonged to the upper middle (professional and intermediate) classes (Table 44). The legal profession was particularly socially exclusive – of our graduates employed here, about two-thirds had fathers with professional or intermediate status occupations and only one in ten had manual working fathers. On the face of it, the administrative class of the Civil Service appeared to be somewhat less socially exclusive: just under half of our graduates employed in this section had fathers in higher grade non-manual posts, while 14 per cent came from working-class homes. And yet if we examine further data in Table 45 it is clear that these graduates were recruited by and large only from certain types of university and were more likely to have been educated at independent schools compared with the graduate body as a whole. Now it will be recalled that the main university groupings could be ranked in terms of social composition and, on the basis of our data, it is clear that the most exclusive (Oxbridge, Scottish and London) were particularly well represented among graduates who obtained posts in the administrative class of the Civil Service. Indeed, nearly 90 per cent came from one or other of these more exclusive institutions, at the expense particularly of graduates from the Smaller or Larger Civic universities who made up 41 per cent of the graduate sample but only 7 per cent of those who took up employment in this field. Incidentally, it is also frequently considered that this key sector of British society by and large recruits only the most able university graduates, but on the basis of our evidence it was difficult to find unqualified support for this view. To be sure, relatively few of these graduates had unclassified degrees, but those who obtained firsts or upper seconds were by no means particularly over-represented.

And yet social exclusiveness was not confined to these

particular professional and managerial fields. There was clear evidence of social differentiation even within the educational sector itself, which, as we have seen, was generally the least socially exclusive field of employment. On the whole the universities appeared to be able to attract large numbers of graduates from professional or intermediate homes whereas the schools were by no means so successful (Table 46). And this is in spite of our previous evidence which suggested a lack of social class bias (either overt or covert) on the part of selection committees in the universities themselves. Thus it would appear that the academically able graduate from a professional or intermediate background will look favourably on a university career which, in his estimation, may even be on a par with employment in, say, the older professions. On the other hand, the less able graduate from a similar background is likely to shun his only real opportunity in education (that is, school teaching) in favour of other careers: hence the marked social class gradient within the educational sector as a whole.

That certain professions are for one reason or another particularly socially exclusive is of course by no means a novel finding. Indeed, in this respect our data supplement several previous studies, some of which we can discuss briefly at this juncture. Early work by one of the present authors showed a considerable measure of actual self-recruitment in a number of professions, as many as one in seven of entrants into teaching, medicine, the Church or law having had 'the advantage of being born into a doctor's, teacher's, minister's, advocate's or solicitor's family'.[39] Although we have no direct evidence on self-recruitment *per se* there are certainly strong grounds for asserting that a considerable measure of social exclusiveness is still characteristic of some of the older professions (such as law), though in respect of teaching there may have been certain long-term changes which merit further discussion.

Considerable light on the social composition of the teaching profession has of course been shed by Floud and Scott, who pointed out that, historically, this profession had always been attractive for the upwardly mobile working-class child.[40] However, although they found that among graduates 'the propensity

G

to teach is still somewhat stronger for those with a working-class background', in their view a change had recently occurred in the social class basis of recruitment involving the growth of interest in teaching among those from middle-class backgrounds which, if perpetuated, would 'mean a gradual transformation of the profession'.[41] Now we have no direct information on non-graduates, but in respect of our graduates it would appear that, if anything, there has been, over a course of time, an intensification of social class influences on the attractiveness of teaching as a profession, and this would appear to run counter to Floud and Scott's prediction. Table 47 contrasts the propensity of graduates from different social origins to enter school teaching. On the basis of our data, therefore, it would appear that school teaching, at least, has become increasingly attractive for the upwardly mobile graduate and the growth of the teaching profession as a whole seems in no way to have resulted in a modification of social class influences on recruitment. Once again, as far as graduates are concerned, those from middle-class homes would appear to have a propensity to shun teaching in favour of other professional, administrative or managerial employment (except, that is, for the most able who frequently set their sights on a university career). Of course we cannot tell whether middle-class children who have not been to university have become increasingly drawn by the prospect of a teaching career but, as we have noted elsewhere, among graduates it is clear that teaching has retained its appeal for those from more humble origins and, for better or worse, the more privileged graduate would still appear to regard it as a somewhat low status profession.[42]

Our findings on the relative social exclusiveness of particular professions also reinforce the view that the Higher Civil Service still recruits largely among graduates from upper-class homes who have attended the most prestigious educational institutions.[43] Again there appears to have been comparatively little change over time, since even the most recent annual report of the Civil Service Commission (for 1969)[44] shows that 47 per cent of open competition entrants in that year came from independent schools, while 71 per cent were graduates of

Oxford or Cambridge. Thus, on balance there would seem to be little doubt that, partly because of the aspirations of graduates with particular social origins, but also partly on account of the preferences and attitudes of the members of the particularly 'prestigious' professional and administrative bodies, recruitment into many key sections of employment depends considerably, but of course by no means entirely, on a number of social class factors.

We are, of course, aware of a wide variety of previous sociological studies which have shown the pervasiveness of social class in our culture and the almost infinite variety of social processes in which it can be seen to operate. Yet here we have observed the importance of social differentiation even between those who are ostensibly academic equals in the highest-ranking sector of education in our society. For the university graduates in this study clearly did not have equal opportunities in the world of work, even if they experienced an identical form of education and had performed equally well or badly. They were (aside from their qualifications) not part of a common culture, but had come up to university with attitudes profoundly influenced by their family backgrounds and these were in many cases reinforced and certainly not attenuated by the process of higher education itself. And when they came to seek employment in the particularly high-status sections, social class influences were reinforced by the images and preferences of prospective employers themselves.

Experiences at work

No study of graduate employment would be complete without some mention being made of the actual experience of graduates at work. After all, the prospect of a high-status occupation, free of a number of the more obvious alienating experiences of manual employment, exerts such a strong pressure on young people as to lead them to undergo long periods of study in schools and universities. Thus before concluding our remarks on the employment of graduates it is worth pausing to look more closely at our graduates' assessment of their actual working environments and, more specifically, the degree to which they considered certain desirable job attributes to be present in their particular occupational fields.

The following discussions are in no way intended to be a definitive statement of the actual satisfactions or otherwise of graduates at work, in spite of the considerable interest among sociologists in this area during the past few years. We have avoided this undertaking because the results of most studies aimed specifically at 'measuring' job satisfaction have by and large been disappointing: indeed, this field has become notorious for its methodological problems and pitfalls. The most important difficulty would appear to be the general inadequacy of survey methods for obtaining any worthwhile measure of satisfaction, largely on account of the unwillingness of respondents to threaten their own self-esteem by giving anything but the most superficial negative replies to any question concerning their experiences at work. For in societies in which status is so dependent on occupation, few will admit or even recognize major deficiencies in the quality of their work situation, for to do so would be in some measure to acknowledge one's own 'inadequacies'. As a result, sociologists have generally sought to overcome this problem by studying a number of behavioural rather than attitudinal indices of 'job satisfaction' or usually, more strictly, 'job dissatisfaction', such as absenteeism, job changes and labour turnover, sickness, accidents, strikes, suicides, and so on. Of course, many of these indices have been designed in the context of studies of the work experience of manual rather than professional workers, while again several have been deduced from certain theoretical propositions concerning the problem of alienation in contemporary industrial societies, and, as a result, are clearly of limited relevance in the present context.[45]

It would have been pretentious to suggest that we had been able to make a realistic appraisal of the 'job satisfaction' of graduates. Rather, we have restricted our effort to an analysis of our respondents' assessment of the extent to which certain job attributes were present in the posts they held at the time of the investigation. This then facilitated certain comparisons between different types of employment; but more importantly, since we derived our list of attributes from a previous study by Morton-Williams and others of final year undergraduates,[46] we were able to compare *undergraduates'* preferred patterns of job characteristics with the actual work experience of our own sample six years after graduation. The list of job attributes is as follows:

1. Congenial colleagues and working conditions (congenial work).
2. Good salary, security, prestige and promotion prospects (salary, security).
3. Opportunities for intellectual development and for increasing one's specialized knowledge (intellectual development).
4. Scope for initiative and freedom to develop one's own ideas (initiative).
5. Novelty and variety in employment (novelty).
6. Socially useful work dealing directly with people (social work).
7. High level administration and planning of operations (administration).
8. Work involving communication with people (other than social work), as in publishing, radio, etc. (communications).
9. Opportunities to rise to the top through one's own efforts (ambition).

It is important at the outset to explain the general nature of the material arising from the Morton-Williams study to which it is proposed to relate certain data from our own investigation. The Morton-Williams material was collected from a national sample of men and women undergraduates in their final year in faculties of pure science and arts/social studies at universities in England and Wales in 1963. In the course of each interview, the respondent was asked to complete a questionnaire touching on a number of aspects of career choice. First, he was asked to indicate on a seven point scale how much he would like or dislike to work for his main career in each of six fields of employment or settings. Secondly, he was asked to do the same thing in respect of work of five different types. Respondents were then asked to say, again on a seven point scale, how important each of thirty different possible career-choice factors was to them. In all, therefore, they were rating the importance to them of forty-one items. By means of factor analysis, these forty-one were grouped into nine clusters of factors in career choice, and the results were presented in terms of these nine.

As far as the undergraduates of 1963 are concerned, therefore, the Morton-Williams material shows, for each of two faculty groups by sex, and also for each 'preferred field of employment' group by sex, the importance they said they attached to each of these nine clusters of factors in choosing which job or career they would opt for, if available. The data represent the characteristics they said they were looking for and the relative weight they gave to each of them. The results are to be interpreted as showing what they thought they would like in their future work, rather than what, realistically, they expected to find.

So far as our graduates of 1960 are concerned, they were asked to make a realistic appraisal of the extent to which the jobs they held in 1966 did or did not possess each of these nine characteristics. What is being related in the analysis that follows, therefore, is the estimate of a group of graduates about the actual characteristics of the posts they held six years after graduation on the one hand, and on the other the expressed views of a younger group, in the final undergraduate year, regarding the features they thought at that time they would look for in their future work.[47]

In our earlier publication we mentioned that the list of nine job characteristics had been included in our questionnaire, respondents being asked to rate, on a three point scale, the degree to which they felt each of these characteristics was present in or absent from the posts they held in 1966.[48] Again, in that report we made certain comparisons between specific employment sectors on the basis of these job attributes. In the present study it is therefore appropriate to go somewhat further by first examining certain faculty differences between the wishes of the undergraduates involved in the Morton-Williams study and our own graduates' realistic appraisals at a later date; and second, by making similar comparisons within a number of different occupational fields irrespective of our respondents' faculties of origin.

Taking first variations among men according to faculty, it seemed that although there was some disjunction between undergraduate wishes and the graduate work experience of scientists, by and large the attributes in their work found by graduates in the humanities matched up reasonably well with the preferred job characteristic patterns of their undergraduate counterparts (see Figure 2.1). More specifically, although scientists found fewer opportunities for high level administration and planning than their undergraduate counterparts had wished, they nevertheless discovered that such characteristics as opportunities for communication, congenial colleagues, scope for initiative and novelty were present to a higher degree than undergraduates in the Morton-Williams survey were looking for. Graduates in the humanities, by contrast, found less scope for initiative and fewer opportunities for communication, but more variety, socially useful activities and high level adminis-tration. All in all, there was little evidence of any widespread gap between the wishes of undergraduates and the experience of graduates.

Moving on to a comparison between particular types of work, it was not surprising that the emphasis undergraduates of both sexes had placed on each aspect of a job varied with the type of career they had in mind. Prospective managers, for example, placed higher value on administrative responsibilities and a good salary than did those aspiring to a university career who, again not surprisingly, laid far greater stress on opportuni-ties for intellectual development. Figure 2.2 contrasts preferred patterns of job characteristics on the part of undergraduates who were planning to take up careers in a number of fields (schools and university teaching, management, social work and research outside universities)[49] with the ratings given by our 1960 graduates who were actually employed in each of these types of work at the time of the survey.

It will be seen, first of all, that school teachers apparently found their colleagues and working conditions much more congenial than the rating given to this factor by prospective

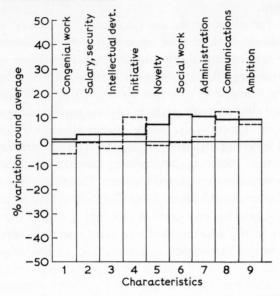

Arts and Social Studies

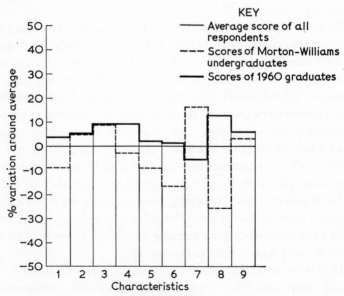

Science

KEY
— Average score of all respondents
--- Scores of Morton-Williams undergraduates
— Scores of 1960 graduates

Figure 2.1

teachers would have required. In some measure, too, both salary and the social utility of their work was also rated more highly by those who were actually working. On the other hand, there were a number of areas which were not quite so satisfactory, especially the administration and communication items together with promotion prospects. It may seem surprising that the salary item received such a high rating from our graduates in view of the recent evidence of militancy among teachers on the issue of pay. This could of course be a result of a more recent feeling that financial rewards from school teaching have declined relative to those in comparable professions. On the other hand, these well publicized complaints on the part of teachers may in large measure be the result of frustration with regard to a number of more intrinsic aspects of their work and the issue of pay a superficial rather than underlying source of their discontent.

The working conditions described by university teachers were different on most items from the preferred patterns of undergraduates hoping to take up academic work. In particular, congenial colleagues and working conditions together with scope for initiative were present to a much greater degree, while opportunities for high level administration and communication received relatively low ratings from the graduates. In many ways this accords with the image of the university setting which allows a considerable degree of freedom to develop intellectual interests in a congenial environment. On the other hand, the lack of opportunities for high level administration and planning might provide some clue to the increasing demands of junior staff, which have been evident recently, for a greater say in the running of departments and in participating in long-term planning decisions in universities generally.

The experience of those working in the universities in 1966 was in many ways remarkably similar to that of graduates who had taken up research careers outside universities. Although among undergraduates somewhat different preference patterns were observable (notably the greater emphasis of the latter on opportunities for high level administration and planning at the expense of the intellectual rewards of work), in the event the

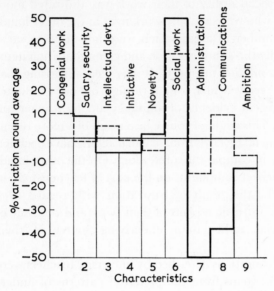

School teaching

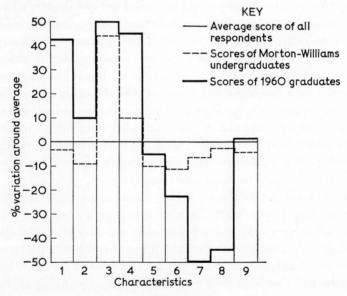

University teaching or research

KEY

—— Average score of all respondents

--- Scores of Morton-Williams undergraduates

—— Scores of 1960 graduates

Figure 2.2

University research

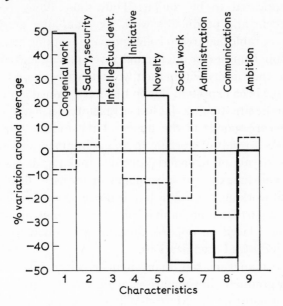

Management

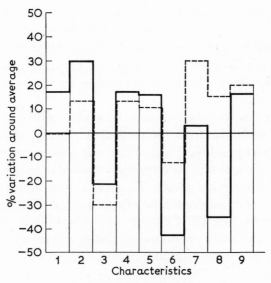

Figure 2.2 (continued)

respective advantages and disadvantages of the two environments appeared to be similar. Thus those doing research, development and production work six years after graduation found favourable features in colleagues and working conditions, salary, opportunities for intellectual development, and scope for initiative and variety within their work to a greater degree than might have been expected. But on the much valued administration item the situation was far less satisfactory. In many respects, too, this corresponds to the image of the industrial research worker. As a result of working in an environment cut off from the main stream of managerial decision making, he would appear to gain unexpected advantages in terms of flexible and congenial working conditions but at the same time suffers from the lack of participation in high level decision making and from limitations placed on opportunities for promotion to the key posts in industrial organizations.

Among managers, too, many items received higher ratings from our graduates in comparison again with the preferences of undergraduates in the Morton-Williams study. On the other hand, three particular items appeared to be present to a lesser degree; namely socially useful work, communications and, oddly enough, high level administration and planning itself. Opportunities for socially useful work were therefore less evident even than the very low level considered important by students; while it is not unexpected that, for junior managers at least, the opportunities for really high level planning are in practice somewhat limited.

In the main, the descriptions social workers gave of their jobs were not dissimilar from the preference patterns of potential recruits (see again Figure 2.2). There was, however, one significant exception, that is the apparently limited opportunities for communication with people. This was a little surprising for, on the face of it, we might have expected social workers to have a considerable amount of contact with others apart altogether from their case work commitments. But by comparison with the expressed needs of undergraduates, at least, this was apparently not the case.

We have examined, therefore, a number of aspects of our

graduates' experiences at work, and would wish to reiterate that it has not been our intention to attempt to say anything definitive on the issue of job satisfaction. Instead, we have identified a number of characteristics and compared the relative weight given to them, first by final year undergraduates thinking of

Social work

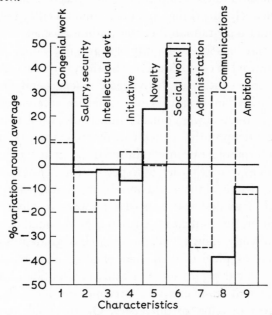

Figure 2.2 (continued)

future careers, and secondly by graduates of six years standing as being present or absent from the actual work on which they were currently engaged. In this way we have hoped to illustrate differing perceptions and evaluations of possible career attributes. In the light of the limitations of our study it would be unreasonable to go further into the complex and difficult field of job satisfaction and it is doubtful, in any case, whether such an exercise would be at all fruitful. By addressing our attention to a more limited, but nevertheless interesting comparison, we hope to have extended our knowledge of aspirations towards specific elements in careers without in any way attempting an infinitely more complex, and from our point of view, impossible task.

Conclusion

Our main aim in this chapter has been to trace some of the more important social influences upon patterns of graduate employment. By way of summarizing these influences we were able to demonstrate, above all, the profound effect of social class on the flow of graduates into particular fields of work.

It was scarcely surprising, first of all, that on entry to university we found our graduates' career ambitions shaped particularly by social class forces. Family background, school and university appeared to complement each other, with the result that graduates from the least 'privileged' backgrounds thought particularly in terms of careers in teaching or research, development and production work outside universities, while their more favoured contemporaries tended to aspire to employment in the established professions or in administrative or managerial work. These findings were regarded as a specific instance of the way in which 'knowledge' of the world and, by inference, perception of the possible and desirable in so far as work is concerned, is created within the context of particular class boundaries. Now we have already shown that working-class graduates in our sample were atypical of their class of origin as a whole, and indeed, we would regard some measure of adoption of middle-class norms and standards as a precondition for a successful school career or entry to university. On the other hand, we would also wish to emphasize, as we have done earlier, that this process of absorption is seldom absolute, with the result that degrees of privilege can still be recognized even among the most educationally successful. Nor did we consider that differences in aspirations could be traced to the varying ambitions of the members of particular classes. Rather we would regard ambition as a relative phenomenon, and on this basis would suggest that if anything it was the working-class rather than the middle-class graduate who was most ambitious, since the latter was only, by and large, consolidating his inherited class advantages. But in any case we would not regard the concept of ambition as being particularly valuable from a sociological point of view: of greater apparent significance are the characteristics of social environments which produce different perceptions of possible and desirable careers.

We then noticed that graduate aspirations changed little during the undergraduate years and certainly that the universities failed generally to provide a 'melting pot' environment in which students' career horizons could be significantly widened. Even if the more immediate influences of home and school declined, these were almost certainly replaced by the structure of students' informal contacts, which effectively reinforced earlier class images and resulted in the same broad class influences in graduates' aspirations being observable at both the beginning and the end of the undergraduate period.

Furthermore, these influences of social class were strengthened when graduates actually sought employment in particular fields. Thus in the instances of older professions and administrative and managerial work, graduates from working-class origins actually competed less successfully than their academic equals from more privileged homes. This does not of course imply any 'conspiracy theory' in the deployment of graduates, but it does suggest that the attitudes of employers in these key sectors are often themselves shaped by certain class perspectives which result in their finding graduates with similar backgrounds to their own slightly more acceptable candidates. And the end result is that the earlier effects of social background are re-affirmed at the point of entry to a particular career.

Sociologists have, of course, been aware for some time of the influence of social background factors on school performance, but here we have demonstrated that these factors still persist at university level and beyond. Indeed, one of the more ironic inferences which can be drawn from our findings is that the most important single destiny of the educationally *successful* working-class child, who has clearly overcome a number of earlier hurdles on the way to a university degree is, as a school teacher, to help prepare the sons of the middle class for those very positions to which, by virtue of his upbringing, he has by and large failed to obtain access.

Naturally these findings are a cause for some concern but we would not wish them to be interpreted simply as grist for the mill of the social reformer. Rather we would emphasize that in a country which relies so heavily on the effective deployment of human talent, it is essential that class factors, such as those we have observed, should be kept at a minimum not only on the grounds of social justice but also for the long-term national economic wellbeing. With this end in mind it would be appropriate, of course, to recommend more effective career guidance, particularly the provision of information about available opportunities, both in schools and universities. Clearly it would appear to be important that university appointments officers become more aware of their duty to awaken students to the wide range of careers open to them: at present it often appears that their responsibilities are largely confined to providing information, or otherwise helping the undergraduate, after he himself has decided upon a particular career.

But such piecemeal reforms, however worth while, are unlikely in our view to effect more than peripheral changes in the outlook of undergraduates themselves. And in any case, we would not regard a 'widening' of the horizons of working-class students as necessarily the most just or the most appropriate solution to the problem,[50] for we have seen that the attitudes of some employers are also in some measure determined by social factors. We would wish, therefore, for a two-way rather than a one-way process of 'education', so that certain established professional, administrative and managerial bodies might profitably examine their own attitudes and selection policies with a view to discovering ways of appealing to a wider social range of candidates who would be selected on the basis of their academic performance, aptitudes, and other rational criteria with the minimum regard for extraneous social considerations. Moreover, just as in another context[51] Jackson and Marsden have argued for changes in the social outlook of schools to make them more appealing to the working-class child, so we too would make a case for comparable changes in the professions and management, again not merely on the grounds of social justice but with a view to a more effective deployment of our available talent.

NOTES

1. A. I. Harris and R. Clausen, *Labour Mobility in Great Britain, 1953–63* (London, H.M.S.O., 1966); E. Ginzberg *et al.*, *Talent and Performance* (New York, Columbia University Press, 1964); S. R. Timperley and A. M. Gregory, 'Some factors affecting the career choice and career perceptions of Sixth Form school leavers', *Sociological Review*, vol. 19 (1971) 95–114.

2. H. L. Wilensky, 'Orderly careers and social participation: the impact of work history on social integration in the middle mass', *American Sociological Review*, vol. 26 (1961) 521–39.

3. W. H. Form and D. C. Miller, 'Occupational career patterns as a sociological instrument', *American Journal of Sociology*, vol. 54 (1949) 317–29; S. M. Lipset and F. T. Malm, 'First jobs and career patterns', *American Journal of Economics and Sociology*, vol. 14 (1955) 247–61.

4. J. R. Butler, *Occupational Choice* (London, H.M.S.O., 1968).

5. S. Cotgrove, 'Education and occupation', *British Journal of Sociology*, vol. 13 (1962) 33–42; A. Collin *et al.*, *The Arts Graduate in Industry* (London, Acton Society Trust, 1962).

6. J. R. Butler, *Occupational Choice*.

7. As defined by, among others, A. Inkeles and P. H. Rossi, 'National comparisons of occupational prestige', *American Journal of Sociology*, vol. 61 (1956) 329–39.

8. E. Ginzberg *et al.*, *Occupational Choice: an Approach to a General Theory* (New York, Columbia University Press, 1951) 29.

9. In particular P. L. Berger and T. Luckmann, *The Social Construction of Reality* (London, Allen Lane, The Penguin Press, 1967).

10. M. L. Kohn, 'Social class and parent–child relationships: an interpretation', *American Journal of Sociology*, vol. 68 (1963) 471–80. The quotation cited is from p. 471.

11. T. Shibutani, 'Reference groups as perspectives', in H. H. Hyman and E. Singer (eds.), *Readings in Reference Group Theory and Research* (New York, Free Press, 1968) 103–13. See p. 106.

12. For evidence, see the works cited in note 43 to Chapter 1.

13. R. H. Turner, 'Some family determinants of ambition', *Sociology and Social Research*, vol. 46 (1962) 397–411. The quotation is from p. 397.

14. A. H. Halsey, 'Education and mobility', in T. R. Fyvel (ed.), *The Frontiers of Sociology* (London, Routledge, 1968) 1–12. See p. 9.

15. B. Jackson and D. Marsden, *Education and the Working Class* (London, Routledge, 1962) 97.

16. D. F. Swift, 'Social class and achievement motivation', *Educational Research*, vol. 8 (1966) 83–95. See p. 83.

17. J. A. Kahl, 'Educational and occupational aspirations of "Common Man" boys', *Harvard Educational Review*, vol. 23 (1953) 186–203.

H

18. See also R. Hoggart, *The Uses of Literacy* (London, Chatto and Windus, 1957) Chapter 5.

19. D. F. Swift, 'Social class, mobility-ideology and 11-plus success', *British Journal of Sociology*, vol. 18 (1967) 165–86.

20. G. Knupfer, 'Portrait of an underdog', *Public Opinion Quarterly*, vol. 11 (1947) 103–14.

21. B. C. Rosen, 'The achievement syndrome: a psychocultural dimension of social stratification', *American Sociological Review*, vol. 21 (1956) 203–11; H. H. Hyman, 'The value systems of different classes: a social psychological contribution to the analysis of stratification', in R. Bendix and S. M. Lipset (eds.), *Class, Status and Power* (Glencoe, Free Press, 1953) 426–42; A. Davis, *Social Class Influences upon Learning* (Cambridge, Mass., Harvard University Press, 1948); S. M. Lipset and R. Bendix, *Social Mobility in Industrial Society* (Berkeley, University of California Press, 1959); C. W. Mills, *White Collar* (New York, Oxford University Press, 1951); J. R. Butler, *Occupational Choice*.

22. B. C. Rosen, 'The achievement syndrome . . .', *op. cit.*, 211.

23. S. M. Lipset and R. Bendix, *Social Mobility in Industrial Society*, 286–7.

24. C. W. Mills, *White Collar*, 259.

25. J. R. Butler, *Occupational Choice*, 9–10.

26. S. Keller and M. Zavalloni, 'Ambition and social class: a respecification', *Social Forces*, vol. 43 (1965) 58–70.

27. Floud and Halsey have suggested that 'education is a process of cultural assimilation through the reconstruction of personalities previously conditioned by class or race'. See A. H. Halsey *et al.* (eds.), *Education, Economy and Society* (Glencoe, Free Press, 1961) 8.

28. Committee on Higher Education, *Higher Education* (London, H.M.S.O., 1963); R. Morton-Williams *et al.*, *Undergraduates' Attitudes to School Teaching as a Career* (London, H.M.S.O., 1966).

29. E. Ginzberg *et al.*, *Occupational Choice*. . . .

30. *Ibid.*, 29.

31. R. Morton-Williams *et al.*, *Undergraduates' Attitudes to School Teaching*. . . .

32. For an explanation of the method used for comparing the increase or decrease in popularity of each type of employment, see J. A. Davis, *Undergraduate Career Decisions* (Chicago, Aldine Publishing Co., 1964).

33. S. Cotgrove, 'Education and occupation', *op. cit.*

34. There was in fact a very slight but not significant *negative* relationship between father's social class and the attraction of a university career (see Table 39).

35. J. Abbott, 'Students' social class in three Northern universities', *British Journal of Sociology*, vol. 16 (1965) 206–19.

36. This underlines Jackson and Marsden's description, in *Education and the Working Class*, of the frustration experienced by working-class university students in contact with ex-public schoolboys, and the result

that such students tended to bunch together in groups from similar backgrounds (p. 147).

37. Much of the data from the present survey pertaining to the patterns of graduate employment have been discussed in detail in an earlier publication. We are therefore concerned here to draw attention to certain influences which underlie those findings rather than to elaborate on the more detailed patterns themselves of graduate employment. See R. K. Kelsall *et al.*, *Six Years After* (Sheffield University, Department of Sociological Studies, Higher Education Research Unit, 1970) Chapters 4, 5 and 6.

38. See p. 9.

39. R. K. Kelsall, 'Self-recruitment in four professions', in D. V. Glass (ed.), *Social Mobility in Britain* (London, Routledge, 1954) 308–20. The quotation is taken from p. 317.

40. J. Floud and W. Scott, 'Recruitment to teaching in England and Wales', in A. H. Halsey *et al.* (eds.), *Education, Economy and Society*, 527–44.

41. *Ibid.*, 539.

42. A more detailed version of this argument appears in R. K. Kelsall *et al.*, 'Still a low status profession', *Times Educational Supplement*, 4 December 1970, 4.

43. The extent to which the administrative class had always tended to be recruited from a narrow range of school and university types and from certain kinds of social background is fully discussed in R. K. Kelsall, *Higher Civil Servants in Britain* (London, Routledge, 1955).

44. Civil Service Commission, *Annual Report, 1969* (London, H.M.S.O., 1970).

45. See, for instance, R. Blauner, *Alienation and Freedom* (Chicago, University Press, 1954).

46. R. Morton-Williams *et al.*, *Undergraduates' Attitudes to School Teaching.* . . . Comparison of the Morton-Williams methodology and findings with American investigations of career choice is made in R. K. Kelsall and H. M. Kelsall, *The School Teacher in England and the United States* (Oxford, Pergamon Press, 1969) Chapter 6.

47. Morton-Williams' interviews were restricted to undergraduates in arts, social science and pure science faculties. For comparative purposes the following discussion also only refers to graduates in those faculties. An average, by faculty and by type of employment, was computed for our data by means of the 'net score' method as a measure of central tendency, since we did not have individual scores from which to calculate a median, which Morton-Williams was able to do. The net score was calculated by subtracting the percentage of respondents saying that the characteristic in question was hardly present at all in their work from those saying it was present to a high degree (ignoring those in the middle who said it was present to a moderate degree): for the graduate data, therefore, variations from the average by subject and industry are

expressed in terms of percentage variations from the net score for that subject or industry.

48. R. K. Kelsall *et al.*, *Six Years After*, Chapter 5.

49. These fields were among those isolated in Morton-Williams' investigation for which comparable data were available from the present survey.

50. Marris makes a similar point: 'why should we want to influence the social behaviour of students and to "indoctrinate" them with the cultural conventions of an elite?'. P. Marris, *The Experience of Higher Education* (London, Routledge, 1964) 119.

51. B. Jackson and D. Marsden, *Education and the Working Class*, Chapter 6.

Chapter Three

SEX, MARRIAGE AND CHILDREN

At the time when our graduates took part in the national follow-up survey, they were all at least twenty-seven years old and had therefore reached a stage in their lives at which most people are married and have started families of their own. Their prolonged full-time education will undoubtedly have militated against marriage and family building during their adolescent years and probably also for some time afterwards, but nevertheless, with the ever-increasing popularity of marriage nowadays it is unlikely to be the case that substantial numbers of university graduates will remain unmarried and childless. Such an observation has profound implications, particularly as regards women graduates; for they will no longer be expected to remain single and devote their whole lives to professional careers, which means that if the abilities of highly educated women are sought after outside the home as well as valued within it, graduate women might either elect to remain childless or alternatively to have only a few children and in a very short space of time, in order to remain in their chosen careers for as much of their working lives as possible. The extent to which this in fact happens remains to be seen in the light of the findings discussed in Chapter 4.

It is unlikely that the repercussions for men graduates of any demographic changes we may observe will be quite so far reaching as this. Marriage and family building must beyond doubt affect the quality of men's lives, but they do not in general change the whole pattern of their existence. However, the fertility of highly educated men and women such as our respondents is of itself an important question, it being well known that the children of professional people are, due to various factors in their environments, more likely than any others to go to a university and to enter professional types of work themselves (as in fact we have shown in Chapter 2). In short, the fertility of today's graduates must, rightly or wrongly, crucially affect the supply of the next generation of professional people.

Clearly, by 1 October 1966, when they had taken their first degrees only six years earlier, few of the married graduates would have completed their families of procreation – even if they had started them. In a sense, therefore, the following discussion is limited by insufficient data, although measures of fertility other than family size have been introduced, and our own findings are also presented in the light of other, more substantive, data on the subject.

Marriages

By six years after their graduation the majority of our graduates were married – a finding which reflects the upward trend in the popularity of marriage during this century among young people in all walks of life[1] – although our respondents were at this point in time somewhat less likely to be married than were people in general in their age group (Table 48), a fact explicable in terms not only of their lengthy exposure to full-time education but also of their relatively high social status, interrelated attributes which are independently associated with the postponement of marriage.[2] However, by the time they were eight years out of university, 85 per cent of the male graduates had married, a figure now exceeding the national proportion for men, while on the other hand the women graduates were still markedly less likely to be married than women of their age in general.[3]

The median time of marriage for men was two years after graduation, and for women, three years after. This, taken together with the fact that in comparison with young women in general in their age group women graduates showed a somewhat low propensity to marry, suggests that these highly educated women were more susceptible than their male counterparts to the delaying effect on marriage of continued full-time education. This is perhaps not surprising in view of the still commonly held notion that for women, marriage and higher education are mutually exclusive: but now that many of the formal obstacles in the way of marriage for the highly educated woman have disappeared – dismissal of women teachers and civil servants on marriage, for instance – we should not be surprised to find that as many as seven in ten of the women who obtained university degrees in 1960 were nevertheless married only six years after graduating. The day of the 'blue-stocking' who, it was held, would rarely have had either the inclination or the opportunity to marry, is very definitely past. Any career obstacles in the way of married women graduates tend now to be covert and not explicitly written into employees' conditions of service, as they once were.

The suggestion that education is a very important factor in the delay of respondents' marriages may be investigated by making control for the continuation or otherwise of full-time study beyond graduation, a strategy which should reveal the extent to which the propensity to marry and the timing of marriage is affected by this variable as well as by the under-graduate study which postponed the marriages of all but 3 per cent of our graduates. Exposure to postgraduate education very plainly has a universal effect on both the propensity to marry and the timing of marriage (Table 49); undoubtedly at least in part because of financial and normative constraints on marriage whilst still a full-time student (only a very few people – twelve women and seventy-six men – had married before coming up to university). It is, of course, also probable that graduates who saw little opportunity or had little desire to marry in the near future would be more likely than others to embark on some form of postgraduate study. In particular, young women who tend to be 'career-oriented' rather than 'home-oriented' (if one can legitimately separate orientations in this way) might well feel the need for a postgraduate qualification while not necessarily counting on finding a suitable husband, and indeed the effect on marriage of postgraduate study is very obviously much stronger for women than it is for men.

Nevertheless, it remains true that women graduates are on the whole more likely to marry, and to do so earlier, than ever before. One needs only to compare Kelsall's findings relating to the marriages of three cohorts of trained graduate women teachers[4] with our own data on the subject (Table 50), to see that over the last thirty years or so there has been a sharp upswing in the popularity of marriage and a greatly increased tendency among these particular women to marry early, a trend which is echoed nationally and thus very probably also by the rest of our graduates, both men and women. This general trend is related to the fact that in younger age groups men now outnumber women, while in the earlier decades of this century there were 'surpluses' of women in all age groups, a fact which, strangely enough, has had some effect on the propensity of men, as well as of women, to marry.

Having established if and when our graduates had married, it remains to ask what kind of partners they chose. Social and educational homogamy is a feature of industrial societies – people tend to choose marriage partners with broadly similar social and educational backgrounds to themselves, and where there are exceptions to this rule, men are more likely to marry 'down' than are women.[5] However, when looking at the marriages of graduates from this point of view, the question of availability should first be considered, since for every woman who graduates there are at present about three men, which plainly signifies that not all graduate men are in a position themselves to marry graduates. If men graduates tend to marry 'down' educationally, it should be remembered that this must be in part a result of the relative shortage of women with university degrees. This proviso does not of course obtain where social class is concerned, and we should expect that in a large proportion of our graduates' marriages the partners would be of similar adult social status, and that where there has been *class* heterogamy there will be agreement in educational level. Table 51 shows that it is indeed the case that graduates marry people similar to themselves in status: six out of ten male respondents had formed unions homogamous in this respect, while as many as nine out of ten of the women had done so, a sex difference in line with expectation. Most of the wives of the men who had married 'down' were in routine white collar occupations when they married. Very few of either the men or the women had married manual workers, despite the fact that about a fifth of these people had themselves come from working-class homes: this would indicate that social origin is of much less significance to the question of class homogamy than is adult social class, a proposition which has already been examined in detail in an earlier chapter.[6]

The education of our respondents will naturally have been of crucial importance to their adult social status, which would suggest that educational homogamy is likely to be a prominent feature of this group of men and women. Each respondent was asked whether his or her marriage partner had had any full-time education since leaving school, and if so, of what type. In 44 per cent of all marriages there was agreement in educational level (that is, both partners had been to a university) but such agreement was far more frequent where married *women* respondents were concerned, as Table 52 indicates. This sex difference is once more in line with expectation, since there are anyway fewer women than men with degrees: however, as many as three-quarters of men respondents' wives had undergone some form of full-time further education, usually a technical, art or teacher training if not a university education, and nearly 90 per cent of the husbands of women graduates were in this position, the majority of these men being, of course, university graduates.

The marriages entered into by 1960 graduates were therefore to people in many ways similar to themselves, and our findings make it abundantly clear that in choosing their marriage partners, the decisive factors were educational level and, in consequence, achieved social class, and that for all graduates, including the upwardly socially mobile, marriage therefore served as a means of consolidating their adult status.[7] However, it is perhaps necessary to be careful not to make our respondents' choice of mates appear too calculated and deliberate, since much of this process is of course an unplanned result of the relational aspect of social class: people are likely to conduct the peer group relationships perceived by them as most salient with people broadly similar to themselves socially, educationally, and in consequence attitudinally, and our graduates are not likely to be any exception to this fundamental sociological principle. In fact, an examination of the characteristics of those graduates who, by marrying manual workers, *did* diverge from this principle is itself most revealing. Among men, marrying 'down' in this way is less unusual than among women, and the ninety-eight graduate women who had formed this kind of union (Table 70) had several interesting features: they tended themselves to be of working-class origin (Table 9), and were slightly more likely than the rest to have married before or during their university courses, both of which findings clearly have implications for the relational aspect of their choices of marriage partners. Moreover, women with manual husbands were rather more likely than other married women graduates to have conceived their first children before marriage, an eventuality which introduces an accidental element into the situation, although the fact that people who conceive children premaritally are usually in some degree emotionally involved with each other means that the relational aspect of such unions cannot be completely set aside.

Families

Graduates' patterns of marriage and their choice of marriage partners have certain implications for their subsequent family building, the most obvious being that the increasing popularity of marriage means that larger proportions of graduates than ever are 'at risk' as far as having children is concerned – because more graduates marry, more are likely to become parents. This prospect is reinforced by the trend to earlier marriage – for the proportion of the childbearing years that women graduates and

the wives of men graduates spend in marriage will be increased –
again augmenting the probability of conceptions. These two
'push' factors to increased fertility among married graduates
may be at least partially offset by the effects of birth control,
which is almost universally employed by people of high status
for spacing births and limiting the size of families.[8]

It is difficult to advance many firm conclusions from our own
data about the fertility of graduates, since in 1966 few respondents had been married longer than six years, so that such
families as they had would more often than not have been still
incomplete at the time of the survey. But it may be possible to
cast some light on the sociological aspects and determinants of
fertility by examining such relevant data as we were able to
collect, particularly those relating to the 5938 men and women
among our graduates who had married and started their
families by 1 October 1966.

An important question in this context is how the graduates
timed the arrival of their first children, an event which, in the
light of the findings discussed below, would seem to have been
fairly deliberately planned by a substantial proportion of them,
at least when premarital conception had not taken place.

The largest single group of graduates with children had had
their first child between one and two years after marrying, although the average intervals between marriage and first birth
(Table 53) indicate that women graduates tended to delay
starting their families rather longer than men, a finding which
echoes their propensity to marry later and to be in general more
susceptible than men to delays to marriage arising from continued exposure to higher education. A plausible explanation
for this rather interesting fact lies in women's – and particularly
highly educated women's – conceptions of their role as mothers
and workers, for these two identities are commonly seen as in
some degree mutually incompatible. Thus for a woman engaged
in work which is salient to her self image to retire even temporarily from employment, as most in fact do when a baby
arrives, is an important step, and a passage from one phase of the
life-cycle to the next involving a disjunction which few men
embarking on parenthood ever experience. This must be so

even though, as we have found, at this stage in their lives few women graduates with children invest their work roles with greater significance than they do their roles as wives and mothers.

That one in eight or nine of the marriages of our graduates was 'precipitated' by the conception of a child is on the face of it rather surprising in the light of the tendency of middle-class people to practise birth control as a matter of course. Indeed, in comparing these figures with Pierce's, which relate to couples married during the 1950s,[9] it would appear that the incidence of premarital conceptions among our graduates was relatively high. Pierce shows that of marriages of non-manual brides aged between twenty and twenty-four, 4·5 per cent were precipitated, and that when such brides were aged twenty-five or over, 5·7 per cent of the marriages were precipitated, while our figure of 11 per cent or so is approximately double both these incidences. However, it is important to bear in mind here the sudden increased freedom and mixing of the sexes which takes place once young people have left school and home and entered university, and also the fact that respondents tended to postpone marriage until after their full-time education was finished, which even in comparison with other young people in non-manual types of occupations was at a relatively late age: nearly all of these men and women, because they married after graduating, must have been at least twenty-one at marriage. Pierce's data show that the premarital conception 'boom' in fact occurred for non-manual women under the age of twenty, more than a quarter of whose marriages were precipitated. It seems, then, that because higher education must have forced many graduates to defer or limit sexual gratification while they were undergraduates, this boom occurred for them at a later age, that is, when they became reasonably free to marry.

When first births were not the outcome of premarital conceptions, it is clear that their timing was much affected by the duration of full-time education: respondents undertaking long-term postgraduate study commitments, particularly if they married soon after their first graduation, put off the arrival of the first child longer than did those who had short-term commitments or none at all. Men and women who undertook studies for doctorates tended to be less likely to have children or if they did, to have their first child later than the Dip.Ed. holders, who in their turn waited longer than those who had undertaken no postgraduate study or training of any kind (Table 54). That the differences between these groups are less marked among the men and women who married more than three years after first graduating is undoubtedly because for the majority of this group postgraduate studies would have come to an end before they married, along with the normative and financial constraints to family building that such studies as a rule bring about.

The net result of the various factors delaying marriage and family building for highly educated men and women is that by October 1966, the time of the survey, when our graduates were nearly all between twenty-seven and thirty years old – ages at which most young people are well into the 'procreation' phase of the life cycle[10] – more than one-third of those who were married still had no children at all,[11] and of those who did very few had more than two. Only five graduates – four men and one woman – had as many as five children.

These observations are, of course, echoed in the average numbers of children born to married graduates by October 1966 – 1·00 to the men, and 0·99 to the women – and also in the finding that six in every ten *first* children were born during or after 1964.[12] These averages compare with the mean of 1·45 children born to all married women between the ages of twenty-five and twenty-nine in 1961,[13] the discrepancy at this stage being at least in part due to our graduates' relatively late ages at marriage, for we find not surprisingly that the longer gradu-ates had been married, the more children they tended to have (Table 55). Although the average numbers of children born to women graduates and to the wives of men graduates were very similar overall, when control is made for time of marriage, in two out of three cases women had on average fewer children than men, and in the third case the averages were identical. This finding is consistent with others already discussed, and it now appears beyond doubt that women graduates are more

susceptible than men to the delaying effect on marriage and
first childbirth of continued full-time education at both undergraduate and postgraduate levels, and that this important sex
difference is very probably due to the conflict or disjunction
between women's roles at home and at work. The arrival of a
child is much more decisive in this connection to a woman than
it is to a man, and especially to a woman who values her work
to some extent.

However, in spite of all this, the fact that highly educated
people are more likely to marry and to do so earlier than ever
before should by no means be understressed when the fertility
of our graduates is compared with that of people of their age in
general, whose marriages and subsequent family building have
not normally been subject to the delays and constraints to which
all recipients of university education are subject in their late
teens and early twenties. Evidence from outside in fact suggests
that the completed family sizes of our graduates will probably
be comparable with, or even larger than, those of many other
groups in the population, but that, because of the various
delaying factors in operation here, their children will tend to be
born rather later in their lives.

The social class 'V-effect' in fertility first noted by David
Glass and Eugene Grebenik in the 1946 Family Census is by
now well known to sociologists and demographers, and has been
discussed more fully elsewhere by one of the present authors.[14]
That there is a reversal in the negative relationship between
social class and fertility at the top end of the social scale is also
suggested by the findings of a national study of three cohorts of
women teachers. In marriages of completed fertility, women
who had embarked on careers in teaching after obtaining postgraduate diplomas in education had on average larger families
for all marriage ages than non-graduate women who had taken
the (then) two-year training course.[15] The 1961 Census returns
also show a direct relationship between fertility and educational
level at the top end of the social scale. Table 56 presents the
mean *complete* family sizes of women married, as were the vast
majority of our married graduates, under the age of twenty-
nine, and shows that the 'highest fertility fell to those couples in

which *both* partners had been in full-time education up to and beyond the age of twenty'.[16] The average completed family of 2·07 children to husbands and wives whose full-time education, like that of all of our graduates and of the majority of their marriage partners, ceased after their twentieth birthdays, is larger than the completed families in all 'socio-economic groups' except manual workers and self-employed professionals.[17] These findings are also in line with those of a small survey of women graduates undertaken by Judith Hubback.[18]

It has in fact been discovered – perhaps unexpectedly – that completed fertility appears to be very closely related to married couples' fertility *intentions*, and that the relationship between intentions and performance is particularly close in the case of high-status people, among whom birth control is in widespread and effective use.[19] The study by Michael Fogarty and his associates of a subsample of our own respondents eight years after they had obtained their first degrees, shows that the married graduates wanted an average of approximately 2·43 children, and that at the time of the survey they had 'on the whole . . . (kept) the family size to the desired level',[20] their average fertility at that time being around 2·46. Both these figures plainly represent relatively high intended and actual fertility, and the additional fact that a group of young men and women who graduated in 1967 said they wanted an average of 2·74 children[21] would add further evidence for the proposition that university graduates are a very fertile group within the middle class, and moreover may even suggest the possibility of an upward trend in such people's fertility.

Despite the fact that graduates tended to postpone marriage and family building until a relatively late age, to a time, that is, when all their educational commitments were at an end, they were still more likely to marry, and to marry earlier, than graduates have ever done before: and although the families of those of them who were married six years after graduation – if indeed they had started families – were still relatively small, it is to be expected that their completed fertility will be high compared with that of others in non-manual occupations. Although there is no lack of data in support of the view that highly educated members of the community are more fertile than other members of the middle class, this fact is perhaps contrary to popular belief which tends to associate large families exclusively with poverty or low status. It is clear, nevertheless, that unless this trend is reversed in the future we can expect our graduates, in spite of their slow start, eventually to catch up with or even to overtake a large number of their less highly educated contemporaries in the family building race.

From what is generally known about the class-related nature of fertility, it could reasonably be inferred that graduates' social backgrounds may be exerting some effect on their own family building patterns. Probably any such effect will be residual, not only because the respondents' marriage partners are themselves overwhelmingly middle class, but more significantly because selective secondary and higher education with their middle-class atmosphere will have at least partially 'resocialized' people of non-middle-class origin to typically middle-class norms, values and behaviour patterns, and many upwardly mobile graduates will in any case have already undergone some anticipatory socialization in this direction in their own homes.[22] The similarities between graduates of varying social origins, at least on these demographic dimensions where a fairly large element of voluntariness is involved, will therefore probably tend to outweigh any differences between them. Indeed, it is already clear that social origin has very little, if any, effect on graduates' choice of marriage partners (Table 9), and that the relationship between social origin and timing of marriage is not very clear cut (Table 11). Other influences arising from their common experiences of higher education intervene here and exert a similar effect on all graduates, regardless of social background.

The timing of the birth of the first child to married graduates is also, as we have shown, subject to postponement due to continued exposure to higher education, so that any differences on this count according to social origin are also likely to be attenuated or even altogether eliminated. This in fact is what Perrucci discovered, but on the other hand, some research by Tien adduces significant support for the hypothesis that upward social mobility is associated with a *longer* interval between marriage and first birth.[23] Our own findings on this count are not quite so clear, however, for despite the fact that the upwardly mobile graduates were consistently less likely than the intergenerationally stable to have any children, in three cases out of four (Table 57) they had nevertheless started families on average rather sooner after getting married. This apparent inconsistency is perhaps most economically explained in terms of Duncan's suggestion that 'a mobile couple's fertility will be a sum of the fertilities of the classes of origin and of destination'.[24]

Because men and women with postgraduate qualifications tended to marry rather later than those with none (see Table 49), the fact that graduates with no such qualifications generally waited longer after marriage to have their first children does not run counter to the proposition that the duration of full-time education is an important determinant of family building patterns, but merely indicates that education exerts its influence here mainly through the timing of graduates' marriages and their tendency to *start* families. Although there are some differences between mobile and stable graduates as regards propensity to have children and timing of first births, these differences are not unilinear, and therefore Tien's hypothesis associating social mobility with postponement of family building is not borne out by the findings of the present survey. On the other hand, the continued exposure to higher education still remains the most important factor indirectly influencing the family building patterns of all university graduates.

Since there is no very clear relationship of any order between graduates' social backgrounds and the timing of either their marriages or the births of their first children, any obvious regression to class gradients of fertility on the part of graduates of different social origins is not to be expected, especially at this early stage in their married lives. In other words, men and women from working-class homes are unlikely to be more fertile than those of higher-status origins; and indeed the picture so far is one of substantial similarity between graduates of all social backgrounds (Table 58). However, the data do point to a very slight re-emergence of the familiar 'V-effect', graduates

I

with routine white collar backgrounds showing relatively low average fertility together with small standard deviations. Whether this small difference will disappear or become accentuated over the years is something about which it is interesting to speculate but impossible to predict: but as far as present evidence shows, the observed pattern here, as with the other demographic patterns discussed, is on the whole one of similarity, there being few consistent social background differences as far as marriage and family building are concerned. It would appear, therefore, that our graduates have in these respects 'formed into a homogeneous group, irrespective of social origin, with behaviour patterns and conventions of its own'.[25]

But are they completely homogeneous? The differences in graduates' fertility according to their social origins are negligible, it is true, but there may very well be significant variations along other important social dimensions. Throughout all our investigations we have seen that graduates' adult environments, whatever their earlier ones, exert considerable direct influence on their present behaviour, which would suggest that there may be a relationship between fertility and *achieved* social class of the type apparent in the class/fertility 'V-effect' repeatedly observed over the past twenty years or so. It will be remembered that high-status professional people are more fertile than men and women in other types of non-manual occupations, particularly routine white collar workers. Although the graduates are very much concentrated at one end of the social scale, they can in fact be separated into the three non-manual classes, and it is evident that when this is done no consistent relationship between class and average family size had emerged by October 1966 (Table 59). This may well be because of the probable relationship between type and length of postgraduate study and subsequent social class, which would explain the unexpectedly low fertility of the professional group in terms of delays to marriage and family building resulting from prolonged study. Because of the complication of the influence of postgraduate study on achieved social class, perhaps the figures given for the average intervals between marriage and first birth may be more indicative of substantive fertility, although this too is not totally free from the effects of continued education, as we discovered earlier. However, the table does make it clear that there is a consistent relationship here of the expected order, in that graduates in professional types of occupations waited a shorter time to have their first children than did those in intermediate non-manual work, who in their turn did not wait as long as those in routine white collar work. The discrepancy between the classes is particularly noticeable among the women graduates, whose fertility in terms of family size was also much influenced by the social classes of their husbands: compared with other women undergraduates, those married to men in routine non-manual occupations were considerably more likely to have one child only or to have no children at all.[26] It would seem, therefore, that although our graduates had barely embarked upon their family building by 1966, their completed family sizes may well ultimately show discrepancies of the type predicted by the 'V-effect' hypothesis.

Social class as we have chosen operationally to define it in this book – that is, in accordance with the Registrar-General's categories for the 1961 Census – is by no means the only salient social dimension along which the fertility of different groups of university graduates may be compared. Indeed, it has certain drawbacks arising on the whole from the fact that the vast majority of our respondents are in the 'top' two or three social classes, while most of the general population, to whom the Registrar-General's classification is intended to apply, are in the remaining manual groups. It may therefore be more fruitful in this particular instance to look at groups of graduates differentiated along dimensions other than social class as defined by the Registrar-General. For instance, when 'professional' is defined as including all graduates in our own 'Work' category called 'Professional Functions',[27] we find that professional men had on average 1·02 children, born 14·84 months after marriage. This makes them appear more fertile in the one respect and less so in the other than the professionals in Table 59, simply because of this shift in definition. The inevitable question of which is the better definition has of course no absolute answer, but here it is probably the case that if a comparison between social classes is not the over-riding prerequisite, a definition which, like our own, specifically relates to the characteristics of the sample or population in question, is preferable. For this reason, the term 'professional' will from now on mean: falling within the 'Professional Functions' category of our own 'Work' classification.

Self-employed professional men have been found to be a very fertile group within the high-status universe of professional work: the 1961 Census, for example, shows that their average complete family size was as high as 2·09, while the corresponding average for professional employees was only 1·83, and for managers of large establishments 1·82.[28] Our own investigations on this count again encounter the obstacle that respondents' families were still incomplete at the time of the survey, so that there was at this time no difference in average family size between professional employees and self-employed professionals (Table 60). However, looking at the interval between marriage and first birth, an indicator of fertility which, for the reasons discussed above, is perhaps more reliable at this stage in our graduates' lives, we find that the self-employed professionals had their first children on average nearly a month and a half earlier than the professional employees. Although it is impossible to predict whether or not this difference will result in larger completed families for the self-employed professional men, it does indicate a greater readiness on their part to embark upon the family building process, and it is most interesting to speculate upon the possible causes of such a phenomenon. Geoffrey Hawthorn suggests several lines of explanation, including the possibility that because the income of self-employed professionals is considerably higher than that of others of similar age and education, such people can afford to have more children. Other explanations point to the high opportunity costs in not working suffered by highly educated wives, and to a possible inefficiency in contraceptive practice due to a greater sense of personal security arising from high income and status. However, as Hawthorn himself points out, these are no more than speculations, and 'simple socio-economic status/fertility associations can only specify questions and not provide answers'.[29]

In spite of the very manifest difficulties attached to any attempt at sociological explanations of differential fertility, other fertility variations along 'socio-economic' dimensions may be interesting to examine in their own right, even if no adequate and plausible explanation for them can be advanced. According to both the measures used here there is a clear negative gradient in fertility from engineers through to men in commerce, and from the academic profession to school teachers (Table 61). This gradient could be explained in terms of differences between the groups in graduate education experience, for as we have seen, delay in family building is positively related to the duration of full-time education or training. However, if this were wholly the case, school teachers, for instance, would be more fertile than university teachers, which they plainly are not. The unexpectedly low fertility of school teachers in fact appears to be a further manifestation of the 'unproductive clerk' syndrome, connected in some way perhaps with their predominantly working- and lower middle-class origins,[30] but more likely the outcome of their present social positions.

The relatively high fertility of engineers is an interesting phenomenon which may in some way be related to their isolation at university from members of the opposite sex, for few women take applied science degrees. This is likely to have repercussions not only on their choice of marriage partners – their lack of contact with women undergraduates means that their brides must usually be chosen from outside the university – but also upon their attitudes towards women in general: engineers may be less prone than other graduates to regard women as their intellectual and physical equals. The conception of women as inferiors is well known to be widespread among working-class men, and it is perhaps significant that men from working-class homes were over-represented among graduates in applied science subjects (see Table 21). The 'tough' and sex-segregated nature of the work of engineers, even that of many graduate engineers, will tend to reinforce this type of attitude towards women, which in extreme cases takes on the nature of the masculine cult of 'machismo'. Machismo is manifested partly in loose conjugal ties and lack of contact between fathers and families, but most importantly in the desire of men to demonstrate their virility by having large numbers of children. It is not, of course, suggested that graduate engineers conform exactly to this ideal type (which is a feature of the so-called 'culture of poverty', a lifestyle in fact of very poorly educated people[31]) but it may well be that the engineers, by virtue of their backgrounds and their experiences at university and in their subsequent jobs, are more likely than any other men graduates to subscribe in some degree to the machismo ideology, a proposition which would explain their relatively high fertility. The rather high fertility of the men who were in commerce in 1966 can by no means be explained in these terms, but is perhaps connected with the self-employed status and secure financial position of many of them: some possible explanations for the high fertility of self-employed professionals have already been suggested above. However, the fact that different explanations have had to be put forward for essentially similar demographic phenomena demonstrates just how difficult it is to attempt a causal sociological analysis of fertility.

Conclusion

At this particular stage in our respondents' lives – six years after their first graduation, when most of them were still under thirty – their behaviour as far as marriage and family building is concerned was on the whole remarkably homogeneous. They married after graduating – that is, somewhat later than most other people of their age; they chose partners broadly similar to themselves in both social class and educational background; and they tended to delay starting their families until after their postgraduate studies, if any, were over and they were embarked on their various careers. Many of the married graduates were still childless six years after graduating, and even those who did have children rarely had more than one or two. But in spite of this overall appearance of similarity, there do emerge certain variations in fertility among the graduates even at this early stage in their married lives. Although differences according to graduates' social origins are not clear, there are more consistent variations in their fertility according to their adult social classes and the types of work they were doing at the time of the survey, self-employed professional men standing out as being more fertile than professional employees, while school teachers, on the other hand, had on average fewer children and delayed the first birth longer than did members of several other occupational groups, in spite of their relatively short postgraduate training – if indeed they underwent any such training at all.[32]

It is significant that throughout all our investigations into the fertility of university graduates, there have emerged certain consistent differences between men and women respondents, differences which can be summed up in the statement that women graduates are considerably more susceptible than men to the delaying effects on marriage and family building of the continued exposure to higher education. The explanation for this is not hard to find, lying as it does at the very heart of the question of the status and role of women in our society. Because of what is expected of women, and the highly educated are no exception, the combination of a career with marriage (and particularly with having children) is not easily managed, and on the arrival of the first child, the majority of women graduates retire from work. If a woman has undergone a lengthy and advanced education culminating in a career which offers her a relatively high degree of personal satisfaction, it is not surprising that she will tend to delay the moment of leaving that career, albeit temporarily, as most women graduates appear to feel they should do in order to look after their children (see Table 75).

There are several factors at work in this situation which influence the marriage and fertility patterns of graduates of both sexes. The most outstanding, and the one which we have had cause to refer to again and again, is the fact that their continued exposure to full-time education has been a crucial influence in this respect on *all* graduates, regardless of other factors in their backgrounds and careers. For most of them, marriage was delayed for several years beyond the national average age, and family building was usually postponed until all full-time education, undergraduate or postgraduate, had ceased.

The notion that people do not marry and have children whilst they are still full-time students has of course attained the status of conventional wisdom, and our findings on this count will therefore surprise nobody. However, there are very sound historical precedents for this pattern of behaviour, for in the Middle Ages and later, scholars were invariably members of Holy Orders and therefore celibate, and their lives were meant to be devoted wholly to the pursuit of learning.[33] As recently as the nineteenth century, the ancient universities were very closely tied to the Established Church, and even to this day, the tradition of the celibate scholar still survives to some extent at Oxford and Cambridge, and dons in all types of universities are often popularly considered to be not quite men of the world. To the extent that universities are taking on more worldly and vocational functions, this tradition will probably tend to die out, but in spite of external changes it still remains in the commonly observed principle that an undergraduate does not marry.

This principle seems to override all other influences to which graduates are subject, even if such influences are in conflict with it. Taking social background as an instance, it is clear that the middle-class tendency to postpone marriage is well in line with the 'celibacy' principle: but in the working class people marry young, a tendency which plainly conflicts with it. However, we have seen that graduates of working-class origin are no less likely than their middle-class counterparts to postpone marriage and family building until after their full-time education is at an end. There are, as we have said, variations in marriage and family building patterns among graduates, but these variations take place when marriage and family building takes place, that is after graduation, which means that the 'celibacy' principle is invariably adhered to. It is significant, though, that the disjunction between learning and the world seems to be sharper for women than for men graduates, so that women tend to delay marriage and the more decisive step of family building longer than men. For them, perhaps, the conflict between scholarship and the world has become the conflict of home and work.

NOTES

1. E. Grebenik and G. Rowntree, 'Factors associated with the age at marriage in Great Britain', *Proceedings of the Royal Society (B)*, vol. 159 (1963) 178–98; General Register Office, *Census 1961 (England and Wales)* (London, H.M.S.O., 1966) Summary, Table 6.

2. E. Grebenik and G. Rowntree, *ibid.*; C. C. Perrucci, 'Social origins, mobility patterns and fertility', *American Sociological Review*, vol. 32 (1967) 615–25.

3. The data quoted in this and the following chapter relating to graduates eight years out of university are taken from a study by M. Fogarty *et al.*, *Sex, Career and Family* (London, Allen and Unwin, 1971). In June 1968, Michael Fogarty, Rhona Rapoport and Robert Rapoport, working for Political and Economic Planning in collaboration with the Tavistock Institute Human Resources Centre, sent questionnaires to a sample of 1071 of our own respondents and received replies from 865 men and women (a response rate of 81 per cent). Their sample was designed to have a greater than representative proportion of women graduates, but otherwise it compares closely in various major respects with the larger group of 1960 graduates who took part in the present survey (see *ibid.*, 554–6).

4. R. K. Kelsall, *Women and Teaching* (London, H.M.S.O., 1963).

5. D. V. Glass (ed.), *Social Mobility in Britain* (London, Routledge, 1954) Chapter 12.

6. See pp. 36–7.

7. B. Jackson and D. Marsden make this point in *Education and the Working Class* (London, Routledge, 1962) 38.

8. R. M. Pierce and G. Rowntree, 'Birth control in Britain', *Population Studies*, vol. 15 (1961) 121–60. Of all informants married between 1950 and 1960, nearly 80 per cent of non-manual couples had at some time used birth control (*ibid.*, 147).

9. R. M. Pierce, 'Marriage in the 'fifties', *Sociological Review*, vol. 11 (1963) 215–40.

10. See C. Rosser and C. Harris, *The Family and Social Change* (London, Routledge, 1965) 165.

11. R. K. Kelsall *et al.*, *Six Years After* (Sheffield University, Department of Sociological Studies, Higher Education Research Unit, 1970) 14, Table 2.10.

12. *Ibid.*, 14, Table 2.9.

13. General Register Office, *Census 1961*, Fertility tables.

14. R. K. Kelsall, *Population* (London, Longmans, 1967) 54–5.

15. R. K. Kelsall, *Women and Teaching*, 42, Table 13.

16. G. Hawthorn, *The Sociology of Fertility* (London, Collier–Macmillan, 1970) 102.

17. General Register Office, *Census 1961*, Fertility tables, Table 14. All the census figures referred to in this chapter are calculated from the returns relating to women married under the age of twenty-nine whose marriages had lasted twenty years or longer.

18. J. Hubback, 'The fertility of graduate women', *Eugenics Review*, vol. 47 (1955) 107–13.

19. G. Hawthorn and J. Busfield, *Some Social Determinants of Family Size: Report of a Pilot Study* (Unpublished, University of Essex, 1968) 4 and 33–4.

20. M. Fogarty *et al.*, *Sex, Career and Family*, 247. The figures are calculated from data presented in Table vii.4, 248.

21. M. Fogarty *et al.*, *Preliminary Report on Sample Survey of 1967 University Graduates* (Unpublished, Political and Economic Planning, 1968) 31.

22. See p. 51.

23. C. C. Perrucci, 'Social origins, mobility patterns and fertility', *op. cit.*; H. Y. Tien, 'The social mobility/fertility hypothesis reconsidered: an empirical study', *American Sociological Review*, vol. 26 (1961) 247–57.

24. See G. Hawthorn and J. Busfield, *Some Social Determinants of Family Size*, 20; and also O. D. Duncan, 'Methodological issues in analysis of social mobility', in N. J. Smelser and S. M. Lipset (eds.), *Social Structure and Mobility in Economic Development* (London, Routledge, 1966) 90–95; J. Berent, 'Fertility and social mobility', *Population Studies*, vol. 5 (1952) 244–60. However, recent research has cast a certain amount of doubt on this proposition, while not actually discrediting it: see, for instance, K. Hope, *Social Mobility and Fertility* (Unpublished, Nuffield Social Mobility Project, 1970).

25. W. Scott, 'Fertility and social mobility among teachers', *Population Studies*, vol. 11 (1958) 251–61.

26. R. K. Kelsall *et al.*, *Six Years After*, 85, Table 7.7.

27. *Ibid.*, 101–2.

28. General Register Office, *Census 1961*, Fertility tables, Table 14.

29. G. Hawthorn, *The Sociology of Fertility*, 85.

30. J. Floud and W. Scott, 'Recruitment to teaching in England and Wales', in A. H. Halsey *et al.*, (eds.), *Education, Economy and Society* (Glencoe, Free Press, 1961) 527–44; R. K. Kelsall *et al.*, 'Still a low status profession', *Times Educational Supplement*, 4 December 1970, 4.

31. See, for instance, N. Dennis *et al.*, *Coal is our Life* (London, Eyre and Spottiswoode, 1956); M. Kerr, *The People of Ship Street* (London, Routledge, 1958). 'Machismo' comes from a Spanish word meaning manly or virile.

32. Twenty-two per cent of graduates teaching in schools held no qualification other than a first degree, which explains any apparent discrepancy between the fertility of school teachers (Table 61) and of Dip.Ed. holders (Table 57).

33. Chaucer's clerk

> 'Ne was so worldly for to have offyce
> For him was lever have at his beddes heed
> Twenty bokes, clad in blake or reed,
> Of Aristotle and his philosophye,
> Than robes, riche, or fithele, or gay sautrye'.
>
> (*The Prologue*, lines 292–6.)

Chapter Four

CAPTIVES BY CHOICE?

. . . Can we ever make young girls and women make real
use of the opportunities that do exist, really make an
issue of equal rights . . . ? [1]

Throughout this study we have been reminded of major social
impediments to the educational and occupational performance
of highly educated men and women. In our second chapter,
for instance, we demonstrated that even among men roughly
equal in terms of measured ability, career aspirations and
experiences varied consistently with social circumstances, with
the result that men from working-class homes were far more
likely to become school teachers than were their colleagues
from more privileged backgrounds, and they were found to be
correspondingly under-represented in the older professions or
in administrative and managerial employment. This led us to
question whether the community was in fact making the most
effective use of its available talent, even among the most highly
educated.

From the evidence on women graduates we are again left
in little doubt that human resources are being most ineffect-
ively used; for highly educated women are, far more than their
male counterparts, greatly restricted in their occupational
achievements by prevailing conditions which bear little relation to their training and capabilities. In the following pages,
therefore, we propose to indicate some of the social conditions
and particularly the ideological climate which give rise to this
situation and which, incidentally, result in few graduate

women being found in the older professions, in management or in any so-called 'high-status' career.[2] Further, we shall see that social class, marital status and the arrival of children each had a limiting effect on the career opportunities of our sample of women. On the other hand, the women themselves appeared to be relatively satisfied with this state of affairs, as a result (as we hope to show) of their acceptance of prevailing attitudes about the 'place' of women in contemporary society.

Our discussion of the status and employment of graduate women begins by an examination of the influence of social class on the aspirations and careers of our female sample. This will then be followed by an account of the effects of both marriage and childbearing on women's employment. Further, in this later analysis, although we shall once more address our attention to social class influences (measured this time, however, in terms of husband's rather than father's occupation) we intend to demonstrate that the ascriptive roles which women had to perform supplemented and, indeed, by and large overshadowed, class influences themselves. In other words, although from one view sex and class are impediments to graduates' achievements and are symptomatic of a more common social problem, from a narrower perspective we would regard sex as having a more significant influence than social class in so far as the employment of women is concerned.

Of course, this is not to deny the importance of social status in shaping the early aspirations and employment of graduate women. Not surprisingly, first of all, women graduates were found to be highly unrepresentative, in terms of social class, of the population of women as a whole. Thus, as many as 67 per cent of the women in the sample of 1960 graduates had fathers in non-manual occupations (Table 1) and even those whose fathers were manual workers had many social characteristics in common with those from higher-status homes, and were atypical of their own class (see Chapter 1). There were, nevertheless, some interesting variations both in attitudes and in behaviour, between women from different social backgrounds towards their studies and careers. The general lack of interest in the vocational rewards of a university degree, for instance, was more marked among women from middle-class than from working-class homes (Table 62), though in any case only a minority of women would have put work completely out of their minds at this time. Indeed, many of our graduates recalled having had an occupation in view when they entered university, several years before employment became inevitable, and although many delayed coming to a firm decision until later and many more changed their minds, it is unlikely that graduates were oblivious of their future work lives; it was rather that they were considering using experiences at university to broaden their knowledge of possible jobs while at the same time coming to grips with their own abilities and aptitudes.

We have seen, however, that social background set certain limits on the career aspirations of graduate men (see Chapter 2). In Table 63, two effects on *women's* attitudes are clear. First, low social origins predisposed an early occupational orientation, for as many as 55 per cent of the daughters of manual workers had a career in mind on going up to university compared with only 48 per cent of those who came from the highest social class. The second significant finding here is that although more than 40 per cent of the women as a whole had a preference for school teaching, this propensity was particularly marked among those from working-class homes, among whom no less than two-thirds with an occupation in mind planned to become teachers and indeed showed little interest in other kinds of work. Again, the comparative disinclination seen here of the graduate from a high-status home to want to take up school teaching is clearly common to both men and women (Tables 30 and 63) and is once more almost certainly a reflection of their low evaluation of school teaching compared with other occupations. For the man or woman from humble home circumstances, on the other hand, school teaching still represents a high-status career and remains a principal channel for upward social mobility.[3] Nevertheless, compared with men, women graduates of whatever social class found school teaching very attractive; after graduation, indeed, between 44 and 63 per cent of all the women stated a clear preference for this work. It is not surprising therefore that when asked about postgraduate study plans, 70 per cent of the women who reported having had such plans were considering a teacher training course. Clearly, then, sex supplemented the influence of social class on the likelihood of graduates thinking in terms of a teaching career; with the result that women generally were far more prone to be attracted by teaching whatever their social origins than their male colleagues with similar aptitudes and levels of educational performance.

Turning more specifically to postgraduate studies, again certain class influences were observable which are worth mentioning. Women with fathers of professional or inter- mediate status were more likely than their colleagues as a whole to have taken a form of professional training (other than teaching) or a course of study which had not resulted in a specific formal qualification (Table 64). Nevertheless, bearing in mind what has been said above about the propensity of women generally to think in terms of, and indeed to take up a career in, teaching, it was scarcely surprising that as many as *one-third* of these high-status graduate women still opted for courses leading to a teaching diploma, compared with only 12 per cent of men with similar backgrounds to their own. As regards reasons for further study, it was noticeable that rather more of the women from non-manual homes gave expressive reasons such as 'a desire for more study for its own sake' than did other women, but in the main instrumental attitudes pre- vailed: indeed, between 54 and 65 per cent of women saw their postgraduate study as preparation for work (Table 65). This kind of orientation, incidentally, stands in marked contrast to their attitudes towards *undergraduate* study, where self develop- ment was the keynote and the intrinsic interest in particular subjects of great importance. At postgraduate level, however, involvement in a subject was rarely mentioned. Clearly, on leaving school, at eighteen plus, the problems of earning a living, marriage, and family responsibilities were for this group of people at a minimum, and they were free to think of the ways in which they personally wanted to develop. But on graduation the situation was rather different, and the decision to postpone earnings for the purpose of study at this time would have been at the expense of preparation for the more or less imminent social responsibilities of adulthood and particularly, of course, marriage. Hence there was a decline in interest in self development at the expense of courses which would be of more immediate benefit to their proposed careers.

It appears, moreover, that the effects of social origins on the attitude of women to study and employment can be regarded as less marked than for men *because of the intense concern of women from all backgrounds for marriage and children.* The highly educated woman is increasingly likely to marry, and to marry at a relatively early age, compared with previous generations of graduates – indeed growing proportions of students are even marrying before their undergraduate studies are completed, a trend which serves as 'insistent pressure' on others to take a similar step.[4]

Now the possibility of marriage (and as we shall see the married state itself) forms a major barrier to women taking up a career commensurate with their talents. In the first instance, apart from the instrumental nature of their interest in post-graduate study the most usual course for women is, as we have seen, a teacher training diploma. Much of the popularity of this training rests on the fact that it takes a relatively short time to complete compared with that required by the elite professions, and so minimizes the time devoted to acquiring vocational training at the expense of a delayed marriage.[5] And indeed most women did in fact put their training to use early on by taking up school teaching, as many as 61 per cent of all women graduates actually working in the education sector in their first post (Table 66). In fact the proportion of women who took up school teaching exceeded the proportion (55 per cent) who had expressed a desire to teach after hearing their finals results (Table 63). As a result, few women were engaged in any other sectors of employment, and were especially unlikely to be in industry or the professions. Again, even when they were employed in these other sectors, there were differences in the types of employment taken up by men and women. For instance, of graduates working in the public service sector, more women than men were in the hospital service (27 per cent compared with 3 per cent) and in libraries, art galleries and museums (12 per cent compared with 3 per cent). Conversely, more men than women were likely to have been in the Civil Service as scientific officers (12 per cent compared with 3 per cent), in public utilities (19 per cent compared with 2 per cent) or working as local government officers (30 per cent compared with 20 per cent). Such differences between the sexes occurred to a greater or lesser extent within all the sectors of employment and remained even when the effect on career of subject studied was taken into account.[6]

But these differences in the career patterns of men and women graduates were even more profound six years after graduation, for by this time only 56 per cent of women were in any gainful employment at all, or, in other words, nearly half were engaged solely in domestic activities. At the same time those still in paid employment were even more solidly bunched in the education sector: indeed, very few at this stage were employed outside teaching, social work or scientific research (see Table 66). In absolute numbers, for example, only four were engaged in production, fifteen in the legal profession, twenty-two in commerce and thirty-six in general management. These data of course confirm that women's talents are being significantly under-utilized in contemporary Britain, and provide further empirical support for the demands for a change in our social structure to prevent such a gross waste of human abilities. For these figures not only reflect a loss to the community of the contribution of highly educated women, but surely in some measure too point to the personal frustration of at least some women who find their interests thwarted by prevailing economic and social conditions.

As we have suggested, women also seemed to be restricted to certain kinds of work according to their social origins, for few women from working-class homes took up employment outside teaching. Those from higher-status homes, by contrast, were more likely to have found professional openings elsewhere. This is vividly demonstrated in Table 67, which shows the women graduates' last work (which could have been at any time up to 1 October 1966) according to social background.

K

Here we see that while 73 per cent of the daughters of manual workers were in professional work (notably teaching) this applied to rather fewer (59 per cent) of those from professional homes, 13 per cent of whom were in 'other' kinds of work, including publishing, journalism and broadcasting. To some graduates these are particularly attractive kinds of employment, offering rather more in the way of glamour and variety than most others. That middle-class graduates of either sex are rather more likely to be in these, and to have a greater breadth of professional experience, serves to demonstrate once more the impact of social class on career achievements (see Chapter 2).

But whereas in the case of our male graduates variations in career opportunities could be accounted for particularly in class terms (see Chapter 2), among women marital status had further profound consequences for their occupational achievements. This is not to deny, of course, the influence of social class in shaping the outlook of women, but it is to assert that these influences were supplemented and, indeed, in most instances substantially modified by ascriptive sex roles themselves. To be sure, degrees of privilege could be observed among women of different backgrounds which affected their career choices and opportunities, but of greater significance was the substantial degree of disadvantage that married women as a whole were observed to suffer from in comparison not only with their academic equals of the opposite sex but also in relation to graduate women who had remained unmarried. In view of this it was scarcely surprising that married women graduates, who made up 70 per cent of our sample of women, were much less likely than women as a whole to be in employment in 1966 (Table 68) and, secondly, that those who were married and still working were much more prone than other working women to be school teachers (Table 69). These data again help to show just how ascriptive sex roles would appear to influence considerably both the chances of women being in employment and the type of work they actually undertake.

It was of interest, too, that the patterns of marriage of our women graduates were essentially homogamous in nature. Few had married men who were not themselves graduates, and fewer still had husbands who were manual workers (see Tables 51 and 52). These findings also had implications for the employment patterns of women graduates, since the vast majority were able to rely on their husband's income to provide a reasonable standard of living for their families, and this in turn fostered specific attitudes towards employment. It was noticeable, first of all, that the small number of women who married men in low status work were far more likely than women graduates generally to be in paid employment and to give financial reasons for working (see Tables 70, 71 and 72).[7] But on the whole graduate women would appear to have had less pressing financial reasons for working and, indeed, by the very nature of their work, had more opportunities for interesting and responsible activities than women in the population as a whole. As a result women graduates, and particularly those whose husbands were in highly paid work, were often able to give expressive reasons, such as mental stimulus, for having (or wanting) a paid job (Tables 73 and 74) and, indeed, were likely to spend more time in employment than married women in general.[8]

Marital status, then, had a major impact on the chances of women working, their type of work and, depending on their husband's financial circumstances, the way they were able to approach employment itself. But the arrival of a child had an even more marked effect upon their chances of being in employment at all. At the time of the survey most married graduate women (62 per cent) had at least one child (see Chapter 3) and, as a consequence of this, a mere 26 per cent of mothers had a paid job six years after graduation.[9]

By and large our women appeared to adapt to and indeed to prefer the prospect of looking after their children in spite of the fact that, because so many were able to rely on their husbands to provide an adequate standard of living, it was quite possible for them to take up employment for intrinsic rather than extrinsic reasons. And again, by virtue of being graduates there was no real prospect of their obtaining only poorly paid or extremely uninteresting work. Thus their choice of a domestic and maternal role cannot be accounted for in terms of the

marked unattractiveness of the alternatives which would presumably be the case for the vast majority of women who have
no high level skills whatsoever. Rather, in order to account for
their choice, and indeed, as we shall see, their generally
favourable attitudes towards a maternal role, we have to look
more at their assimilation of a broad set of attitudes towards
motherhood and domesticity generally. In short, we have to
examine the influence of an ideology about the 'place of
women' in home and society. This ideology, indeed, is so
pervasive that a woman's positive appraisal of her domestic
role has rapidly become conventional and statistically normal
among graduate women generally, and this in turn, more
than anything else, helps to explain the major impact of childbirth on the work participation of graduate women in contemporary Britain.

That such an ideology has major repercussions on women's,
and indeed on highly educated women's, assessment of the
respective advantages of domestic and occupational roles is of
course by no means a new discovery. In this respect our data
merely supplement a number of studies which have purported
to, and have indeed actually shown, that so far as 'Western'
women are concerned, their greatest aim in life is to be a 'good'
parent and in consequence they are 'decidedly familistic in
their values'.[10] A very recent study of 1967 graduates showed,
for instance, that 73 per cent of women expected family relationships to give them their greatest satisfaction in life, while
only 12 per cent expected such rewards from their careers.
Incidentally, this study further reveals that the majority of
graduate men (53 per cent) also saw the family as their prime
source of satisfaction although, not surprisingly, a higher
percentage than among women (30 per cent) expected this to
come from their career.[11] This emphasis of both men and
women on the home as their primary source of satisfaction has
further significance as we shall suggest, for it implies that some
greater interchangeability of domestic and career roles between
married partners could in certain instances be welcomed by
both parties. But in respect of women generally, and highly
educated ones in particular, the vast majority undoubtedly

perceive their lives to be dominated by having children and looking after a home. This is not to say, of course, that paid work has no place in the life plans of graduate wives and mothers – indeed on present trends it would appear that the higher the level of education received the more likely a woman is to be at work – but it is to suggest that for the most part our women will perceive work to be of secondary, and family of primary, significance to them. And this order of priorities, of course, acts as a major barrier to the full use of their high level educational qualifications in some form of gainful employment.

Not surprisingly, the varying preferences of women generally for particular aspects of their lives has been expressed more formally in conceptual terms. The majority of women, it would appear, and this includes our sample of graduates, accord to what Dahlstrom[12] has called the 'moderate' conception of the role of women which has elsewhere been described as the 'three phase' or 'conventional' model.[13] This is a popular half-way house between two extremes. It ostensibly avoids the pitfalls of, on the one hand, the conservative position which idealizes a family system in which the wife devotes herself exclusively to her home, her husband being her sole means of support; but, on the other hand, it rejects many of the alternatives of the 'radicals' who would wish to see a redistribution of work within the family, so that tasks previously assigned to the wife are assumed and shared by the husband jointly so that the wife can have a more equal responsibility for earning the family's living.[14] The people who take an 'intermediate' position in this debate,[15] *though not necessarily an intermediate position if all possible distributions of work are taken into account,* thus aim to effect ways and means by which women can participate in work while continuing many of their traditional obligations at home. They accept that children need security and a regular way of life, and interpret this to mean that the child's physical mother must always be at hand when needed (and should not work outside the home when the child is very young), but they also recognize the valuable contribution which women can make in outside work once children are at school and such participation should, they feel, be encouraged by the provision of appropriate domestic help, community facilities, etc.

The so-called moderate ideology is indeed the most common one held by highly educated women in contemporary Britain. It was expressed particularly by a group of 1967 graduates who planned, on the whole, to work until they had children, drop out completely while their children were very young, return to work part time when their children were at primary school and then seek full time employment when their children reached secondary school or adulthood.[16] Now our own sample of women were particularly interesting in this respect since they were actually at the family building stage of their lives at the time of the investigation. During this period and consistent with the expectations of the later cohort of graduates, the majority (three-quarters of mothers, 60 per cent of the sample) had given up paid work to look after their children (Table 75), and having no paid employment were therefore more or less wholly dependent on their husband's income. There is little doubt, however, that the majority of graduate women perceived this to be a temporary phase and that they hoped to be engaged in some form of paid work alongside their familial obligations for a considerable part of their future lives.[17]

And yet the so-called 'moderate' ideology, however ostensibly reasonable in principle, appears to have more far-reaching consequences for our graduate women's employment than at first sight appears obvious. In fact it would seem to imply that the obligations of women as mothers are not, as so many women think likely, confined to a comparatively short period of full-time domesticity, but actually circumscribe their whole working lives in a number of important ways. Furthermore, unless there are substantial changes in the nature of 'high-status' careers, which on the face of it seems improbable, or employers outside teaching are prepared to adapt their working environments to facilitate female participation or, again, there is a major reshuffling of domestic duties between husband and wife, the moderate ideology seems to us to imply the permanent relegation of women to 'second-rate' careers, or certainly to ensure that it will be almost impossible for them to compete successfully with men in 'high-ranking' occupations.

In the first place, any combination of work and home which requires a woman to opt out completely from paid work, even for perhaps only six or seven years, is largely inconsistent with success in many 'high-status' occupations. For these years are important for selection and appraisal within a career structure, while at the same time the rapidly changing state of knowledge in these fields makes it difficult even for those who remain to keep up, let alone those who return.[18] Moreover, the preservation of the traditional responsibilities of women in the home puts an almost intolerable strain on those women who do take up professional employment, even when their children are at school.[19] Of course many wives of middle-class men employ other women to help with their domestic chores; indeed, while about half the working women paid for such assistance, so did one in five of the women who were fully occupied at home, a sign perhaps of the relative affluence of their husbands (Table 76), but this barely scratches the surface of the problem.

Again, the second main implication of the moderate ideology as far as women's employment is concerned is that whenever there is any conflict between domestic and work responsibilities, it is consistent with this ideology as well as with the overall emphasis of women on obtaining their prime satisfaction from the home, that the career will always take second place. What happens is that women seek types of employment which are best adjusted to the possible strain of combining their home duties with those of any paid activities. And this is precisely why, in spite of certain important social class variations, the prospect of a career in teaching appeals so strongly to women generally, since no other occupation is so clearly adapted to their domestic duties. Yet even in teaching, of course, women compete far less successfully than men in terms of obtaining key posts in that profession.[20] All in all, as we have seen, as many as two-thirds of the women in our sample who had an occupation in mind on entering university were actually planning to teach, and the popularity of this profession continued undiminished throughout the undergraduate years. In the event, as many as 60 per cent of women graduating in 1960 actually took up a teaching post; and by the time of the survey almost seven out of ten of those who were still working were school teachers.[21] Moreover, the popularity of teaching was particularly evident among the small number of graduates who were full-time workers despite having young children: indeed, as we shall see, three-quarters of those so placed were in fact teachers.

The merits of a teaching career from a woman's standpoint rest on the fact that it is at present the best adapted of all main professional occupations to their domestic responsibilities. Indeed it is such a good example of the way in which the moderate ideology encourages women only to seek employment which is already in some measure adapted to their domestic role that it is worth considering in some detail. Later on in our discussion we shall note, however, that even teaching was not entirely suited to all a married woman's requirements, and in other respects was clearly far from an ideal career.

Of course it is almost a tautology, at least on the basis of the moderate ideology, to say that teaching is a particularly congenial career for the married woman. After all, it is because children are at home during the comparatively long school holidays that other forms of employment are generally unsuited to a woman successfully pursuing her dual responsibilities. However, there are other aspects of a teaching career which are also advantageous to the married woman. First of all, teaching is believed to be exceptional in its lack of a 'specialized and rapidly changing knowledge base'[22] (a large proportion of women teachers in any case work in primary schools), with the result that women can quite easily be absent for a few years while raising a family without the necessity for a period of retraining. To be sure there have been of late many changes in teaching techniques and in school curricula, but these are probably less marked than in most other specialist professional fields. Again, 'lack of accumulated experience on the job is no bar to resumption of work in teaching after a prolonged absence',[23] and teaching still includes a large number of opportunities for part-time work (which is a very popular solution for women who want to combine paid work with domestic responsibilities). Furthermore, employment opportunities in this field are generally widespread throughout the country and this facilitates easy job changes in the event of the husband moving on account of his own career. At the same time school teaching is said to be commensurate with the socially developed interests of many women, most of whom express concern that their jobs should be useful to the community and personally rewarding to themselves. Since women can afford in general to be less concerned than men with the financial rewards of work, they do not consider that school teaching is badly paid. And finally, perhaps most important of all, the working hours and, as we have mentioned, the holidays of teachers clearly suit the daily and yearly routine of children of school age.[24]

But these advantages of a teaching career are by no means an unmixed blessing in the eyes of those who would like to see a more even spread of talent in different fields of employment regardless of social class or sex differences. Because of the particularly well-adapted nature of teaching to a married woman's role requirements, coupled with her essentially domestically biased ideology, there has been comparatively little pressure for substitute care arrangements or for comparable working arrangements in other types of employment. Indeed, the school teaching profession is so well-adapted to the problems of working mothers that it has actually served to dampen the demands of highly educated women for changes in other occupations, or in domestic structures which would further their occupational chances in these other fields. For an opportunity to become a teacher is, on these grounds, more attractive to a graduate wife and mother than is the chance of competing, say, for a job in management which is at the present time extremely ill-adjusted to her other commitments. The end result is clearly that neither the occupational structure nor family organization are forced to undergo the modification necessary for graduate women to have a variety of outlets for their occupational interests and, in effect, teaching provides a safety valve which allows the *status quo* both in other fields of employment and in domestic arrangements to be preserved.

And yet on the basis of our data it would appear that even teaching was by no means an ideal career for the married woman. Certainly we found strong grounds for the claim that graduate women working as school teachers (clearly of course the great majority of graduate women workers) were relatively dissatisfied with their working lives compared with similarly employed men. In Table 77, for example, it can be seen that although there was a substantial agreement between men and women who were school teachers in 1966 in the rating of their jobs for congenial colleagues and working conditions, for salary and for the social utility of their work, on each of the other items women rated their education posts very much more adversely than their male colleagues. The difference was particularly marked in respect of opportunities for intellectual development and, not surprisingly in view of our concern about the implications of the 'moderate' ideology, for opportunities to rise to the top. As we observed in our previous report

in both these cases a positive net score on the men's side contrasts with a negative one on the women's side, and this also occurs, though to a less marked degree, for novelty and variety of employment. Another striking case, where their work is much less favourably regarded by the women than by the men, is in respect of the scope it offers for initiative and freedom to develop one's own ideas.[25]

It will be recalled that in Chapter 2 we compared these main job characteristics with the findings of the Morton-Williams survey on undergraduate attitudes. Taking women as a whole, it is worth mentioning here that the working conditions of those who were still in employment six years after graduation substantially failed to meet the ideals of undergraduates, and this was in marked contrast with the considerable conjunction between wishes and reality in the case of men (see Figure 2.1, p. 104). On *each* of the nine job characteristics (congenial work, salary and security, intellectual development, initiative, novelty, social work, administration, communication, ambition) the working conditions described by the *women* who were still working six years after graduation failed to come up to the standards which undergraduate women were hoping to find in their work (Figure 4.1).[26]

Thus whatever the advantages that teaching (or for that matter any other form of employment) would appear to bring to the married woman in respect of her domestic role, it is clear that from a career point of view the graduate woman teacher undoubtedly suffers by comparison with her male contemporaries of presumably equivalent academic and technical competence.

We have dealt with our graduate women teachers at some length, not only because the vast majority of working women in our sample were in fact in this profession, but also because it exemplifies the way in which even highly skilled and intelligent women seek employment which is best adapted to their domestic responsibilities. But another interesting group of women, who were involved in a variety of occupations *on their own account*, are also worth a brief mention. They were few in number (thirty-two) and they were also highly atypical of graduate women generally; obviously, too, they had chosen other means of combining domestic and paid activities. They were found (Table 78) to have particularly favourable educational and social backgrounds, being far more likely than other graduate women to have attended independent schools or Oxbridge. They tended to have better educated and higher-status parents than other graduate women while their husbands, too, seemed to be of a somewhat higher social status. The possibility of being self-employed in a variety of fields (only 22 per cent were in education) appeared, then, to be to an important extent a function of a privileged social position, and is illustrative of one of the means used by those of high status, who in the main look unfavourably on a teaching career, to combine home and work while preserving intact a primary emphasis on family obligations.

Any investigation of the problems faced by married women in combining a career with considerable domestic responsibilities should examine more closely the position of the full-time working mother, for she, above all, should exemplify the problems of effectively combining two roles and might indeed

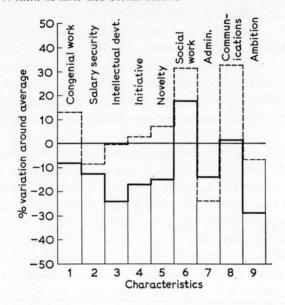

Women in Arts and Social Studies

Women in Science

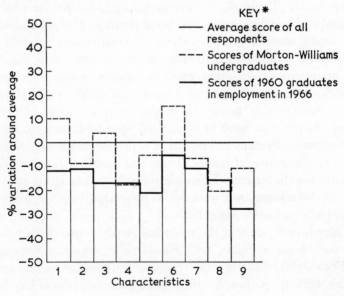

KEY *

—— Average score of all respondents

--- Scores of Morton-Williams undergraduates

—— Scores of 1960 graduates in employment in 1966

Figure 4.1

be considered to be an instance of a person with a particularly high career, as opposed to domestic, commitment. In the event, however, we found comparatively little support for this argument, for while it was true that these working mothers had a slightly higher career commitment than graduate women generally, they nevertheless had somewhat different family building patterns which appeared to facilitate participation in work activities, and certainly they did not generally seek careers in fields which were untypical of graduate women as a whole.

First of all, graduate mothers who had a full-time job did appear to be relatively more interested in using their abilities to the full than were their contemporaries. Moreover, they were more highly educated than women graduates as a whole, as many as 16 per cent having attempted a doctorate compared with only 3 per cent of full-time housewives (Table 78). Again, only a third had undertaken *no* post-graduate studies, compared with 43 per cent of fully domesticated women. All in all, they seemed to exemplify the pattern that the more education a woman receives the more likely she is to engage in paid activities.

On the other hand, there were certain important differences in their family building patterns compared with the house-bound women in our sample, and these differences were probably of decisive importance in accounting for their participation in full-time work. Nearly two-thirds (61 per cent), for example, had only one child, and their median family size was generally smaller than that of full-time housewives (1·45 compared with 1·60). On balance, too, they were more likely to have had their children somewhat earlier (again compared with full-time housewives): indeed, 11 per cent actually had their first child before graduation. In general, therefore, their family building arrangements were more conducive to their engagement in paid work than were those of the majority of graduate women. Indeed, in many circumstances they may actually have had no children under school age; and where they did, their children were usually few in number which almost certainly made it more easy to obtain either nursery facilities or some substitute care arrangements which would presumably be more difficult for women with larger families.

Other data, too, suggest that these women by and large shared the common ideology; thus, for example, *full-time working mothers were in fact far more concentrated in the education sector than graduate women as a whole* (Table 78). In so far as their first posts were concerned, 72 per cent were employed in teaching compared with 59 per cent of presently housebound mothers and 53 per cent of the self-employed, and by 1966 three-quarters of the women who had children and a full-time job were in teaching posts. So in our view, full-time working mothers could not be regarded as displaying many different characteristics from graduate women as a whole. Certainly they did not appear to underemphasize their role as mothers at the expense of a career orientation, and in consequence they failed to seek a variety of openings in professions which have always been traditional preserves of the male. Rather, they exemplified certain overall tendencies among married women to look for work in teaching because this is the best adapted profession to their domestic responsibilities and they appeared to take on full-time paid activities because their family situation was more conducive to this possibility than that of graduate women as a whole.

Even among full-time working mothers, therefore, we found comparatively little evidence in favour of the view that there is a widespread feeling of frustration among young graduate women as a result of a primary emphasis being placed on their home lives. Rather, the 'moderate' (or 'conventional') ideology, as we have seen, effectively shelters women from any potential feelings of this type, with the result that few women seek openings in employment which are not adjusted to the demands of a family. If anything, as we shall see, the working rather than the non-working mothers appeared to be the least (rather than the most) contented with their conditions. This argument is worth pursuing more fully at this juncture.

Graduate mothers generally – the majority of whom retire from paid work once they have children – appeared to be relatively more contented with their lives in comparison with those who remained single or childless, and who in most cases, therefore, kept working. For example, the study by Fogarty and others of a subsample of our own respondents eight years after they graduated,[27] revealed that graduate women with children seemed to be more sure that their university education had had beneficial effects on their lives than others who had not married or had no children (Table 79). Nearly one-third (31 per cent) of the single women were equivocal about the advantages of higher education for their social life and friendship patterns, describing its influence as 'mixed', compared with only 13 per cent and 23 per cent respectively of graduate women who were married with or without children. This can actually be explained on the grounds that women who marry and produce children are following the most conventional pattern, making social intercourse for them relatively easier than for the women who have deviated from the normal by remaining childless or single. Similar explanations may account for the fact that, compared with their married counterparts, single women were more likely to feel that their university experience had been rather less beneficial to their own self image. In the face of neutrality and even hostility from those around them, such women might be subject to greater self-analysis and possibly find a scapegoat for their self-doubt in the higher education they received. Again, women graduates who had married and had children had, to a greater extent than the other two groups, experienced improved social relations with their parents since taking their degree. We know, from the research of Komarovsky and of Wallin,[28] that parents of female undergraduates encourage their daughters in both the academic and social aspects of their lives but again, in line with the conventional ideology, place particular emphasis on marriage. It is likely, therefore, that women who have, apparently successfully, achieved both these ends will be happier in their relations with parents and perhaps with their lives in general than those who are seen to have 'failed' in either or both areas. Other items of data point to the same conclusion. Among married women graduates there was almost unanimous agreement that a degree had had positive benefits for employment, although among single women a small but important minority (more than one in ten) doubted that this was the case. Interestingly enough, however, very few women in the total sample of 1960 graduates, whether married or single, felt really strongly about *their treatment at work*. There were admittedly certain important exceptions, and notably the minority who had rejected traditionally 'feminine' work and were working in industry or commerce.[29] But even in these instances their at times vociferous complaints were most atypical of the silent majority who were mainly school teachers or housewives and were, on balance, uncomplaining about their experiences at work (Tables 80, 81 and 82). These women were presumably more concerned to achieve a happy home life and in consequence did not feel very strongly about any absence of opportunity at work even if, as we have seen earlier, they were able to perceive unsatisfactory elements in their work. Again it was significant that full time housewives by no means indicated that their early retirement resulted from lack of opportunities, employer's intolerance or husband's disapproval. This was prompted, rather, by their own acceptance and 'internalization' of an ideology which supported such conduct and, indeed, by their own genuine desires which implied a disruption of their careers in favour of domestic responsibilities.

Here, as we have suggested, lies the chief impediment to women's professional success and the main explanation for their general lack of antipathy or hostility to an order which not only channels their activities into certain specific areas but also, within these areas, deprives them of equal opportunities to compete with their male contemporaries. For a belief in a secondary commitment to work effectively restrains a woman from taking advantage of scarce educational resources which in other circumstances would lead to interesting, high-status work. Indeed, in our society few people are able to find fulfilling work consistent with their talents and aptitudes, although higher education has been seen to provide a small proportion of each age group with such an opportunity. There is little doubt, moreover, that many male graduates value a university degree primarily for career reasons, since it provides them with a key to interesting, secure and financially rewarding lifetime opportunities. But women graduates, by contrast, ignore many of these opportunities and make only half-hearted preparations for work which may or may not be consistent with their abilities. For them the attraction of a university degree is ultimately bound up with the desirability of such a step in the eyes of an 'appropriate' male.[30] Their preparation for work therefore takes the form of contingency planning in case they should find it necessary to take a paid job, and their principal concern is for marriage and children, with the result that their job has to be adjusted to the demands that wifehood and motherhood make. Of course, a university education offers other advantages for women: they benefit from the joy of learning while developing interests and attitudes which are compatible with those of prospective partners. At the same time they are thrown into contact in the university milieu with men whom they consider to be suitable as potential husbands and who, in the way of things, are set for secure and high-status careers. But all these advantages are far more related to the domestic than to the career aspects of their lives.

Of course the attitudes of female undergraduates towards their studies and careers are frequently congenial to and may be encouraged by their male colleagues, who are thus protected from feminine competition for the highest examination results and the most prestigious career openings. In fact, university women seem to avoid being too competitive, thereby being careful not to prejudice their chances of attracting the 'right' man by either spending too much time on work activities or appearing to men to be too successful in worldly events and therefore in their eyes unlikely to make a desirable marriage companion. Many women believe that men actually dislike intellectual women, though in this they may well be mistaken.[31] But there are certain obvious advantages in a man having a girlfriend whose intellectual level is similar to his own. Or, as Rousseau remarked, 'a man who thinks should not ally himself with a woman who does not think, for he loses the chief delight of social life if he has a wife who cannot share his thoughts'.[32]

In practice, in any case, a highly intelligent woman is

L

seldom a threat to her husband because highly educated married couples tend to preserve a division of labour on traditional lines and this arrangement appears to be generally regarded as satisfactory by both partners. Indeed, in present circumstances marital harmony is subject to greater strain if the married pair attempt any other allocation of tasks, particularly when childrearing is highly salient for them. The graduate wife finds her education valuable not only in her relations with her husband but also in the socialization of her children. One woman in a study of graduates by Judith Hubback expressed it thus: 'we married graduates can use our training, I think, to run our homes more efficiently, give our husbands more intelligent companionship and help our children more effectively in their lives and in their studies'.[33] By the same token, if the occupational system is unjust or unfair or if their opportunities for a variety of jobs are effectively restricted, women appear to accept the situation.

So far we have examined a number of reasons why married women in contemporary Britain are not making use of their undoubted talents and training in a variety of occupations. Up to this point, our account has been somewhat pessimistic with regard to the possibility of any alteration in this situation, since we have seen that, by and large, the women themselves accept these limitations on their employment opportunities. However, more recently there have been a number of trends which would appear to run counter to the general tendencies which we have observed throughout this chapter and these are worth dealing with at this point.

To begin with, there have been a number of signs of frustration among middle-aged women who, in the 'empty nest' stage of their lives, when their children have left home, begin to question their usefulness both to themselves and to their families.[34] This is a comparatively new phenomenon since it is only recently that a number of important demographic changes have coincided with the growing educational opportunities for girls. In the past, of course, when families were larger but were started later, while marriages too were later and less frequent, and when life expectancy was much lower than it is today, comparatively few women suffered from the increasingly important social problem of underemployment for as many as twenty years of their lives, from the time their children leave home to retirement. Now it is true that only the more astute of the young women in our sample will have really given these issues much thought, but by failing to do so they may well in fact foster their own future unhappiness. Approximately 60 per cent of our full-time housewives felt they would want opportunities for paid work later on in their lives, yet by that time not only may employment be difficult to obtain but it may also be in extremely restricted fields and involve work in no way commensurate with graduate women's capacities and training. And thus a combination of demographic tendencies, together with the high level of education which women are increasingly receiving, may well lead to the emergence of a powerful and eloquent group who are extremely discontented with their situation. There are likely to be, then, major demands for change during the next few decades from this group of women.

We have suggested that middle-aged women are likely increasingly to examine their own contribution to society once their children are relatively independent. There is also already a minority of younger women who are demanding changes in social conditions which at present perpetuate the relative subordination of women to family life, while others are actively demonstrating that other options are available to women who wish for more satisfying careers alongside family life. To begin with, women's liberation groups are becoming more numerous among contemporary undergraduates: their basic demands include such changes as twenty-four hour nurseries, equal pay, equal education and job opportunities, and free abortion on demand. This militancy among young women, while not obvious among our own sample, may well be the vanguard of a new interpretation by women of their position in society. Again, *some* highly qualified women, while accepting the obvious advantages of married life and children, are not content to make this their whole existence, they and their husbands both having a high career commitment. These women, who have been called[35] 'continuous-in workers', while being at present only a 'statistically minor variant' are nevertheless the very women who are likely in the future to hold responsible senior positions. They therefore represent a 'creating minority' in terms of family and work roles, and may be setting the scene for the emergence of new attitudes by working out with their husbands new patterns of relationships between work and family that will facilitate the wife's pursuit of an effective career if she wants this. For the patterns of work and family life judged appropriate today are not those approved of by an earlier generation and by the same token they are quite likely to change in the future. Indeed, social approval may one day support the woman who chooses work and family patterns which can lead to highly responsible jobs in a variety of fields.[36]

There are, then, tendencies which offer some hope for a greater utilization of the talents of highly qualified women in the future. At present, however, there is no doubt that women's abilities are being used exceptionally poorly in contemporary Britain in so far as the occupational system is concerned. We have already seen that the women graduates of 1960 who were still working were doing so in a restricted number of occupations and were especially concentrated in the teaching profession.[37] Other key sectors of employment were dominated by men. While six men graduates had become Members of Parliament not one of their female contemporaries had been so fortunate; and perhaps more importantly, while 618 of our graduate men were in management only thirty-six women were so engaged. There is, furthermore, real fear for the status of women at present even though the proportion of married women at work is growing, for certain advances made by women in the early part of this century are probably on the decline and, indeed, men are if anything increasingly getting hold of key positions which were once traditionally reserved for women. Wilensky, for example, has made the important point that while more married women are going out to work they are entering low-status male occupations such as clerical posts but do not control them, while men have entered *and are gaining control* of the more attractive female occupations such as school teaching, social work, and librarianship.[38] Again, it seems that in America even fewer women now enter the most prestigious and lucrative professions, and in assessing the situation as regards women in science and engineering in the United States in 1960, Rossi found that only 9 per cent of scientists and less than 1 per cent of engineers were women.[39] In these fields, and in medicine and law, women lost rather than gained ground *vis-à-vis* men between 1950 and 1960, and since then the position has not improved.[40] Knudsen, too, suggests that women are losing the footholds they once had, that their status is declining absolutely and relatively to men in certain fields – notably chemistry and biology – and argues forcibly that women themselves are to blame, being largely indifferent to occupational success.[41] It is evident from our own data that the majority of graduate women in Britain are doing little to change the situation, which might support the McNally view that 'it is hard to believe that if a strong desire to break into other types of work had prevailed among women in general, they would not have achieved it in the past ten or twenty years'.[42]

The declining importance of women in a number of professions – not least being those which were once their traditional preserve – may be in some measure dependent on certain demographic changes. In particular, the spinster is of course increasingly rare on account of the growing popularity of marriage[43] and, as a result, the old style career woman has become progressively less common. Moreover, since demographic changes have been accompanied by the growth of ideologies which encourage women to place career second to family, the upshot has certainly been a decline in the number of career-oriented women who are eager to reach 'the top' or at least do well in their respective professions; and without this orientation, as we have noted earlier, it is in practice extremely difficult for women to compete successfully with men, at least under present circumstances.

In view of these changes, it is scarcely surprising that a number of facilities which make female participation in the labour force a more easy process have if anything declined during the postwar period, and until recently there has been comparatively little opposition from women themselves against these developments. The provision of nurseries, particularly, has woefully declined since the end of World War II and it has become, in consequence, extremely difficult for a woman whose marriage is intact to place her child in existing nurseries even for a few hours daily because preference has to be given to unmarried mothers, deserted wives and widows whose financial problems are clearly more pressing.[44] In any case, the charges for a child so placed may be so high as to make it financially unrewarding to go out to work. Further, apart from technical changes which have considerably reduced some of the more arduous household chores,[45] there has been very little attention paid to other ways of lightening the domestic responsibilities of married women and, above all, to the possibility of creating a social climate which would be more supportive to a mother who wanted more than a 'little job'. For example, cheap family restaurants, more shopping facilities in the workplace, more flexible opening hours for all community services and so on, are still somewhat distant prospects. But in some ways it is the lack of pressure from women themselves for rather simple and obvious changes of this type which is so remarkable and, indeed, reflects very well their acceptance of, and belief in, an ideology which they themselves serve to perpetuate.

All this does not imply, of course, that the talents of our highly qualified women are completely wasted as a result of concentrating on the domestic aspects of their lives at the expense of wider interests. But we would most certainly wish to echo the view expressed in a recent book by Fogarty, Rapoport and Rapoport for working out more flexible arrangements at home and at work to ease the strain on married partners, when both are intensely involved in a career while raising a family.[46] In concentrating on dual career families and the ways in which men and women in these circumstances reconciled work and family life, they found that mutual accommodation of needs was paramount and that on balance the benefits of the lifestyle so achieved tended to outweigh the costs. Nevertheless, it was clear that 'the support provided for one another by the dual career couples should not be idealized. There were many strains and stresses involved, ambivalence and undercutting, conflict and so on.'[47] On the whole, however, these families tended to cope with household tasks without a total reversal of traditional roles, usually by delegating certain of their responsibilities to paid helpers and by reapportioning the remainder between husband, wife and children. These arrangements, incidentally, appeared to have certain important benefits in so far as children were concerned, for they were brought into their parents' lives to a striking degree and were encouraged 'to participate in many of the interests and concerns of the parents, becoming part of the egalitarian ethos of the families'.[48] But in the absence of publicly organized child care, parents had to seek the assistance of outsiders for which they had to pay quite heavily and, apart from the financial cost of *ad hoc* arrangements such as these, working couples constantly feared an imminent domestic crisis in the event of one or more of their helpers letting them down. But all in all the dual career family type would appear to bring significant advantages to the domestic unit as a whole in spite of certain obvious difficulties which, as we have suggested, owe much to the lack of support from local and central authorities.

Thus, if these and other forms of family structure which permit the greater participation of women in the labour force are to become more common, the provision of practical support of various kinds is essential. Furthermore, there should be an introduction of employment conditions in which leave of absence, generous maternity grants and so on are the rule, in recognition of the essentially different life cycle of women employees. It may be necessary to introduce measures which positively discriminate in favour of female employees, in order to counteract the current pressure against them.

Yet the working out of new structures in the workplace and in the home could also, as has recently been recognized, be for the benefit of men as well as ensuring that trained and talented women are able to use their skills more fully.[49] We have already seen that the majority of men derive their greatest satisfaction in life from the home and from family life generally; so they too would appear to be likely beneficiaries from alternative arrangements which would leave them free to spend more time in these activities. Furthermore, while many men *and* women enjoy the excitement of a top job, this kind of pressure has a price in time as well as in mental and physical stress. 'Why not, then, work less or rather work differently with a better balance of time and effort between interests on and off the job?'[50]

It is clear that there is no shortage of ideas for developing more flexible family relationships, more support for the woman who wants to keep her career even though she has children, and for the more effective use of available female talent generally. But in our view the major stumbling block is still the dominance of an ideology which continues to place greater emphasis on the family life of a woman at the expense of her interests and obligations elsewhere. And, indeed, without a substantial change in this set of attitudes we cannot be hopeful that major changes will take place in the status of women, at least in the short run.

This becomes fairly obvious if we recapitulate some of the main findings and themes of this chapter. Six years after graduation the majority of women graduates were married, and more than half of these had no paid activity whatsoever, while those at work were heavily concentrated in the education sector (largely because, as we have suggested, careers in teaching were so well adapted to their domestic responsibilities). To be sure there were important class differences in the pattern of female employment, with the result that graduate women whose fathers were manual workers were particularly concentrated in education, a tendency which was slightly less marked among their middle-class contemporaries. But, in general, these class differences were heavily outweighed by the tendency of women generally to think in terms of, and indeed to obtain employment in, the education sector. To some extent, the comparatively small proportion of women in employment six years after taking their first degree could be regarded as the *temporary* result of childbearing, for though the arrival of a child was usually accompanied by a woman giving up her job altogether, a large proportion of full-time housewives said they would wish to return to some form of paid work at a later stage in their lives. This and other studies of highly educated women confirm the view that few women in this position consider it desirable that they should be full-time wives and mothers all their lives but that they would certainly, on balance, abandon a career in favour of domestic responsibilities wherever there was a clash between these two aspects of their lives. On the surface this appears to be a tolerable compromise between two more extreme positions, but given the current nature of the occupational structure and the high degree of competition for posts among the more educated, this inevitably results in women being only able to choose certain types of career, and within these, competing on unfavourable terms with men. And while the 'moderate' ideology prevails, with its implicit bias in favour of a notion that a woman's 'place' is primarily in the home, there would appear to be little prospect of any major alteration in the employment status of women.

On balance, too, the full-time housewives were the most contented with their lot. Women in teaching and, indeed, in most kinds of work were aware of certain deficiencies in their work environment, and as a result, undergraduate hopes for satisfying careers noted in another survey seemed to be unfulfilled among the majority of graduate women. But in spite of these difficulties they appeared to accept such conditions to a considerable degree because of the emphasis they placed on home and family as their prime source of satisfaction. Our evidence on the full-time working mothers in our sample did little to suggest that a sizeable number of women were seeking to compete successfully alongside men in a number of different kinds of work: rather, this group was even more concentrated in the teaching profession than graduate women as a whole and appeared simply to have certain distinct family building patterns which facilitated their full-time employment.

We thus saw little chance of the vast majority of graduate women being a force for change, at least in the short run. This is not to suggest, however, that we take an entirely pessimistic view of the future. To begin with, there is increasing evidence of a highly unsatisfactory state of affairs developing among older groups of graduate women. We saw that a combination of demographic changes and the increasing education of women as a whole is likely to lead to a substantial and highly articulate number of women emerging in the future who, when their children are relatively independent, will almost certainly demand employment commensurate with their high level training and abilities. Moreover, evidence is accumulating of the militancy of young women who are currently at university, while some young married couples are in any case experimenting with new patterns of family life and may well become the pacesetters of the future.

But, all in all, unless there is a major change in the dominant ideology which women themselves generally subscribe to and actually foster, backed by considerable government and employer action to make available facilities which will encourage women not to view work as a relatively peripheral aspect of their lives, we cannot be particularly optimistic at present. Yet how long, it may be asked, will the country be able to tolerate the considerable wastage of highly educated women as a result of their grossly ineffective and irrational deployment in the labour market; and for how long will women themselves accept a state of affairs which inevitably depresses their status *vis-à-vis* men?

NOTES

1. E. Figes, *Patriarchal Attitudes: Women in Society* (London, Faber, 1970) 178.

In our previous report, it may be recalled that a considerable amount of material of a factual nature was supplied on the graduate women in our sample, and although we have included some important additional details and findings here, we have deliberately reduced the material of this type to a minimum in order to avoid overlap. Those wanting additional details on the work experiences of graduate women should see R. K. Kelsall *et al.*, *Six Years After* (Sheffield University,

Department of Sociological Studies, Higher Education Research Unit, 1970) Chapters 4 and 7.

2. Political and Economic Planning, *Women and Top Jobs* (London, P.E.P., 1969).

3. R. K. Kelsall *et al.*, 'Still a low status profession', *Times Educational Supplement*, 4 December 1970, 4.

4. K. H. Mueller, 'The cultural pressures on women', in O. P. David (ed.), *The Education of Women* (Washington, American Council on Education, 1959) 49–63.

5. T. Leggatt, 'Teaching as a profession', in J. A. Jackson (ed.), *Professions and Professionalization* (Cambridge, University Press, 1970) 153–77.

6. R. K. Kelsall *et al.*, *Six Years After*, Chapter 4.

7. The British Federation of University Women, in a study of graduate women of all ages, found a consistent relationship between husband's income and wife's employment. See C. E. Arregger (ed.), *Graduate Women at Work* (London, B.F.U.W., 1966).

8. A. Hunt, *A Survey of Women's Employment* (London, H.M.S.O., 1968), vol. 1.

9. In Eastern Germany, by comparison, 73 per cent of women aged 25–39 with children were in the workforce in 1964. See M. P. Fogarty *et al.*, *Sex, Career and Family* (London, Allen and Unwin, 1971) Chapter 2.

10. *Ibid.*, 239.

11. *Ibid.*, 199.

12. E. Dahlstrom (ed.), *The Changing Roles of Men and Women* (London, Duckworth, 1967) 175.

13. M. P. Fogarty *et al.*, *Sex, Career and Family*, Chapter 3.

14. See E. Dahlstrom (ed.), *The Changing Roles of Men and Women*.

15. See, for instance, A. Myrdal and V. Klein, *Women's Two Roles*, 2nd edition (London, Routledge, 1968), especially Chapters 9 and 10.

16. M. Fogarty *et al.*, *Preliminary Report on a Sample Survey of 1967 University Graduates* (Unpublished, P.E.P., 1968) 35. Quoted by kind permission of the authors.

17. As we saw in our earlier publication, 47 per cent of non-working married women graduates wanted a part-time job, 13 per cent a full-time job. R. K. Kelsall *et al.*, *Six Years After*, 88.

18. A. S. Rossi, 'Women in science: why so few?', *Science*, vol. 148 (1965) 1196–1202. This point was also made by senior managers in a company studied by Isobel Allen. See M. P. Fogarty *et al.*, *Women in Top Jobs* (London, Allen and Unwin, 1971) 53.

19. See M. P. Fogarty *et al.*, *Sex, Career and Family*, especially Chapter 9.

20. Central Office of Information, *Women in Britain* (London, H.M.S.O., 1964) 12.

21. See Table 66.

22. T. Leggatt, 'Teaching as a profession', *op. cit.*, 163–5.

23. *Ibid.*, 164.

24. C. E. Arregger in *Graduate Women at Work* and A. Myrdal and V. Klein in *Women's Two Roles* support the view that school teaching is in many ways 'ideal' for women.

25. R. K. Kelsall *et al.*, *Six Years After*, 72.

26. One minor exception was among women scientists on the communications item, where a small positive difference between wishes and actual working conditions could be seen.

27. See note 3 in Chapter 3.

28. M. Komarovsky, 'Cultural contradictions and sex roles', *American Journal of Sociology*, vol. 52 (1946) 184–9; P. Wallin, 'Cultural contradictions and sex roles – a repeat study', *American Sociological Review*, vol. 15 (1950) 288–93.

29. M. Rendel, 'Do women have trouble getting jobs?', *New Society*, 27 August 1964, 17–18.

30. G. Psathas, 'Toward a theory of occupational choice for women', *Sociology and Social Research*, vol. 52 (1968) 253–68.

31. A small-scale study of men and women undergraduates at Sheffield University revealed that while women thought men disliked an 'intellectual' woman, men in fact did not agree. S. Whitely, *A Study of Latent Role Conflict among Female University Students* (Unpublished dissertation, Sheffield University, Department of Sociological Studies, 1968).

32. Quoted in E. Figes, *Patriarchal Attitudes . . .*, 97.

33. J. Hubback, *Wives who went to College* (London, Heinemann, 1957) 75.

34. As described by B. Friedan, *The Feminine Mystique* (London, Gollancz, 1964).

35. M. P. Fogarty *et al.*, *Sex, Career and Family*, Chapter 9.

36. *Ibid.*, 485–6.

37. See again R. K. Kelsall *et al.*, *Six Years After*, Chapter 4.

38. H. L. Wilensky, 'Woman's work: economic growth, ideology, structure', *Industrial Relations*, vol. 7 (1968) 235–48.

39. A. S. Rossi, 'Women in science: why so few?', *op. cit.*

40. Cf. C. F. Epstein, *Woman's Place* (Berkeley, University of California Press, 1970).

41. D. D. Knudsen, 'The declining status of women: popular myths and the failure of functionalist thought', *Social Forces*, vol. 48 (1969) 183–93.

42. G. B. McNally, 'Patterns of female labour force activity', *Industrial Relations*, vol. 7 (1968) 204–18.

43. R. K. Kelsall, *Population* (London, Longmans, 1967).

44. M. Ramelson, *The Petticoat Rebellion* (London, Lawrence and Wishart, 1967); M. Rendel *et al.*, *Equality for Women* (London, Fabian Society, 1968). Recently Dr Colin Hindley described the shortage of nursery school places in Britain as 'a national scandal . . . in Britain it is almost as difficult to get a child into nursery school as it is into Eton'. *Sunday Times*, 4 April 1971, 3.

45. Though Goode makes the important point that 'the substantial development of laboursaving devices and technology has not lightened labour in the modern United States home. . . . Most of these devices merely raise the standards for cleanliness and repairs'. W. J. Goode, *World Revolution and Family Patterns* (Glencoe, Free Press, 1963) 15.

46. M. P. Fogarty *et al.*, *Sex, Career and Family.*

47. *Ibid.*, 341.

48. *Ibid.*, 341.

49. This point is also made by M. P. Fogarty *et al.*, in *ibid.*, Chapter 13.

50. *Ibid.*, 491.

TABLES

37. Class of degree, social origin and occupational plans on graduation (men only)
38. Type of secondary school attended and occupational plans on graduation (men only)
39. University, social origin and occupational plans on graduation (men only)
40. Class of degree and employment sector (men only)
41. Subject of degree and employment sector (men only)
42. Work in 1966 and social origin (men only)
43. Social origin and the realization of occupational aspirations (men only)
44. Social origins of men in 'prestigious' occupations in 1966
45. Academic characteristics of Higher Civil Servants and of all men graduates
46. Social origins of men in education in 1966
47. Propensity of graduate men to take up a teaching career
48. Proportions of men and women married
49. Postgraduate study and the timing of marriage
50. Timing of marriage by graduate women teachers
51. Social classes of graduates' marriage partners
52. Full-time further education of graduates' marriage partners
53. Timing of first births
54. Postgraduate study and the timing of first birth
55. Fertility and the timing of marriage
56. Fertility and level of education
57. Social mobility and the timing of first birth
58. Fertility and social origin
59. Fertility and achieved social class
60. Fertility of employed and self-employed professional men
61. Fertility of men in four occupational groups
62. Women's social origins and their motives for wanting higher education
63. Social origin and occupational plans (women only)
64. Social origin and postgraduate study (women only)
65. Social origin and motives for undertaking postgraduate study (women only)
66. First and 1966 employment sectors of men and working women

M

Table 1. Social classes of graduates' fathers*

Registrar-General's social class groupings	Men graduates	Women graduates
	%	%
I : Professions	12	15
II : Intermediate	34	39
III Non-manual: Other non-manual	14	13
TOTAL NON-MANUAL	60	67
III Manual: Skilled manual	19	14
IV : Semi-skilled manual	6	5
V : Unskilled manual	1	—
TOTAL MANUAL	26	19
Forces	—	1
No answer	14	12
ALL GRADUATES	100	100
No.	9404	3582

* At the time respondents entered university in all tables unless otherwise stated.

Table 2. Social classes displaying highest intergenerational associations of status

Authors*	Highest index	Designation of father's class
Glass	13·2	Professional, administrative
Centers	20·0	Large business
Davidson and Anderson	4·9	Professional
Rogoff	4·5	Professional
Jackson and Crockett	5·4	Professional
Janowitz	22·0	Upper middle

* D. V. Glass (ed.), *Social Mobility in Britain* (London, Routledge, 1954) 199; R. Centers, 'Occupational mobility of urban occupational strata', *American Sociological Review*, vol. 13 (1945) 197–203; P. E. Davidson and H. D. Anderson, *Occupational Mobility in an American Community* (Stanford, University Press, 1937); N. Rogoff, *Recent Trends in Occupational Mobility* (Glencoe, Free Press, 1953); E. F. Jackson and H. J. Crockett, 'Occupational mobility in the U.S.', *American Sociological Review*, vol. 29 (1964) 5–15; M. Janowitz, 'Social stratification and mobility in Western Germany', *American Journal of Sociology*, vol. 64 (1958) 6–24. Where necessary, indices have been calculated by the present author from the data given.

Table 3. Sources of elite heterogeneity

Social origin	Men	Women	Total
	%	%	%
Routine non-manual	16	15	16
Skilled manual	22	16	20
Semi-skilled manual	7	6	7
Unskilled manual	1	1	1
TOTAL INFLOW	46	38	44
No. (father's social class known)	8030	3134	11164

Table 4. Class opportunities to enter the elite stratum

Social class	(a) Class distribution of population (England and Wales) 1961* %	(b) Expected no. of fathers in each class in a situation of perfect mobility	(c) Actual no. of fathers in each class	(d) Index of opportunity $(c \div b)$
Professional	2·4	268	1669	6·23
Intermediate non-manual	22·9	2556	4567	1·79
Routine non-manual	9·8	1094	1789	1·64
Skilled manual	29·4	3282	2245	0·68
Semi-skilled manual	20·9	2333	772	0·33
Unskilled manual	14·6	1631	122	0·07
ALL CLASSES	100·0	11164	11164	1·00

* *Source:* General Register Office, *Census 1961 (England and Wales)* (London, H.M.S.O., 1966).

Table 5. Intragenerational mobility of graduates' fathers

Social class of father at respondent's entry to university	Social class of father at respondent's birth																	No.
	Professional		Intermediate		Routine non-manual		Skilled manual		Semi-skilled manual		Unskilled manual		Forces		Unknown		
		%		%		%		%		%		%		%		%	
Professional	1401	72	73	2	108	4	21	1	10	1	0	—	24	6	32	6	1669
Intermediate	270	14	2823	79	844	31	310	11	127	14	9	7	73	18	111	20	4567
Routine non-manual	16	1	112	3	1384	51	105	4	52	6	8	7	70	17	42	8	1789
Skilled manual	11	—	62	2	72	3	1851	69	126	14	22	18	42	10	59	11	2245
Semi-skilled manual	1	—	33	1	45	2	152	6	482	52	9	7	24	6	26	5	772
Unskilled manual	0	—	6	—	9	—	31	1	7	1	66	54	1	—	2	—	122
Forces	3	—	3	—	7	—	5	—	0	—	0	—	62	15	0	—	80
Unknown	255	13	488	13	244	9	222	8	120	12	9	7	119	27	285	50	1742
No.	1957	100	3600	100	2713	100	2697	100	924	100	123	100	415	100	557	100	12986

Table 6. Degree of mobility of fathers from the birth of respondents to their entry to university

Social class of father at respondent's birth	Average distance mobile*
Professional	−0·23
Intermediate	−0·09
Routine non-manual	+0·36
ALL NON-MANUAL	+0·03
Skilled manual	+0·23
Semi-skilled manual	+0·80
Unskilled manual	+0·99
ALL MANUAL	+0·39
ALL CLASSES	+0·15

* A minus sign denotes downward mobility, a plus sign upward: 1 = one step in the class scale.

Table 7. Intergenerational changes of status* in three generations: sons

Grandfather–father	Father–son				
	Ascent	Observed ÷ Expected (O/E)	Stability	Observed ÷ Expected (O/E)	Total
Ascent	392 (652·7)†	0·60	1886 (1625·3)	1·16	2278
Stability	936 (1183·3)	0·79	3194 (2946·7)	1·08	4130
Descent	712 (204·0)	3·49	0 (508·0)	0·00	712
TOTAL	2040	1·00	5080	1·00	7120

* Distinction is made in all generations between non-manual, skilled manual, and unskilled manual classes only: all sons are in the non-manual category, and fathers in semi-skilled occupations are here designated unskilled.

† Bracketed numbers represent expected values, in Tables 7, 8 and 9.

Table 8. Intergenerational changes of status in three generations: daughters

Grandfather–father	Father–daughter				
	Ascent	*O/E*	*Stability*	*O/E*	*Total*
Ascent	79 (196·5)	0·40	815 (697·5)	1·16	894
Stability	267 (364·1)	0·73	1390 (1292·9)	1·07	1657
Descent	275 (60·4)	4·13	0 (214·6)	0·00	275
TOTAL	621	1·00	2205	1·00	2826

Table 9. Social origins of graduates and achieved social classes of their marriage partners

	Father's social class					
	Professional and intermediate	O/E	Routine non-manual	O/E	Manual	O/E	Total
MEN GRADUATES: Wife's class*							
Professional and intermediate	1588 (1502)	1·06	537 (504)	1·07	836 (955)	0·88	2961
Routine non-manual	860 (903)	0·95	286 (303)	0·94	634 (574)	1·10	1780
Manual	98 (141)	0·70	32 (47)	0·68	148 (90)	1·64	278
TOTAL	2546	1·00	855	1·00	1618	1·00	5019†
WOMEN GRADUATES: Husband's class*							
Professional and intermediate	1226 (1216)	1·01	302 (302)	1·00	440 (450)	0·98	1968
Routine non-manual	71 (70)	1·01	15 (17)	0·88	28 (26)	1·08	114
Manual	45 (56)	0·80	16 (14)	1·14	29 (20)	1·45	90
TOTAL	1342	1·00	333	1·00	497	1·00	2172†

* Wife – on marriage: husband – since marriage.
† Number of marriages in which respondent's class of origin and present class of spouse known.

Table 10. Social and educational homogamy of 1960 graduates

Marriages in which	Percentage of cases in which both variables are known	No. of cases in which both variables are known
1. Spouse's achieved social class and respondent's class of origin were the same	40	7191
2. Partners had similar educational level:		
(a) Spouse had higher or further education	78	9298
(b) Spouse had university education	44	9298
3. Partner's achieved social classes were the same	70	8194

Table 11. Social origins and the timing of marriage: graduates with teaching diplomas and with first degrees only

Father's social class	Men						Women					
	Dip.Ed.			First degree only			Dip.Ed.			First degree only		
	(a)	(b)	(c)	(a)	(b)	(c)	(a)	(b)	(c)	(a)	(b)	(c)
	%	%	%	%	%	%	%	%	%	%	%	%
Professional	24	33	43	42	31	27	33	38	29	59	28	13
Intermediate non-manual	36	30	33	40	33	27	35	34	31	61	22	17
Routine non-manual	42	30	28	52	27	22	31	39	30	62	22	16
Skilled manual	45	30	27	49	30	21	30	37	33	65	18	17
Semi-skilled	37	34	29	50	33	17	30*	39*	30*	47*	30*	23*
Unskilled	54*	23*	23*	42*	42*	17*	25*	37	38*	40*	40*	20*
ALL CLASSES	39	31	31	44	30	25	33	36	31	59	22	18
No.	484	382	382	988	682	526	368	411	347	599	227	166

* Numbers of graduates in these cells are very small.
(a) Married up to 2 years after first graduation.
(b) Married 2–6 years after.
(c) Not married on 1 October 1966.

Table 12. Social class and family size: I

	Non-manual	Manual
Graduates' families of origin: average number of children	2·24 (2·30*)	2·24
Average number of live births to women married 1920–4† (completed families)	1·89	2·67
Marriages 1925–9‡	2·16	2·89

* Corrected average, excluding mobile non-manual (father's social class, III, Non-manual).

† Data from D. V. Glass and E. Grebenik, *The Trend and Pattern of Fertility in Great Britain* (*Family Census 1946*, vol. 6) (London, H.M.S.O., 1954). Status is that of husbands at the time of interview.

‡ Source: J. Berent, 'Fertility and social mobility', *Population Studies*, vol. 5 (1952) 244–60.

Table 13. Social class and family size: II

Father's social class	Average size of family of origin	Number of graduates
Professional	2·39	1669
Intermediate	2·27	4567
Routine non-manual	2·01	1789
Skilled manual	2·18	2245
Semi-skilled manual	2·37	772
Unskilled manual	2·42	122

Table 14. Type of school last attended by parents of upwardly mobile graduates*

Type of school	Father	Mother
	%	%
Grammar, High, Senior Secondary	16	20
Technical School, Central School	10	7
Elementary, Junior Secondary	67	64
Independent, Direct Grant	3	4
Overseas Schools	1	1
Other	—	—
No answer	4	4
ALL SCHOOLS	100	100

* Of manual working-class origin throughout, unless otherwise stated.

Table 15. Terminal education age of parents of upwardly mobile graduates

Terminal education age	Father	Mother
	%	%
14 or under	69	63
Over 14	21	25
Unknown	10	12
ALL AGES	100	100

Table 16. Further education of parents of upwardly mobile graduates

Whether either parent had further education	%
Yes	24
No	76
No answer	—
ALL	100

Table 17. Social class of paternal grandfathers of upwardly mobile graduates

Grandfather's social class if known	%
Non-manual	26
Skilled manual	46
Unskilled manual	28
ALL CLASSES	100

Table 18. Major influences on upwardly mobile graduates

Person(s) stated to be major influence on career and education	Men	Women
	%	%
Parent(s)	32	46
Other family	6	5
Friend(s)	5	2
Teacher at school	44	40
University (lecturers or Appointments Boards)	8	5
Others*	5	2
ALL	100	100
No. answering	1086	347

* Includes Youth Employment Officers, potential employers and miscellaneous persons.

Table 19. Attitudes to university of parents of upwardly mobile graduates

Attitude	Fathers	Mothers
	%	%
Active encouragement	58	65
Friendly interest	28	25
Neutral	8	6
Rather opposed	2	2
No answer, unknown	4	2
ALL	100	100
No. of upwardly mobile graduates	3139	3139

Table 20. Major influences on intergenerationally stable graduates*

Person(s) stated to be major influence on career and education	Men	Women
	%	%
Parent(s)	52	56
Other family	3	3
Friend(s)	3	1
Teacher at school	31	33
University (lecturers or Appointments Boards)	7	5
Others	4	2
ALL	100	100
No. answering	2228	1060

* Father in professional or intermediate non-manual work (Registrar-General's classes I and II) when respondent entered university.

Table 21. Subjects studied by intergenerationally mobile and stable graduates

| | Men | | Women | |
	Stable	Mobile	Stable	Mobile
	%	%	%	%
Arts	27	29	58	63
Social Science	18	9	11	7
Science	26	33 }	29 }	28
Technology	27	28		
Other	2	1	2	2
ALL SUBJECTS	100	100	100	100
No.	4292	2422	1944	717

Table 22. Graduates of working-class origin in different university groups

| University group * | Percentage of working-class origin | |
	Men	Women
Oxbridge	13	6
London	24	18
Scottish	24	20
Smaller Civic	30	22
Larger Civic	35	23
Wales	43	34
ALL UNIVERSITIES	26	20
No.	2422	717

* See R. K. Kelsall *et al.*, *Six Years After*, 91, for a list of institutions included in the survey.

Table 23. Academic performance of stable and mobile graduates in two university groups

	Percentage obtaining good* degrees			
	Oxbridge		Wales	
	Stable	Mobile	Stable	Mobile
MEN *Faculty*				
Arts	29 (8)	30 (6)	39 (12)	37 (11)
Social Science	18 (8)	16 (8)	50 (—)†	— (—)†
Science	28 (16)	41 (21)	50 (27)†	48 (22)†
Technology	32 (14)	42 (25)†	23 (5)	15 (—)
WOMEN *Faculty*				
Arts	28 (8)	25 (5)†	37 (7)	15 (2)
Social Science	29 (11)†	— (—)†	— (—)†	— (—)†
Science	12 (9)	67 (17)	39 (10)†	35 (6)†

* Firsts and upper seconds. The percentage of firsts only is given in brackets.

† No. (in this cell) < 50.

Table 24. Motives of intergenerationally mobile and stable graduates wanting higher education

Motive*	Stable graduates	Mobile graduates
	%	%
Instrumental	28	33
Expressive	49	45
BOTH TYPES	77	78
No. keen to go to university	5005	2539

* *Instrumental:* to qualify for a career, for a better chance to get on, to better myself socially, etc.

Expressive: to broaden my education, pursue my subject, develop academically, for family reasons (e.g. tradition), for the fun of university life, etc.

N

Table 25. Social origins and achieved social classes

Respondent's social class	Father's social class					
	Professional	Intermediate non-manual	Routine non-manual	Skilled manual	Semi-skilled manual	Unskilled manual
	%	%	%	%	%	%
MEN*						
Professional	40	35	31	31	29	21
Intermediate non-manual	57	62	67	67	69	77
Routine non-manual	1	1	2	2	2	2
Other or unknown	2	2	—	—	—	—
ALL CLASSES	100	100	100	100	100	100
No.	1132	3160	1316	1738	580	104
WOMEN*						
Professional	11	10	7	7	6	6
Intermediate non-manual	77	80	83	86	85	88
Routine non-manual	12	10	10	7	9	6
Other or unknown	—	—	—	—	—	—
ALL CLASSES	100	100	100	100	100	100
No.	537	1407	473	507	192	18

* Men's classes are based on their occupations on 1 October 1966, and those of the women on their first jobs after graduation.

Table 26. Men's* occupational aspirations at three points in time

Type of occupation in mind	On entering university	Before finals	On graduating
	%	%	%
Teaching in school or further education	22	20	22
Teaching or research in a university	9	17	16
Research development or production *not* in a university	25	21	20
Administrative or managerial	13	16	16
Professional services	20	17	17
Other specified types	11	9	9
ALL MEN WITH AN OCCUPATION IN MIND	100	100	100
No.	5782	7478	8074
PROPORTIONS HAVING AN OCCUPATION IN MIND	55	80	86
No.	9404	9404	9404

* Data in Tables 26 to 47 refer to male respondents only.

Table 27. Subject of degree and occupational plans on entry to university

Type of occupation in mind	Arts	Social Science	Science	Technology
	%	%	%	%
Teaching in school or further education	45	6	23	4
Teaching or research in a university	6	5	20	5
Research development or production *not* in a university	1	1	39	50
Administrative or managerial	14	24	4	14
Professional services	15	56	8	18
Other specified types	19	8	5	9
ALL MEN WITH AN OCCUPATION IN MIND	100	100	100	100
No.	1440	768	1356	1512
PROPORTIONS HAVING AN OCCUPATION IN MIND	51	56	50	64
No.	2810	1366	2690	2382

Table 28. Type of secondary school attended and occupational plans on entry to university

Type of occupation in mind	Independent	Direct Grant	LEA
	%	%	%
Teaching in school or further education	11	23	26
Teaching or research in a university	5	11	10
Research development or production *not* in a university	16	23	30
Administrative or managerial	20	13	9
Professional services	31	21	16
Other specified types	16	9	9
ALL MEN WITH AN OCCUPATION IN MIND	100	100	100
No.	1290	926	2924
PROPORTIONS HAVING AN OCCUPATION IN MIND	55	55	56
No.	2330	1674	5222

Table 29. University group and occupational plans on entry to university

Type of occupation in mind	Scottish	Wales	Larger Civic	Smaller Civic	Oxbridge	London
	%	%	%	%	%	%
Teaching in school or further education	22	37	20	35	17	16
Teaching or research in a university	7	6	8	5	12	13
Research development or production *not* in a university	27	28	33	26	12	30
Administrative or managerial	14	6	11	9	17	12
Professional services	22	17	19	11	27	19
Other specified types	8	6	8	13	16	9
ALL MEN WITH AN OCCUPATION IN MIND	100	100	100	100	100	100
No.	540	334	1604	584	1428	758
PROPORTIONS HAVING AN OCCUPATION IN MIND	62	56	57	58	51	59
No.	870	600	2802	1024	2818	1290

Table 30. University, social origin and occupational plans on entry to university

Type of occupation in mind	Scottish				Wales				Larger Civic			
	Prof.	Int.	Routine non-man.	Man.	Prof.	Int.	Routine non-man.	Man.	Prof.	Int.	Routine non-man.	Man.
	%	%	%	%	%	%	%	%	%	%	%	%
(1) Teaching in school or further education	15	11	24	30	9	26	32	43	10	16	24	23
(2) Teaching or research in a university	3	9	9	8	9	11	4	6	8	8	8	10
(3) Research development or production *not* in a university	18	24	32	37	36	34	12	31	27	29	33	41
(4) Administrative or managerial	18	17	9	10	27	3	12	5	12	15	12	7
(5) Professional services	36	26	21	10	9	16	32	9	35	22	17	12
(6) Other specified types	9	12	6	5	9	9	8	6	8	10	5	7
(7) ALL MEN WITH AN OCCUPATION IN MIND	100	100	100	100	100	100	100	100	100	100	100	100
(8) No.	66	196	68	134	22	76	50	134	148	502	236	524
(9) PROPORTIONS HAVING AN OCCUPATION IN MIND	60	68	66	64	73	49	68	53	63	60	57	53
(10) No.	110	288	122	208	30	156	74	256	236	842	412	986

Table 30—*continued*

	Smaller Civic				Oxbridge				London				ALL UNIVERSITIES			
	Prof.	*Int.*	*Routine non-man.*	*Man.*	*Prof.*	*Int.*	*Routine non-man.*	*Man.*	*Prof.*	*Int.*	*Routine non-man.*	*Man.*	*Prof.*	*Int.*	*Routine non-man.*	*Man.*
	%	%	%	%	%	%	%	%	%	%	%	%	%	%	%	%
(1)	19	29	46	40	9	13	33	24	6	12	26	21	10	16	29	28
(2)	—	2	5	6	8	11	11	19	6	10	9	15	7	9	9	10
(3)	38	32	15	22	11	12	15	14	42	29	30	30	22	23	24	32
(4)	14	8	10	11	14	21	11	11	10	18	9	12	14	16	11	9
(5)	10	13	10	12	39	27	20	18	28	19	13	15	33	23	18	13
(6)	19	15	15	9	18	16	9	15	8	12	13	6	13	13	9	8
(7)	100	100	100	100	100	100	100	100	100	100	100	100	100	100	100	100
(8)	42	186	82	190	294	592	178	160	100	250	92	168	672	1802	706	1310
(9)	44	60	47	61	58	51	54	45	64	60	45	54	59	57	64	54
(10)	96	308	176	310	506	1156	330	354	156	414	204	310	1134	3164	1318	2424

Table 31. Social origin and type of secondary school and university attended

Father's social class	School type					University							
	Independent	Direct Grant	LEA	ALL SCHOOLS	No.*	Scottish	Wales	Larger Civic	Smaller Civic	Oxbridge	London	ALL UNIVERSITIES	No.
	%	%	%	%		%	%	%	%	%	%	%	
Professional	50	17	30	100	1132	10	3	21	8	45	14	100	1132
Intermediate	31	19	48	100	3160	9	5	27	10	37	13	100	3160
Routine non-manual	15	19	65	100	1316	9	6	31	13	25	16	100	1316
Manual	6	16	77	100	2422	9	10	41	13	14	13	100	2422

* Includes graduates who attended other types of school.

Table 32. **Subject and university group**

	Scottish	Wales	Larger Civic	Smaller Civic	Oxbridge	London
	%	%	%	%	%	%
Arts	34	34	19	38	42	15
Social Science	7	. 5	12	11	22	18
Science	26	24	30	35	24	35
Technology	33	35	37	15	11	30
Other subjects or unknown	—	1	2	1	1	2
ALL MEN	100	100	100	100	100	100
No.	870	600	2802	1024	2818	1290

Table 33. Gains in aspiring recruits to each occupation

Type of occupation in mind	(a) On entering university	(b) On graduating	(c) Net gain (b)−(a)	Percentage gain
Teaching in school or further education	1118	1774	656	59
Teaching or research in a university	478	1294	816	171
Research development or production *not* in a university	1318	1648	330	25
Administrative or managerial	654	1268	614	94
Professional services	1048	1362	314	30
Other specified types	566	728	162	29

Table 34. Subject of degree and occupational plans on graduation

Type of occupation in mind	Arts	Social Science	Science	Technology
	%	%	%	%
Teaching in school or further education	41	7	21	8
Teaching or research in a university	10	8	32	9
Research development or production *not* in a university	1	3	30	42
Administrative or managerial	19	30	6	15
Professional services	14	42	7	17
Other specified types	15	9	4	8
ALL MEN WITH AN OCCUPATION IN MIND	100	100	100	100
No.	2370	1156	2380	2076
PROPORTIONS HAVING AN OCCUPATION IN MIND	84	85	89	87
No.	2810	1366	2690	2382

Table 35. Class of degree and occupational plans on graduation

Type of occupation in mind	First	Upper second	Undivided second	Lower second	Other honours	Ordinary
	%	%	%	%	%	%
Teaching in school or further education	9	18	24	26	24	25
Teaching or research in a university	48	34	17	11	3	3
Research development or production *not* in a university	21	18	13	23	17	25
Administrative or managerial	8	12	18	15	22	16
Professional services	9	12	19	18	20	20
Other specified types	5	5	9	8	14	12
ALL MEN WITH AN OCCUPATION IN MIND	100	100	100	100	100	100
No.	810	1682	880	1754	1312	1620
PROPORTIONS HAVING AN OCCUPATION IN MIND	89	88	84	84	85	87
No.	908	1910	1050	2080	1548	1862

Table 36. Subject, social origin and occupational plans on graduation

Type of occupation in mind	Arts				Social Science				Science				Technology			
	Prof.	Int.	Routine non-man.	Man.	Prof.	Int.	Routine non-man.	Man.	Prof.	Int.	Routine non-man.	Man.	Prof.	Int.	Routine non-man.	Man.
	%	%	%	%	%	%	%	%	%	%	%	%	%	%	%	%
Teaching in school or further education	27	34	45	53	2	7	7	12	16	18	28	22	3	6	4	14
Teaching or research in a university	16	9	9	10	3	6	12	14	35	32	31	30	5	9	11	11
Research development or production *not* in a university	1	1	1	—	1	3	1	5	31	27	28	37	38	39	48	47
Administrative or managerial	20	21	21	15	34	32	19	29	4	10	6	5	22	18	14	9
Professional services	15	19	12	10	54	42	49	34	9	8	5	5	21	18	17	14
Other specified types	22	16	13	12	5	10	12	6	5	5	3	2	10	10	7	5
ALL MEN WITH AN OCCUPATION IN MIND	100	100	100	100	100	100	100	100	100	100	100	100	100	100	100	100
No.	296	722	364	588	182	462	136	192	248	736	390	690	236	766	218	604
PROPORTIONS HAVING AN OCCUPATION IN MIND	87	87	80	84	87	84	81	86	87	90	88	89	88	88	88	88
No.	342	832	454	704	212	554	154	224	286	820	446	778	268	890	248	690

Table 37. Class of degree, social origin and occupational plans on graduation

Type of occupation in mind	First or upper second				Other second				Other honours				Ordinary			
	Prof.	Int.	Routine non-man.	Man.	Prof.	Int.	Routine non-man.	Man.	Prof.	Int.	Routine non-man.	Man.	Prof.	Int.	Routine non-man.	Man.
	%	%	%	%	%	%	%	%	%	%	%	%	%	%	%	%
Teaching in school or further education	13	11	19	18	16	22	29	31	13	19	34	34	9	16	29	33
Teaching or research in a university	33	34	35	40	14	11	14	10	3	2	3	3	1	2	4	3
Research development or production *not* in a university	22	21	20	20	15	17	15	28	12	14	21	26	21	23	24	32
Administrative or managerial	12	14	9	9	19	18	15	13	28	27	18	14	23	20	17	11
Professional services	13	13	13	9	22	22	18	13	26	22	12	13	38	24	15	13
Other specified types	7	6	4	4	14	9	9	5	18	16	12	9	9	15	11	9
ALL MEN WITH AN OCCUPATION IN MIND	100	100	100	100	100	100	100	100	100	100	100	100	100	100	100	100
No.	278	820	366	686	366	882	374	656	182	498	194	258	164	566	190	486
PROPORTIONS HAVING AN OCCUPATION IN MIND	90	89	87	90	88	88	84	84	84	86	86	86	87	96	85	86
No.	310	924	422	760	418	1020	444	786	218	580	226	300	188	628	224	568

Table 38. Type of secondary school attended and occupational plans on graduation

Type of occupation in mind	Independent	Direct Grant	LEA
	%	%	%
Teaching in school or further education	13	22	26
Teaching or research in a university	9	17	18
Research development or production *not* in a university	13	19	24
Administrative or managerial	26	16	11
Professional services	26	16	13
Other specified types	13	9	7
ALL MEN WITH AN OCCUPATION IN MIND	100	100	100
No.	1994	1468	4556
PROPORTIONS HAVING AN OCCUPATION IN MIND	86	88	87
No.	2330	1674	5222

Table 39. University, social origin and occupational plans on graduation

Type of occupation	Scottish				Wales				Larger Civic			
	Prof.	Int.	Routine non-man.	Man.	Prof.	Int.	Routine non-man.	Man.	Prof.	Int.	Routine non-man.	Man.
	%	%	%	%	%	%	%	%	%	%	%	%
(1) Teaching in school or further education	14	17	33	33	27	24	26	46	8	18	23	23
(2) Teaching or research in a university	16	15	15	18	27	32	26	16	28	16	19	17
(3) Research development or production *not* in a university	16	21	19	21	27	21	16	19	20	25	24	35
(4) Administrative or managerial	20	13	12	10	13	6	10	10	15	15	11	8
(5) Professional services	31	26	13	13	7	9	13	5	23	17	18	11
(6) Other specified types	2	8	8	5	—	8	10	5	6	9	5	5
(7) ALL MEN WITH AN OCCUPATION IN MIND	100	100	100	100	100	100	100	100	100	100	100	100
(8) No.	98	266	104	182	30	132	62	218	208	752	352	856
(9) PROPORTIONS HAVING AN OCCUPATION IN MIND	89	94	85	88	100	86	81	85	88	90	85	87
(10) No.	110	288	122	208	30	156	74	256	236	842	412	986

Table 39—continued

O

	Smaller Civic				Oxbridge				London				All Universities			
	Prof.	Int.	Routine non-man.	Man.	Prof.	Int.	Routine non-man.	Man.	Prof.	Int.	Routine non-man.	Man.	Prof.	Int.	Routine non-man.	Routine Man.
	%	%	%	%	%	%	%	%	%	%	%	%	%	%	%	%
(1)	22	29	40	36	15	16	26	26	11	9	19	19	14	17	27	28
(2)	8	17	17	17	11	10	15	15	12	13	15	24	15	14	17	17
(3)	19	15	16	19	10	11	12	13	35	30	26	25	17	19	19	26
(4)	22	11	15	9	21	28	19	22	18	18	12	10	19	19	14	11
(5)	8	14	7	13	28	23	17	14	11	20	16	14	23	20	15	12
(6)	22	14	5	6	16	12	11	10	12	9	12	7	12	10	8	6
(7)	100	100	100	100	100	100	100	100	100	100	100	100	100	100	100	100
(8)	74	264	156	276	448	972	286	296	132	374	170	270	990	2758	1124	2096
(9)	77	87	89	89	89	84	87	84	85	90	85	87	87	87	85	86
(10)	96	308	176	310	506	1156	330	354	156	414	204	310	1134	3164	1318	2424

Table 40. Class of degree and employment sector

Employment sector (1 October 1966)	Classified degrees					Unclassified degrees	ALL CLASSES
	First	Upper second	Undiv. second	Lower second	Third, fourth and pass inc. Aegrotat		
	%	%	%	%	%	%	%
Public administration	8	10	10	10	8	11	10
Education	51	41	39	36	28	28	36
Industry	24	29	22	29	28	31	28
Commerce	2	5	7	5	10	6	6
Private practice	3	5	7	8	9	7	7
Churches and others	6	8	10	7	13	13	9
Not employed on 1 October 1966 or no details given	5	3	4	5	4	3	4
ALL SECTORS	100	100	100	100	100	100	100

Table 41. Subject of degree and employment sector

Employment sector (1 October 1966)	Arts	Social Science	Science	Techno-logy	Other Subjects	ALL SUBJECTS
	%	%	%	%	%	%
Public administration	11	10	8	12	22	10
Education	53	19	46	19	46	36
Industry	11	20	31	50	13	28
Commerce	6	14	4	4	1	6
Private practice	2	27	1	5	10	7
Churches and others	13	7	6	6	10	9
Not employed on 1 October 1966 or no details given	4	4	4	4	7	4
ALL SECTORS	100	100	100	100	100	100

Table 42. Work in 1966 and social origin

	Professional	Intermediate	Routine non-manual	Manual
EMPLOYMENT SECTOR:	%	%	%	%
Public administration	10	9	11	11
Education	28	29	40	44
Industry	27	30	27	29
Commerce	6	8	5	3
Private practice	12	7	5	4
Churches and others	12	12	8	6
Not employed on 1 October 1966 or no details given	4	4	3	3
ALL SECTORS	100	100	100	100
TYPE OF WORK:				
Production	4	4	4	4
Commercial	9	10	8	6
Research	27	27	28	28
Professions	44	40	47	49
Management	7	8	4	5
Others	4	6	6	5
Not employed on 1 October 1966 or no details given	4	4	3	3
ALL TYPES	100	100	100	100
No.	1132	3160	1316	2422

Table 43. Social origin and the realization of occupational aspirations

| | Occupation in mind on graduation | | | | | | | | | | | | | | | |
| | University teaching or research | | | | School teaching | | | | Administrative or managerial | | | | Other professions | | | |
	Prof.	Int.	Routine non-man.	Man.	Prof.	Int.	Routine non-man.	Man.	Prof.	Int.	Routine non-man.	Man.	Prof.	Int.	Routine non-man.	Man.
% who achieved their ambitions by 1966	46	46	38	49	82	85	89	85	53	60	62	44	61	60	62	52
No.	70	182	74	178	110	408	266	492	100	312	96	102	138	328	102	130
TOTALS	152	398	194	366	134	478	300	578	188	524	156	232	226	546	164	248

Table 44. Social origins of men in 'prestigious' occupations in 1966

Type of employment	Professional and intermediate	Other non-manual	Manual	Other*	ALL CLASSES	No.
	%	%	%	%	%	
Legal profession	64	11	11	14	100	414
General management	56	9	19	15	100	618
Administrative class of the Home Civil Service	45	14	14	26	100	84
ALL MEN	46	14	26	14	100	9404

* Including cases in which father's social class is unknown.

Table 45. Academic characteristics of Higher Civil Servants and of all men graduates

	Men in the Administrative Class in 1966 (No. = 84)	All 1960 men graduates (No. = 9404)
	%	%
UNIVERSITY GROUP:		
Scottish	21	9
Oxbridge	57	30
Wales	5	6
London	10	14
Larger Civic	7	30
Smaller Civic	—	11
TYPE OF SECONDARY SCHOOL:		
Independent	40	25
Direct Grant	17	18
LEA	43	56
Other	—	1
CLASS OF DEGREE:		
First	12	10
Upper second	19	20
Undivided second	29	11
Lower second	24	22
Other classified	10	17
Unclassified	7	20

Table 46. Social origins of men in education in 1966

Type of educational institution		Professional and intermediate	Routine non-manual	Manual	Other	ALL CLASSES	No.
		%	%	%	%	%	
Universities	%	43 (35)	14 (27)	27 (26)	16 (32)	100	1038
Other further education institutions	%	39 (14)	17 (15)	31 (13)	13 (12)	100	454
Schools	%	33 (51)	17 (59)	34 (60)	15 (56)	100	1880
ALL EDUCATIONAL INSTITUTIONS		(100)	(100)	(100)	(100)		
No.		(1252)	(534)	(1062)	(524)		3372

Table 47. **Propensity of graduate men to take up a teaching career**

Social origin	Floud and Scott* (1947–51)	Kelsall, Poole and Kuhn (1966)†
	%	%
Working class	18·5	26·6
Other	15·5	17·7
ALL CLASSES	16·3	20·0

* *Source:* J. Floud and W. Scott, 'Recruitment to teaching in England and Wales', in A. H. Halsey *et al.* (eds.), *Education, Economy and Society*, 539.

† Before drawing any points of comparison one cautionary remark is in order. Floud and Scott's study only covered recruitment into teaching from England and Wales, whereas we have included graduates from Scottish universities. However, since Scottish universities have among the lowest proportion of graduates from working-class backgrounds and Scottish graduates as a whole have quite a marked propensity to enter school teaching we have probably, as a result, underestimated rather than over-estimated the particular tendency of working-class graduates in England and Wales to embark on a teaching career.

Table 48. **Proportions of men and women married**

	Men	Women
	%	%
Population aged 25–34 in 1966*	78	87
1960 graduates:		
(a) in 1966	72	71
(b) in 1968†	85	76

* *Source: Annual Abstract of Statistics, 1967 (England and Wales)* Table 25.

† *Source:* M. Fogarty *et al.*, *Sex, Career and Family* (London, Allen and Unwin, 1971) 239.

Table 49. Postgraduate study and the timing of marriage

Time of marriage after first graduation	Doctorate	Dip.Ed.	First degree only
	%	%	%
Men graduates:			
Up to 2 years	34	38	44
2–6 years	41	31	30
Not married 6 years after	26	31	25
Women graduates:			
Up to 2 years	30	32	59
2–6 years	34	36	22
Not married 6 years after	34	31	18

Table 50. Timing of marriage by graduate women teachers

Year of starting to teach	Percentage married		Percentage unmarried 5 years later
	Up to 1 year later	2–5 years later	
1936*	3	33	64
1949*	4	34	62
1954*	25	34	41
1961	32	36	32

* Source: R. K. Kelsall, *Women and Teaching* (London, H.M.S.O., 1963) 38, Table 11.

Table 51. Social classes of graduates' marriage partners

Wives* of men graduates			*Husbands† of women graduates*		
		%			%
Professional and inter-mediate non-manual	3502	61	Professional and inter-mediate non-manual	2217	91
Routine non-manual	2042	36	Routine non-manual	129	5
Skilled manual	140	2	Skilled manual	77	3
Semi-skilled and unskilled manual	66	1	Semi-skilled and unskilled manial	21	1
No.	5750	100	No.	2444	100

* Based on wife's occupation at marriage.
† Based on husband's main occupation since marriage.

Table 52. Full time further education of graduates' marriage partners

	Wives of men graduates	*Husbands of women graduates*
	%	%
None	25	13
University	32	78
Commercial, Technical, Art, Agricultural	14	5
Teacher training	16	2
Nursing training	9	—
Some other type	4	2
ALL TYPES	100	100
No.	6748	2550

Table 53. Timing of first births

Interval between marriage and first birth	Men graduates	Women graduates
	%	%
Less than 8 months (premarital conception)	12	11
9–12 months	18	17
1–2 years	33	30
2–3 years	18	21
3–4 years	11	13
4–6 years	6	7
6–10 years	1	—
Average interval (months)	14·98	15·73
ALL MARRIED GRADUATES WITH CHILDREN	100	100
No.	4320	1618

Table 54. Postgraduate study and the timing of first birth

Interval	Doctorate	Dip.Ed.	First Degree
	%	%	%
Married from first graduation to 2 years later:			
9–12 months	10	12	14
1–2 years	17	19	22
2–3 years	17	15	17
3–4 years	13	14	14
4–6 years	11	6	7
6–10 years	—	—	1
No children	25	25	16
ALL BIRTHS*	100	100	100
Married from 2 to 6 years after graduation:			
9–12 months	8	8	8
1–2 years	16	14	23
2–3 years	5	10	7
3–4 years	1	2	2
4–6 years	—	—	—
6–10 years	—	—	—
No children	64	58	51
ALL BIRTHS*	100	100	100

* Including premarital conceptions.

Table 55. Fertility and the timing of marriage

Married	Average number of children	
	Men graduates	Women graduates
Before university or during course	1·95	1·42
On graduation or up to 2 years after	1·38	1·34
2–6 years after	0·54	0·54
ALL MARRIAGES	1·00	0·99

Table 56. Fertility and level of education

Terminal education age	Mean number of children
Husband 17–19, wife ≥ 20	1·94
Husband ≥ 20, wife 17–19	2·06
Both ≥ 20	2·07

Source: Census 1961, Fertility tables, Table 18: marriages of twenty or more years' duration only.

Table 57. Social mobility and the timing of first birth

	Average interval between marriage and first birth (*months*)			
	Men graduates		Women graduates	
	Stable	Mobile*	Stable	Mobile*
Dip.Ed.	14·09	12·94	14·30	12·88
First degree	16·61	17·83	18·43	18·00

* Of manual working-class origin only.

Table 58. Fertility and social origin

Father's social class	Men graduates			Women graduates		
	Average no. children	S.D.	No.	Average no. children	S.D.	No.
Professional and intermediate	1·01	0·92	2998	1·04	0·93	1398
Routine non-manual	0·99	0·89	984	0·88	0·93	346
Skilled manual	0·98	0·94	1320	0·94	0·94	362
Semi-skilled and unskilled manual	1·01	0·92	528	0·84	0·99	149

Table 59. Fertility and achieved social class

	Men graduates		Women graduates	
Social class*	Average number of children	Average interval between marriage and first birth (months)	Average number of children	Average interval between marriage and first birth (months)
Professional	0·98	14·21	0·81	11·64
Intermediate non-manual	1·03	15·66	0·97	16·08
Routine non-manual	0·98	16·48	0·96	18·06

* Men – based on 1966 occupation; women – based on first occupation after graduation.

Table 60. Fertility of employed and self-employed professional men

	No. married	Average number of children	Average interval between marriage and first birth (months)
Self-employed	272	1·02	13·69
Employees	2660	1·02	14·96

Table 61. Fertility of men in four occupational groups

Occupational group, 1 October 1966	No. married	Average number of children	Average interval between marriage and first birth (months)
Engineering	1522	1·09	14·89
Commerce	588	1·08	15·07
University and further education: teaching and research	1110	1·00	15·17
School teaching	1166	0·96	15·54

Table 62. Women's* social origins and their motives for wanting higher education

Motive†	Father's social class			
	Professional	Intermediate	Routine non-manual	Manual
	%	%	%	%
Expressive	62	59	63	55
Instrumental	17	20	18	25
Other	4	5	4	5
No answer	15	15	14	14
ALL	100	100	100	100

* Unless otherwise stated, data in Tables 62 to 82 refer to women respondents only.

† Answers included in the expressive category were 'to pursue a subject', 'parents encouraged me', 'school influence', 'it was natural', 'to get away' etc.: those included in the instrumental category were 'career reasons', 'to better myself', etc.

P

Table 63. Social origin and occupational plans

	Professional		Intermediate		Routine non-manual		Manual		ALL WOMEN	
	(a)* %	(b)† %	(a) %	(b) %	(a) %	(b) %	(a) %	(b) %	(a) %	(b) %
Teaching in school or further education	38	44	52	52	60	61	66	63	54	55
Teaching or research in a university	9	13	7	10	6	7	4	9	6	10
Research development or production *not* in a university	11	7	10	8	8	7	9	6	9	7
Administrative or managerial	5	6	4	5	5	4	2	4	4	5
Professional services	25	17	19	14	14	15	12	11	17	14
Other	12	13	9	11	7	6	7	8	9	9
ALL WOMEN WITH AN OCCUPATION IN MIND	100	100	100	100	100	100	100	100	100	100
No.	256	416	651	1128	247	393	395	592	1772	2846
PROPORTIONS HAVING AN OCCUPATION IN MIND	48	77	46	80	52	83	55	83	49	79
No.	537		1407		473		717		3582	

* (a) On entry to university.   † (b) On graduation.

Table 64. Social origin and postgraduate study

Highest qualification attempted	Professional and intermediate	Routine non-manual	Manual
	%	%	%
Doctorate	4	4	3
Masters	5	4	4
Teacher training	33	40	42
Other professional training	19	15	14
Further first degree	1	2	—
No paper qualification	7	5	3
No postgraduate study	31	29	33
ALL	100	100	100
No.	1944	473	717

Table 65. Social origin and motives for undertaking postgraduate study

Motive*	Professional and intermediate	Routine non-manual	Manual
	%	%	%
Instrumental	54	65	63
Expressive	20	23	19
None	26	12	18
No.	1324	334	484

* The categories with an expressive orientation were 'a desire for more study for its own sake', 'a desire to continue to participate in student life', etc.: those with a predominantly instrumental character were 'a need to obtain particular professional qualifications', 'a need to obtain a higher degree for career reasons', 'attractive offer of postgraduate finance', etc.

Table 66. First and 1966 employment sectors of men and working women

Employment sector	First employer		1966 employer	
	Men	Women	Men	Women
	%	%	%	%
Public administration	11	14	10	13
Education	33	61	36	68
Industry	33	8	28	5
Commerce	5	4	6	3
Private practice	8	1	7	1
Churches and others	9	7	8	10
No employment	1	3	4	—
ALL SECTORS	100	100	100	100
No.	9404	3852	9404	2014

Table 67. Last jobs* and social origins

Type of work	Professional	Intermediate	Routine non-manual	Manual
	%	%	%	%
Production	1	—	1	—
Commercial	2	1	1	—
Research	14	15	12	12
Professions	59	63	71	73
Management	8	7	7	6
Others	13	11	—	7
No employment up to 1 October 1966	2	3	7	2
ALL TYPES	100	100	100	100
No.	537	1407	473	717

* i.e. before retirement if not employed on 1 October 1966.

Table 68. Civil status and propensity to work

Civil status	No.	Proportion in paid employment 1 October 1966
Single	976	91
Married	2550	42
Divorced, widowed, separated	56	92
ALL WOMEN	3582	56

Table 69. Civil status and employment sector

Employment sector (1 October 1966)	Single	Married	ALL WOMEN WORK-ING IN 1966*
	%	%	%
Public administration	17	10	13
Education	63	71	68
Industry	4	5	5
Commerce	4	3	3
Private practice	2	2	1
Others	10	8	10
ALL SECTORS	100	100	100
No.	893	1082	2014

* Including separated and divorced women.

Table 70. Employment status and husband's social class

Husband's social class	Wife's employment status 1 October 1966				ALL MARRIED WOMEN	No.
	Employed full-time	Employed part-time	Housewife	Others*		
	%	%	%	%	%	
Professional	24	14	58	3	100	1112
Intermediate	26	16	56	1	100	1105
Routine non-manual	38	14	48	—	100	129
Manual	33	14	50	3	100	98
Forces	16†	8†	76†	—	100	37
No answer	31	19	47	3	100	69
ALL MARRIED WOMEN	26	15	56	3	100	2550

* Includes self-employed women and students.
† Numbers on which percentages are based are unreliably small.

Table 71. Employment status of graduate mothers and their husbands' earnings

Husband's earnings p.a.	Employed full-time	Employed part-time	Self-employed	Housewife full-time	ALL MOTHERS	No.
	%	%	%	%	%	
£1000 or less	7	17	3	72	100	69
£1001–£1500	7	16	1	77	100	370
£1501–£2000	4	17	1	78	100	541
£2001–£2500	4	18	3	75	100	249
£2501 or more	5	18	3	75	100	247
Not known	10	12	4	75	100	142
No.	100	264	32	1212		1618*

* Includes ten mothers who were students.

Table 72. Employment status and husband's income

Husband's income	Graduate wives working	Graduate wives working full-time
	%	%
£1000 or less	81	74
£1001–£2000	64	59
£2001–£3000	61	49
£3000 or more	46	51

Source: C. E. Arregger, *Graduate Women at Work* (London, British Federation of University Women, 1966) 23.

Table 73. Mothers' reasons for working and their husbands' earnings

Motive*	Husband's annual income				
	£1500 or less	£1501–£2000	£2001–£2500	£2501 or more	ALL WORKING MOTHERS
	%	%	%	%	%
Instrumental	55	36	33	25	38
Expressive	38	56	57	70	44
Other	7	8	10	5	18
ALL	100	100	100	100	100
No.	105	118	61	70	396†

* Motives included in the instrumental category were 'family financial reasons', 'to have money of my own', etc.: those of a predominantly expressive nature were 'to continue career interests', 'to make use of my education', 'need of company', 'for enjoyment', 'for mental stimulus', etc.

† Includes cases in which husband's income is unknown.

Table 74. Reasons* for wanting to work given by full-time housewives

	%
Instrumental	34
Expressive	48
Other	18
ALL	100
No. answering	897

* Reasons included in the instrumental category were 'family financial', 'to have money of my own', etc.: those of a mainly expressive character included 'to be useful', 'need for mental stimulus', 'for interest', 'to make use of my education', 'need of company', etc.

Table 75. Main reason given by married women graduates for not working

Reason for not working 1 October 1966	Without children	With at least one child
	%	%
No one to look after my children	—	18
Prefer to look after my own children	—	68
Pregnancy	59	—
Husband's work entails frequent moves	5	6
Looking for post	15	4
Just moved house	9	1
Transport difficulties	3	—
Too busy	3	1
Health reasons	2	—
Full-time student	2	1
Other reasons	2	—
ALL MARRIED WOMEN NOT IN PAID EMPLOYMENT ANSWERING	100	100
No.	131	780

Table 76. Paid domestic help received by graduate mothers

Help received	Employment status 1 October 1966				ALL MOTHERS
	Self-employed	Employed full-time	Employed part-time	Full-time housewife	
	%	%	%	%	%
Some	41	46	39	20	26
None	59	54	61	80	74
ALL	100	100	100	100	100
No.	32	100	264	1212	1618*

* Includes ten women who were students

Table 77. Perceived job characteristics of women and men employed full-time in education in 1966

	Women (net score*)	Men (net score*)
Congenial colleagues, etc.	56	62
Good salary etc.	23	24
Opportunities for intellectual development	−8	27
Scope for initiative	30	49
Novelty	−3	12
Socially useful work	50	42
High level administration	−72	−64
Other work involving communication with people	−44	−32
Opportunities to rise to the top	−25	5

* For details of 'net score', see Chapter 2, note 47.

Table 78. Characteristics of graduate mothers

	Employment status 1 October 1966			
Characteristics	Self-employed No. 32	Employed full-time No. 100	Full-time housewife No. 1212	ALL MOTHERS No. 1618*
	%	%	%	%
SCHOOL ATTENDED				
Independent	34	16	19	19
LEA	50	66	62	62
Others	16	18	19	19
UNIVERSITY ATTENDED				
Scottish	6	10	16	15
Wales	3	8	8	8
Larger Civic	22	28	29	28
Smaller Civic	9	19	18	17
Oxbridge	31	13	11	13
London	28	21	18	19
WHETHER PARENTS CONTINUED THEIR EDUCATION AFTER LEAVING SCHOOL				
Yes	69	59	64	63
No	31	40	36	36
Other answers	—	1	—	1
FATHER'S SOCIAL CLASS ON RESPONDENT'S ENTRY TO UNIVERSITY				
Professional	19	15	15	16
Intermediate	38	43	41	41
Routine non-manual	9	9	13	13
Skilled manual	16	12	14	14
Other manual	3	8	5	5
Others	16	13	11	11
WHETHER HUSBAND UNDERTOOK FURTHER FULL-TIME EDUCATION				
Yes	94	87	89	89
No	6	11	11	11
Other answers	—	2	—	—

* Includes students and part-time workers.

Table 78—*continued*

	Employment status 1 October 1966			
	Self-employed	*Employed full-time*	*Full-time housewife*	ALL MOTHERS
	%	%	%	%
HUSBAND'S FURTHER EDUCATION				
University	97	74	81	80
Commercial, Art, etc.	—	6	5	5
Teacher training	—	6	1	2
Other answers	—	—	2	2
None	3	14	11	11
HUSBAND'S SALARY ON 1 OCTOBER 1966				
Under £2000 p.a.	41	54	61	60
Over £2001 p.a.	43	23	30	30
No answer	16	23	9	10
NUMBER OF CHILDREN				
One only	50	61	49	51
Two	41	33	43	42
Three	9	6	7	6
Four or more	—	—	1	1
Mean number of children	1·59	1·45	1·60	1·57
FIRST CHILD BORN				
Before graduation	—	11	1	2
6 months after graduation	—	2	—	—
1 year after graduation	3	5	1	2
18 months after graduation	3	2	4	4
2 years after graduation	3	12	5	6
3 years after graduation	22	20	16	16
3–6 years after graduation	66	42	67	65
No answer	3	5	4	4
Median time after graduation	3–6 yrs	2–3 yrs	3–6 yrs	3–6 yrs

Table 78—*continued*

| | Employment status 1 October 1966 | | | |
	Self-employed	Employed full-time	Full-time housewife	ALL MOTHERS
	%	%	%	%
HIGHEST POSTGRADUATE QUALIFICATION ATTEMPTED				
Doctorate	3	16	3	4
Masters	6	6	4	4
Teacher training	16	33	31	31
Other professional training	16	6	15	14
Other answers	6	6	4	6
None	53	33	43	42
OWN FIRST EMPLOYER				
Education	53	72	59	60
Public administration	3	13	15	14
Industry	6	3	9	8
Private practice	3	3	1	1
Communications	19	3	3	4
Others	15	6	8	9
None	—	—	5	4
EMPLOYER 1966				
Education	22	75	—	17
Public administration	—	7	—	1
Industry	6	3	—	1
Private practice	6	3	—	—
Communications	34	6	—	2
Others	22	6	—	2
None or no answer	9	—	100	76

Table 79. Benefits of a university degree*

	Single women	Married women	
		Without children	With children
	No.	*No.*	*No.*
	109	69	278
	%	%	%
IN SOCIAL LIFE AND FRIENDSHIP			
Has been beneficial	43	49	52
Has not made any difference	26	28	34
Has had mixed effects	30	23	13
Has been detrimental	1	—	—
TO FEELINGS ABOUT ONESELF			
Has been beneficial	61	61	67
Has not made any difference	20	26	20
Has had mixed effects	17	12	13
Has been detrimental	3	—	—
FOR RELATIONS WITH PARENTS AND RELATIVES			
Has been beneficial	19	19	24
Has not made any difference	61	54	52
Has had mixed effects	18	22	21
Has been detrimental	2	5	3
FOR EMPLOYMENT			
Has been beneficial	83	100	92
Has not made any difference	6	—	4
Has had mixed effects	11	—	3

* Data in this table were supplied by Dr Robert Rapoport from the findings of his survey of a subsample of our graduates: see Chapter 3, note 3.

Table 80. Difficulties experienced by graduate women because of their sex

Type of difficulty	Employment sector in 1966							ALL EMPLOYED	OTHER WOMEN
	Public administration	Education	Industry	Commerce	Private practice	Communi-cations	Others		
	%	%	%	%	%	%	%	%	%
In access to jobs or training	9	7	14	10	10	13	8	8	4
In promotion prospects	5	7	14	10	7	7	7	7	2
Hostility of employer	2	3	14	6	3	1	7	3	3
In pay and working conditions	2	—	8	6	10	5	3	2	1
Other forms of prejudice	7	4	9	4	10	7	10	5	3
None	75	79	41	64	60	67	65	75	87
ALL WOMEN	100	100	100	100	100	100	100	100	100
No.	258	1359	99	67	30*	109	92	2014	1568

* Number on which percentages based unreliably small.

Table 81. Difficulties experienced by married graduate women because of their marital status

Type of difficulty	Employment sector in 1966					ALL EMPLOYED	OTHER MARRIED WOMEN
	Public administration	Education	Industry and Commerce	Communications	Others		
	%	%	%	%	%	%	%
Employer's fear of loss through pregnancy, child's illness, etc.	17	18	26	7	21	18	13
Little prospect of promotion	3	3	2	—	2	3	1
Finding post difficult	7	5	3	5	7	5	3
Children under 5	—	3	2	12	5	4	7
Difficult to balance home and work	8	5	6	7	2	5	5
Other difficulties	6	4	8	7	7	5	3
None	59	62	53	62	56	60	68
ALL MARRIED WOMEN	100	100	100	100	100	100	100
No.	106	768	88	59	61	1082	1468

Table 82. Difficulties experienced by graduate women arising from inability to move about due to family responsibilities

Type of difficulty	Employment sector in 1966							ALL EMPLOYED	OTHER WOMEN
	Public administration	Education	Industry	Commerce	Private practice	Communications	Others		
	%	%	%	%	%	%	%	%	%
Transport	1	1	1	—	3	1	1	1	1
Husband's employment entails frequent moves	19	19	13	9	12	11	19	18	20
Children and other responsibilities	2	6	2	9	10	9	1	4	9
Difficult to find work	—	1	—	1	—	1	1	1	1
None	78	73	84	81	75	78	78	76	69
ALL WOMEN	100	100	100	100	100	100	100	100	100
No.	258	1359	99	67	30*	109	92	2014	1568

* Number on which percentage based unreliably small.

Q

Appendix

METHODS OF MEASURING
SOCIAL MOBILITY

To render possible empirical research into social mobility, the concept needs to be operationalized. To this end the criteria according to which social status and hence social mobility are defined should first of all be decided upon, and here it is usual, for the reasons discussed in Chapter 1, to use occupation as the sole or principal criterion. Secondly, the point in time from which mobility, if any, is to be measured must be decided upon: for instance, when considering *intragenerational mobility* the statuses of one individual at at least two points in time are compared, it being common to take as the base the outset of the working life of that individual, and as the terminal point the time of the survey. There are, however, several variations to this pattern, and indeed we ourselves, in attempting to measure the intragenerational mobility of our graduates' fathers, have compared their statuses at the birth of their children and at the time these children entered university.

More problems arise when attempting to measure *inter-generational mobility*, mainly because at least two people are involved here, and the time spans in question can often be considerable. The point in time at which the status of a member of an earlier generation can be considered definitive is open to debate, and different operational solutions have been offered by different researchers: the status of the father at the time of the survey, at his death or retirement, when the respondent was born, and at the same age as the respondent have variously been used as starting points, while perhaps the most common solution has been to base the father's status on his 'main paid occupation'. In the present survey, intergenerational mobility has been measured by using as a starting point fathers' social classes based on their occupations at the time our respondents entered university and the paternal grandfathers' classes based on their main paid occupations. Graduates' social classes are usually based on their occupations at the time of the survey (October 1966), or if they were not employed then, at earlier points in time: those of their marriage partners are based on the occupations of these partners either at the time of marriage in the case of wives of men graduates, or since marriage in the case of husbands of women graduates. The social class categories of the respondents, their fathers and their spouses are those used by the Registrar General in the 1961 Census:

Social class		*Occupations*
I		⎰ Professions
II	non-manual ⎨	Intermediate
III Non-manual		⎱ Routine non-manual
III Manual		⎰ Skilled manual
IV	manual ⎨	Semi-skilled manual
V		⎱ Unskilled manual

Most of our graduates are in classes I and II.

In the measurement of both types of mobility, intragenerational and intergenerational (but more particularly the latter), the question of recall is always a problem. Not everyone, for instance, will know what his grandfather's job was, and even if he does, his recollection of it may well be inaccurate, while the tendency to 'upgrade' is by now well established. The same also applies when a respondent is asked to state his father's occupation at the time he (the respondent) was born. A few people will even have lost touch with their fathers when relatively young. Inaccuracies and non-response resulting from faulty recall can be offset to some extent by asking for fairly detailed information, which was the strategy adopted here. Not only was each graduate asked to state his father's main occupation at two points in time, but he was also requested to indicate for both occasions whether his father was self-employed or not, whether he had any people working directly under him (and if so, how many), what industry or profession he was in, and in what capacity he worked. It would have been impossible to elicit that amount of detail about our graduates' paternal grandfathers, and so a three-category occupational classification (non-manual, skilled manual and unskilled manual) was used to which the respondents themselves assigned their grandfathers. Consequently, in spite of the obstacles in the way of obtaining the information required, response to the questions was good. The social classes of fathers at both points in time – the birth of graduates and their entry to university – is known for 10676 of the 12986 respondents (82 per cent), while 9946 men and women were able to assign their fathers' fathers to one of the three categories given (77 per cent). Moreover, of the 9298 married respondents, 8194 (88 per cent) gave details of their spouses' occupations.

With information to hand about the social classes of the graduates, their marriage partners, their fathers and their grandfathers, various calculations as to the extent and degree of mobility can be made when these classes are compared for each individual. It almost goes without saying that the result of such an investigation will depend to a great extent upon the nature and number of the class categories used: basically, the fewer the categories, the lesser will be the degree and extent of social mobility recorded.

Various statistical calculations have been made on the raw mobility data, the first of which is the index of association, a statistical model arising from the hypothesis of perfect mobility. This model permits an estimate to be made of the relative chances of social mobility available to people of different social class origins: 'the question of *relative* mobility, or the different opportunities of gaining high status available to individuals of different social origin, is part of the problem of the recruitment of *elites*' (D. V. Glass). The hypothesis of perfect mobility in turn enables us to calculate the 'expected frequency', or the number of people we should expect to find in any one status group if there were random association between the statuses of, say, fathers and sons, or if chances of intergenerational ascent, descent and stability were randomly distributed. In the former situation, if a certain proportion of fathers is in status category X, we should expect on the hypothesis of perfect mobility that an equal proportion of their sons would be in that same category, a situation which would be represented statistically by an index of 1. To the extent that the proportion of sons exceeds that expected, the index of association rises above 1, since it is calculated by dividing the observed number of sons in the same status category as their fathers by the expected number, i.e.,

$$\text{Index of association} = \frac{\text{Observed No.}}{\text{Expected No.}}$$

For example, if 5 per cent of fathers are in category X, and these fathers have 100 sons, then we should expect 5 per cent (i.e. 5) of these sons to be in the same category in a situation of perfect mobility. If there are in fact 10 sons in category X the index of association is:

$$O/E$$
$$= 10/5$$
$$= 2,$$

which represents some degree of intergenerational association of status. The 'index of opportunity' (Table 4) is calculated in the same way as this and has a similar meaning. Where there is a two-value table of observations, as in Table 7, the expected values are calculated as in a chi-square test, that is by dividing the product of the corresponding marginal totals of the table by the grand total: for instance, in Table 7:

$$\text{Expected value} = \frac{2278 \times 2040}{7120}$$
$$= 652 \cdot 7$$

From this value the index is calculated in the usual way. Clearly the perfect mobility situation is a statistical model, an ideal type, and no judgment as to the desirability or possibility of such a situation is intended. The index provides a common standard whereby relative chances of mobility out of – or stability within – different status groups can be assessed.

Another statistical artefact used here is the measure of the average distance mobile, or degree of mobility. In order to calculate this coefficient, it is assumed operationally that the distance from one status category to the next over the whole scale equals 1. With this premiss in mind, it then becomes possible to calculate the average number of categories over which a population or a sample has been mobile, and the overall direction of this mobility. The stable, the downwardly mobile and the upwardly mobile are separated out, and the mobile are classified according to the number of categories through which they have passed in either direction. For instance, on the basis of the Registrar General's social class scale, movement from a 'skilled manual' to an 'intermediate non-manual' occupation would be movement upwards over two categories. Calculation of the average distance mobile is thus as follows:

Distance mobile (direction and number of categories) (X)	No. in each group (f)	fX
Up { etc. +2 +1		
Stable 0		
Down { −1 −2 etc.		
	Σf	ΣfX

$$\text{Average distance mobile} = \frac{\Sigma fX}{\Sigma f}$$

Because in any stratification system a large proportion of the population is invariably stable, this coefficient for the average distance mobile is usually low; in the last column, the fX for the stable is of course always zero.

BIBLIOGRAPHY

The four hundred or so items included in this bibliography by no means constitute an exhaustive list of readings within the wide range of general and specific topics covered by our research. Instead, the references are restricted to works which have proved directly or indirectly useful in the writing of this book and which are more or less readily available to the reader in that they are all English-language works which have been published at sometime or another, and which if out of print should be obtainable in, or with the help of, any university, college or large public library in Britain.

I. General sociology, philosophy and methodology

BERGER, P. L. AND LUCKMANN, T., *The Social Construction of Reality*. London, Allen Lane, The Penguin Press, 1967.

BLALOCK, H. M., *Causal Inferences in Non-experimental Research*. Chapel Hill, University of North Carolina Press, 1961.

CARSTAIRS, G. H., *This Island Now (B.B.C. Reith Lectures 1962)*. London, Hogarth Press, 1963.

FYVEL, T. R., *The Frontiers of Sociology*. London, Routledge, 1968.

GERTH, H. H. AND MILLS, C. W., *From Max Weber*. London, Routledge, 1948.

HOGGART, R., *The Uses of Literacy*. London, Chatto and Windus, 1957.

KLEIN, J., *Samples from English Cultures*. London, Routledge, 1965.

MARSHALL, T. H., *Sociology at the Crossroads*. London, Heinemann, 1963.

MERTON, R. K. AND LAZARSFELD, P. F. (eds.), *Continuities in Social Research*. Glencoe, Free Press, 1950.

RUSSELL, B., *Principles of Social Reconstruction*. London, Allen and Unwin, 1916.

RUSSELL, B., *Unpopular Essays*. London, Allen and Unwin, 1950.

RYDER, N. B., The cohort as a concept in the study of social change. *American Sociological Review*, **30** (1965) 843–61.

WELFORD, A. T., *et al.* (eds.), *Society: Problems and Methods of Study*. London, Routledge, 1962.

II. Demographic data

BARGER, B. AND HALL, E., The interrelationships of family size and socio-economic status for parents of college students. *Journal of Marriage and the Family*, **28** (1966) 186–7.

BERENT, J., Fertility and social mobility. *Population Studies*, **5** (1952) 244–60.

BLAKE, J., Reproductive ideals and educational attainment among white Americans. *Population Studies*, **21** (1967) 159–74.

CENTRAL STATISTICAL OFFICE, *Annual Abstract of Statistics*, no. 104. London, H.M.S.O., 1967.

CHRISTENSEN, H. T. AND BOWDEN, O. P., Studies in child spacing – II: the time interval between marriage of parents and birth of their first child, Tippecanoe County, Indiana. *Social Forces*, **31** (1953) 346–51.

GENERAL REGISTER OFFICE, *Census 1961 (England and Wales)*. London, H.M.S.O., 1966.

GIBSON, J. B., Biological aspects of a high socio-economic group. *Journal of Biosocial Sciences*, **2** (1970) 1–16.

GLASS, D. V. AND GREBENIK, E., *The Trend and Pattern of Fertility in Great Britain (Family Census 1946, vol. 6)*. London, H.M.S.O., 1954.

GREBENIK, E. AND ROWNTREE, G., Factors associated with the age at marriage in Great Britain. *Proceedings of the Royal Society (B)*, **159** (1963) 178–98.

HAWTHORN, G., *The Sociology of Fertility*. London, Collier–Macmillan, 1970.

HAWTHORN, G. AND BUSFIELD, J., A sociological approach to British fertility. In GOULD, J. (ed.), *Penguin Social Sciences Survey 1968*. Harmondsworth, Penguin, 1968, 168–210.

HUBBACK, J., The fertility of graduate women. *Eugenics Review*, **47** (1955) 107–13.

KELSALL, R. K., *Population*. London, Longmans, 1967.

KELSALL, R. K., *et al.*, Marriage and family building patterns of university graduates. *Journal of Biosocial Science*, **3** (1971) 281–7.

PERRUCCI, C. C., Mobility, marriage and child spacing among college graduates. *Journal of Marriage and the Family*, **30** (1968) 273–82.

PERRUCCI, C. C., Social origins, mobility patterns, and fertility. *American Sociological Review*, **32** (1967) 615–25.

PIERCE, R. M., Marriage in the 'fifties. *Sociological Review*, **11** (1963) 215–40.

PIERCE, R. M. AND ROWNTREE, G., Birth control in Britain: Part II. *Population Studies*, **15** (1961) 121–60.

POWERS, M. G., Socio-economic status and the fertility of married women. *Sociology and Social Research*, **50** (1966) 472–82.

SCOTT, W., Fertility and social mobility among teachers. *Population Studies*, **11** (1958) 251–61.

TIEN, H. Y., The social mobility/fertility hypothesis reconsidered: an empirical study. *American Sociological Review*, **26** (1961) 247–57.

WESTOFF, C. F. AND POTVIN, R. H., *College Women and Fertility Values*. Princeton, University Press, 1967.

WESTOFF, C. F., *et al.*, *The Third Child*. Princeton, University Press, 1963.

WRONG, D. H., Class fertility differentials in England and Wales. *Millbank Memorial Fund Quarterly*, **38** (1960) 37–47.

III. Family and socialization

(a) Sociology of the family

BAILYN, L., Career and family orientations of husbands and wives in relation to marital happiness. *Human Relations*, **23** (1970) 97–113.

BANKS, J. A., *Prosperity and Parenthood*. London, Routledge, 1954.

BAYER, A. E., Marriage plans and educational aspirations. *American Journal of Sociology*, **75** (1969) 239–44.

BERGER, P. L. AND KELLNER, H., Marriage and the construction of reality. *Diogenes*, **46** (1964) 1–24.

BLOOD, R. O. AND WOLFE, D. M., *Husbands and Wives*. New York, Free Press, 1960.

FOGARTY, M. P., *et al.*, *Sex, Career and Family*. London, Allen and Unwin, 1971.

FOLSOM, J. K., *The Family and Democratic Society*. London, Routledge, 1948.

FOOTE, N. N., The appraisal of family research. *Journal of Marriage and the Family*, **19** (1957) 92–9.

GOODE, W. J., *World Revolution and Family Patterns*. Glencoe, Free Press, 1963.

HILL, R., Sociology of marriage and family behaviour, 1945–56. *Current Sociology*, **7** (1958) 1–33.

MACE, D. AND MACE, V., *The Soviet Family*. London, Hutchinson, 1964.

ROSSI, A. S., Transition to parenthood. *Journal of Marriage and the Family*, **30** (1968) 26–39.

(b) Socialization

BARRY, H., *et al.*, A cross-cultural survey of some sex differences in socialization. *Journal of Abnormal and Social Psychology*, **55** (1957) 327–32.

BATES, F. L., Position, role, status: a reformulation of concepts. *Social Forces*, **34** (1956) 313–21.

BOSSARD, J. H. AND BOLL, E. S. *The Sociology of Child Development*, 4th ed. New York, Harper, 1966.

BRIM, O. G., Family structure and sex role learning by children . . . *Sociometry*, **21** (1956) 1–16.

CLAUSEN, J. A., Recent developments in socialization theory and research. *Annals of the American Academy of Political and Social Science*, **377** (1968) 139–55.

COTTRELL, L., The adjustment of an individual to his age and sex roles. *American Sociological Review*, **7** (1942) 617–20.

DAHLSTROM, E. (ed.), *The Changing Roles of Men and Women*. London, Duckworth, 1967.

DAVIS, A., American status systems and the socialization of the child. *American Sociological Review*, **6** (1941) 345–56.

EISENSTADT, S. M., Reference group behaviour and social integration: an explorative study. *American Sociological Review*, **19** (1954) 175–85.

ELDER, G. H. AND BOWERMAN, C. E., Family structure and child-rearing patterns: the effect of family size and sex composition. *American Sociological Review*, **28** (1963) 891–905.

FROMM, E., Sex and character. In ANSHEN, R. N., *The Family: its Function and Destiny*. New York, Harper and Row, 1949.

HARTLEY, R. E., Some implications of current changes in sex-role patterns. *Merrill Palmer Quarterly*, **6** (1960) 153–63.

HEILBRUN, A. B., Sex role identity and achievement motivation. *Psychological Reports*, **12** (1963) 483–90.

HYMAN, H. H. AND SINGER, E. (eds.), *Readings in Reference Group Theory and Research*. New York, Free Press, 1968.

HYMAN, H. H., Reflections on reference group behaviour. *Public Opinion Quarterly*, **24** (1960) 383–96.

KOMAROVSKY, M., Cultural contradictions and sex roles. *American Journal of Sociology*, **52** (1946) 184–9.

KOMAROVSKY, M., Functional analysis of sex roles. *American Sociological Review*, **15** (1950) 508–16.

LINTON, R., Age and sex categories. *American Sociological Review*, **7** (1942) 589–603.

LYNN, D. B., The process of learning parental and sex-role identification. *Journal of Marriage and the Family*, **28** (1966) 466–70.

LYNN, D. B., Sex differences in identification development. *Sociometry*, **24** (1961) 372–83.

MCCLELLAND, D. C., *et al.*, *Talent and Society*. Princeton, Van Nostrand, 1958.

MACCOBY, E. E., The choice of variables in the study of socialization. *Sociometry*, **24** (1961) 357–71.

MURDOCK, G. P., Comparative data on the division of labour by sex. *Social Forces*, **15** (1936–7) 551–3.

NEIMAN, L. J. AND HUGHES, J. W., The problem of the concept of role: a re-survey of the literature. *Social Forces*, **30** (1951–2) 141–9.

NEWSON, J. AND NEWSON, E., *Infant Care in an Urban Community*. London, Allen and Unwin, 1963.

PACKARD, V., *The Sexual Wilderness*. London, Longmans, 1968.

PARSONS, T., Age and sex in the social structure of the United States. *American Sociological Review*, **7** (1942) 604–16.

ROSEN, B. C., Family structure and achievement motivation. *American Sociological Review*, **26** (1961) 575–85.

ROSEN, B. C., The psychosocial origins of achievement motivation. *Sociometry*, **22** (1959) 185–218.

ROSENKRANTZ, P., *et al.*, Sex-role stereotypes and self concepts in college students. *Journal of Counselling and Clinical Psychology*, **32** (1968) 287–95.

SARBIN, T. R., Role theory. In LINDZEY, G. AND ARONSON, E. (eds.), *The Handbook of Social Psychology*, vol. I. Reading, Mass. Addison-Wesley, 1954.

SCHNEIDER, L. AND LYSGAARD, S., The deferred gratification pattern: a preliminary study. *American Sociological Review*, **18** (1953) 142–9.

SEWELL, W. H., Some recent developments in socialization theory and research. *Annals of the American Academy of Political and Social Science*, **349** (1963) 163–81.

SHUVAL, J. T., Occupational interests and sex-role congruence. *Human Relations*, **16** (1963) 171–82.

WALLIN, P., Cultural contradictions and sex roles – a repeat study. *American Sociological Review*, **15** (1950) 288–93.

IV. Sociology of education

(a) General

ABRAMS, M., Rewards of education. *New Society*, 9 July 1964, 26.

BENN, C. AND SIMON, B., *Half Way There: Report on the British Comprehensive School Reform*. London, McGraw-Hill, 1970.

BORDUA, D. J., Educational aspirations and parental stress on college. *Social Forces*, **38** (1960) 262–9.

CENTRAL ADVISORY COUNCIL FOR EDUCATION, *Early Leaving*. London, H.M.S.O., 1954.

CENTRAL ADVISORY COUNCIL FOR EDUCATION (England), *Fifteen to Eighteen*. London, H.M.S.O., 1959.

COHEN, E., Parental factors in educational mobility. *Sociology of Education*, **38** (1964–5) 404–25.

COTGROVE, S., Education and occupation. *British Journal of Sociology*, **13** (1962) 33–42.

DOUGLAS, J. W. B., *The Home and the School*. London, MacGibbon and Kee, 1964.

DOUGLAS, J. W. B., *et al.*, *All Our Future: a Longitudinal Study of Secondary Education*. London, Davies, 1968.

ELDER, G. M., Family structure and educational attainment: a cross-national analysis. *American Sociological Review*, **30** (1965) 81–96.

FLOUD, J. AND HALSEY, A. H., The sociology of education. *Current Sociology*, **7** (1958) 165–93.

HALSEY, A. H., Education and equality. *New Society*, 17 June 1965, 13–15.

HALSEY, A. H., Genetics, social structure and intelligence. *British Journal of Sociology*, **9** (1958) 15–28.

HALSEY, A. H., *et al.* (eds.), *Education, Economy and Society*. Glencoe, Free Press, 1961.

HANS, N., Independent schools and the liberal professions. *Yearbook of Education*, (1950) 219–38.

HANSEN, D. A. AND GERSTL, J. E. (eds.), *On Education: Sociological Perspectives*. New York, Wiley, 1967.

JACKSON, B., *Streaming: an Education System in Miniature*. London, Routledge, 1964.

KALTON, G., *The Public Schools*. London, Longmans, 1966.

MCDILL, E. L. AND COLEMAN, J., Family and peer influences on college plans of high school students. *Sociology of Education*, **38** (1965) 112–16.

MACLURE, J. S., *Educational Documents: England and Wales, 1816–1963*. London, Chapman and Hall, 1965.

REHBERG, R. A. AND WESTBY, D. L., Parental encouragement, occupation, education and family size . . . *Social Forces*, **45** (1967) 362–74.

SEWELL, W. H. AND SHAH, V. P., Parents' education and children's educational aspirations and achievements. *American Sociological Review*, **33** (1968) 191–209.

SEWELL, W. H., *et al.*, The educational and early occupational attainment process. *American Sociological Review*, **34** (1969) 82–92.

SWIFT, D. F. (ed.), *Basic Readings in the Sociology of Education*. London, Routledge, 1970.

SWIFT, D. F. AND ACLAND, H., The sociology of education in Britain, 1960–1968: a bibliographical review. *Social Science Information*, **8** (1969) 31–64.

WEINBERG, I., *The English Public Schools: the Sociology of Elite Education*. New York, Atherton Press, 1967.

(b) Higher education

CLARK, B. R., The 'cooling-out' function in higher education. *American Journal of Sociology*, **65** (1960) 569–76.

COMMITTEE ON HIGHER EDUCATION, *Higher Education*. London, H.M.S.O., 1963.

COUPER, M. AND HARRIS, C., CAT to University: the changing student intake. *Educational Research*, **12** (1970) 113–20.

FURNEAUX, W. D., *The Chosen Few*. London, Oxford University Press, 1961.

HALMOS, P. (ed.), *Sociological Studies in British University Education* (Sociological Review Monograph no. 7). Keele, University Press, 1963.

HAVEMAN, E. AND WEST, P. S., *They Went to College*. New York, Harcourt, Brace, 1952.

KELSALL, R. K., *Applications for Admission to Universities*. London, Association of Universities of the British Commonwealth, 1957.

KELSALL, R. K., *et al.*, *Six Years After*. Sheffield University, Department of Sociological Studies, Higher Education Research Unit, 1970.

KLINGENDER, F. D., Students in a changing world. *Yorkshire Bulletin*, **6** (1954) 1–33.

MACLAY, I., A random sample of university undergraduates. *Universities Quarterly*, **23** (1968) 80–94.

MARRIS, P., *The Experience of Higher Education*. London, Routledge, 1964.

MUSGROVE, F., University freshmen and their parents' attitudes. *Educational Research*, **10** (1967) 78–80.

PAYNE, G. AND BIRD, J., The newest universities – 2: what are their students like? *New Society*, 23 October 1969, 641–3.

ROSS, J. M. AND CASE, P., Who goes to Oxbridge? *New Society*, 19 May 1966, 11–13.

ROTHBART, G. S., The legitimation of inequality: objective scholarship vs. black militance. *Sociology of Education*, **43** (1970) 159–74.

ZWEIG, F., *The Student in the Age of Anxiety*. London, Heinemann, 1963.

V. Social stratification and mobility

(a) General

BENDIX, R. AND LIPSET, S. M. (eds.), *Class, Status and Power*. Glencoe, Free Press, 1953.

BOTT, E., Class as a reference group. *Human Relations*, **7** (1954) 259–85.

BOTTOMORE, T. B., *Classes in Modern Society*. London, Allen and Unwin, 1965.

BOTTOMORE, T. B., *Elites and Society*. London, Watts, 1964.

CENTERS, R., Occupational mobility of urban occupational strata. *American Sociological Review*, **13** (1948) 197–203.

CENTERS, R., *The Psychology of Social Classes*. Princeton, University Press, 1949.

CHINOY, E., Social mobility trends in the United States. *American Sociological Review*, **20** (1955) 180–6.

COLE, G. D. H., *Studies in Class Structure*. London, Routledge, 1955.

DAVIDSON, P. E. AND ANDERSON, D. H., *Occupational Mobility in an American Community*. Stanford, University Press, 1937.

DAVIES, I., *Social Mobility and Political Change*. London, Pall Mall, 1970.

GLASS, D. V. (ed.), *Social Mobility in Britain*. London, Routledge, 1954.

HIMMELWEIT, H. T., *et al.*, The views of adolescents on some aspects of the social class structure. *British Journal of Sociology*, **3** (1952) 148–72.

INGHAM, G. K., Social stratification. *Sociology*, **4** (1970) 105–13.

JACKSON, E. F. AND CROCKETT, H. J., Occupational mobility in the United States. *American Sociological Review*, **29** (1964) 5–15.

JANOWITZ, M., Social stratification and mobility in Western Germany. *American Journal of Sociology*, **64** (1958) 6–24.

KAHAN, M., *et al.*, On the analytical division of social class. *British Journal of Sociology*, **17** (1966) 122–32.

KAHL, J. A., *The American Class Structure*. New York, Holt, Rinehart and Winston, 1960.

KINLOCH, G. C. AND PERUCCI, R., Social origins, academic achievement, and mobility channels: sponsored and contest mobility among college graduates. *Social Forces*, **48** (1969) 36–45.

KLUCKHOHN, F., Dominant and substitute profiles of cultural orientations: their significance for the analysis of social stratification. *Social Forces*, **28** (1950) 376–93.

KNUPFER, G., Portrait of an underdog. *Public Opinion Quarterly*, **11** (1947) 103–14.

LIPSET, S. M. AND BENDIX, R., *Social Mobility in Industrial Society*. Berkeley, University of California Press, 1959.

LIPSET, S. M., AND ROGOFF, N., Class and opportunity in Europe and the U.S. *Commentary*, **18** (1954) 562–8.

MCGUIRE, C., Social stratification and mobility patterns. *American Sociological Review*, **15** (1950) 195–204.

MARSH, R. M., Values, demand and social mobility. *American Sociological Review*, **28** (1963) 565–75.

MILLER, S. M., Comparative social mobility: a trend report and a bibliography. *Current Sociology*, **9** (1960) 1–89.

ROGOFF, N., *Recent Trends in Occupational Mobility*. Glencoe, Free Press, 1953.

SMELSER, N. J. AND LIPSET, S. M. (eds.), *Social Structure and Mobility in Economic Development*. London, Routledge, 1966.

SVALASTOGA, K., *Prestige, Class and Mobility*. London, Heinemann, 1959.

TURNER, R. H., Acceptance of irregular mobility in Britain and the United States. *Sociometry*, **29** (1966) 334–52.

TURNER, R. H., Sponsored and contest mobility in the school system. *American Sociological Review*, **25** (1960) 855–67.

VEBLEN, T., *The Theory of the Leisure Class*. London, Allen and Unwin, 1925.

WIRTH, L., Social stratification and social mobility in the United States. *Current Sociology*, **2** (1953–4) 279–303.

(b) Social psychological correlates

ANDERSON, C. A., *et al.*, Intelligence and occupational mobility. *Journal of Political Economy*, **60** (1952) 218–39.

BEILIN, H., The pattern of postponability and its relation to social class mobility. *Journal of Social Psychology*, **44** (1956) 33–48.

BERNSTEIN, B., Elaborated and restricted codes: their social origins and some consequences. *American Anthropologist*, **66** (1964) 55–69.

BERNSTEIN, B., Some sociological determinants of perception. *British Journal of Sociology*, **9** (1958) 158–74.

CROCKETT, H. J., The achievement motive and differential occupational mobility in the United States. *American Sociological Review*, **27** (1962) 191–204.

ELDER, G. H., Achievement motivation and intelligence in occupational mobility. *Sociometry*, **31** (1968) 327–54.

ELLIS, E., Social psychological correlates of upward mobility

R

among unmarried career women. *American Sociological Review*, **17** (1952) 558–63.

ROSEN, B. C., The achievement syndrome: a psychocultural dimension of social stratification. *American Sociological Review*, **21** (1956) 203–11.

STACEY, B., Achievement motivation, occupational choice and intergeneration occupational mobility. *Human Relations*, **22** (1969) 275–81.

STACEY, B., Some psychological aspects of intergeneration occupational mobility. *British Journal of Social and Clinical Psychology*, **4** (1965) 275–86.

SWIFT, D. F., Social class and achievement motivation. *Educational Research*, **8** (1966) 83–95.

(c) Class and outlook

ABRAMS, M., British elite attitudes and the European Common Market. *Public Opinion Quarterly*, **29** (1965) 236–46.

CARO, F. G. AND PIHLBLAD, C. T., Aspirations and expectations . . . *Sociology and Social Research*, **49** (1965) 465–75.

EMPEY, L. T., Social class and occupational aspiration. *American Sociological Review*, **21** (1956) 703–9.

JAHODA, G., Social class attitudes and levels of occupational aspiration among secondary school leavers. *British Journal of Psychology*, **44** (1953) 95–107.

KAHL, J. A., Educational and occupational aspirations of 'Common Man' boys. *Harvard Educational Review*, **23** (1953) 186–203.

KATZ, F. M., The meaning of success: some differences in value systems of social classes. *Journal of Social Psychology*, **62** (1964) 141–8.

KELLER, S. AND ZAVALLONI, M., Ambition and social class: a respecification. *Social Forces*, **43** (1965) 58–70.

KOHN, M. L., Social class and parent–child relationships: an interpretation. *American Journal of Sociology*, **68** (1963) 471–80.

KOHN, M. L., Social class and parental values. *American Journal of Sociology*, **64** (1959) 337–51.

KOHN, M. L. AND SCHOOLER, C., Class, occupation and orientation. *American Sociological Review*, **34** (1969) 659–78.

LOCKWOOD, D., Sources of variation in working-class images of society. *Sociological Review*, **14** (1966) 249–67.

MUSGROVE, F., Social class and levels of aspiration in a technological university. *Sociological Review*, **15** (1967) 311–22.

REISSMAN, L., Levels of aspiration and social class. *American Sociological Review*, **18** (1953) 233–42.

SEWELL, W. H., *et al.*, Social status and educational and occupational aspiration. *American Sociological Review*, **22** (1957) 67–73.

SWIFT, D. F., Social class, mobility-ideology and 11-plus success. *British Journal of Sociology*, **18** (1967) 165–86.

TURNER, R. H., *The Social Context of Ambition*. San Francisco, Chandler Publishing Co., 1964.

(d) Class, mobility and education

ABBOTT, J., Students' social class in three Northern universities. *British Journal of Sociology*, **16** (1965) 206–19.

BROCKINGTON, F. AND STEIN, Z., Admission, achievement and social class. *Universities Quarterly*, **18** (1963) 52–73.

CARO, F. G. AND PIHLBLAD, C. T., Social class, formal education and social mobility. *Sociology and Social Research*, **48** (1964) 428–39.

DAVIS, A., *Social Class Influences upon Learning*, Cambridge, Mass., Harvard University Press, 1948.

ELLIS, R. A. AND LANE, W. C., Structural supports for upward mobility. *American Sociological Review*, **28** (1963) 743–56.

FLOUD, J., Educational opportunity and social mobility. *Yearbook of Education*, (1950) 117–35.

FLOUD, J., *et al.*, *Social Class and Educational Opportunity*. Melbourne, Heinemann, 1956.

FORD, J., *Social Class and the Comprehensive School*. London, Routledge, 1970.

JACKSON, B. AND MARSDEN, D., *Education and the Working Class*. London, Routledge, 1962.

JENCKS, C., Social stratification and higher education. *Harvard Educational Review*, **38** (1968) 277–316.

KRAUSS, I., Sources of educational aspirations among working class youth. *American Sociological Review*, **29** (1964) 867–79.

LAWTON, D., *Social Class, Language and Education*. London, Routledge, 1968.

LITTLE, A. AND WESTERGAARD, J., The trend of class differentials in educational opportunity in England and Wales. *British Journal of Sociology*, **15** (1964) 301–16.

MULLIGAN, R. A., Socioeconomic background and college enrolment. *American Sociological Review*, **16** (1951) 188–96.

SANDFORD, C. T., *et al.*, Class influences in higher education. *British Journal of Educational Psychology*, **35** (1965) 183–94.

SEWELL, W. H. AND SHAH, V. P., Social class, parental encouragement and educational aspirations. *American Journal of Sociology*, **73** (1968) 559–72.

SEWELL, W. H. AND SHAH, V. P., Socioeconomic status, intelligence and attainment of higher education. *Sociology of Education*, **40** (1967) 1–23.

SIMPSON, R. L., Parental influence, anticipatory socialization and social mobility. *American Sociological Review*, **27** (1962) 517–22.

VI. Sociology of occupations

(a) General

BLAU, P. M. AND DUNCAN, O. D., *The American Occupational Structure*. New York, Wiley, 1967.

CAPLOW, T., *The Sociology of Work*. Minneapolis, University of Minnesota Press, 1957.

DAVIES, A. F., Prestige of occupations. *British Journal of Sociology*, **3** (1952) 134–47.

DUBIN, R., *The World of Work*. Englewood Cliffs, Prentice-Hall, 1958.

HUSEN, T., *Talent, Opportunity and Career*. Stockholm, Almqvist and Wiksell, 1969.

INKELES, A. AND ROSSI, P. H., National comparisons of occupational prestige. *American Journal of Sociology*, **61** (1956) 329–39.

ROE, A., *The Psychology of Occupations*. New York, Wiley, 1956.
ROSENBERG, M., *Occupations and Values*. Glencoe, Free Press, 1957.
WILENSKY, H. L., Work, careers and social integration. *International Journal of Social Science*, **12** (1960) 543–60.

(b) *Aspirations and choice*

BECKER, H. S. AND CARPER, J., The elements of identification with an occupation. *American Sociological Review*, **21** (1956) 341–8.
BELL, G. D., Processes in the formation of adolescents' aspirations. *Social Forces*, **42** (1963–4) 179–86.
BERDIE, R. F., Factors associated with vocational interests. *Journal of Educational Psychology*, **34** (1943) 257–77.
BLAU, P. M., *et al.*, Occupational choice: a conceptual framework. *Industrial and Labour Relations Review*, **9** (1956) 531–43.
BOX, S. AND COTGROVE, S., Scientific identity, occupational selection and role strain. *British Journal of Sociology*, **17** (1966) 20–8.
BUTLER, J. R., *Occupational Choice*. London, H.M.S.O., 1968.
BRUNKAN, R. J., Perceived parental attitudes and parental identification in relation to problems in vocational choice. *Journal of Counselling Psychology*, **13** (1966) 394–402.
CARPER, J. W. AND BECKER, H. S., Adjustment to conflicting expectations in the development of identification with an occupation. *Social Forces*, **36** (1957–8) 51–6.
COULSON, M. A., *et al.*, Towards a sociological theory of occupational choice: a critique. *Sociological Review*, **15** (1967) 301–9.
DUFTY, N. F., The relationship between paternal occupation and occupational choice. *International Journal of Comparative Sociology*, **2** (1961) 81–7.
DYNES, R. R., *et al.*, Levels of occupational aspiration: some aspects of family experience as a variable. *American Sociological Review*, **21** (1956) 212–15.
ESKOLA, A., Level of aspiration in career selection. *Acta Sociologica*, **5** (1961) 239–49.

FORD, J. AND BOX, S., Sociological theory and occupational choice. *Sociological Review*, **15** (1967) 287–99.

GARDNER, J. W., The use of the term 'level of aspiration'. *Psychological Review*, **47** (1940) 59–68.

GINZBERG, E., *et al.*, *Occupational Choice: an Approach to a General Theory*. New York, Columbia University Press, 1951.

HUTCHINS, D., *Technology and the Sixth Form Boy*. Oxford, University Department of Education, 1963.

JENSON, P. G. AND KIRCHNER, W. K., A national answer to the question 'do sons follow their fathers' occupations?'. *Journal of Applied Psychology*, **39** (1955) 419–21.

KATZ, F. E. AND MARTIN, H. W., Career choice processes. *Social Forces*, **41** (1962) 149–54.

KUVELSKY, W. P. AND BEALER, R. C., A clarification of the concept occupational choice. *Rural Sociology*, **31** (1966) 265–76.

LAMBERT, W. AND KLINEBERG, O., Cultural comparisons of boys' occupational aspirations. *British Journal of Social and Clinical Psychology*, **3** (1964) 56–65.

LIPSET, S. M., *et al.*, Job plans and entry into the labour market. *Social Forces*, **33** (1955) 224–32.

LOGAN, R. F. L. AND GOLDBERG, E. M., Rising 18 in a London suburb: a study of some aspects of the life and health of young men. *British Journal of Sociology*, **4** (1953) 323–45.

MOORE, W. E., Occupational socialization. In GOSLIN, D. A. (ed.), *Handbook of Socialization Theory and Research*. Chicago, Rand McNally, 1969.

MOWSESIAN, R., *et al.*, Superior students' occupational preferences and their fathers' occupations. *Personnel and Guidance Journal*, **45** (1966) 238–42.

MUSGRAVE, P. W., Continuities in the sociological theory of occupational choice. *Sociological Review*, **16** (1968) 93–7.

MUSGRAVE, P. W., Towards a sociological theory of occupational choice. *Sociological Review*, **15** (1967) 33–46.

ROBERTS, K., The entry into employment: an approach towards a general theory. *Sociological Review*, **16** (1968) 165–84.

SLOCUM, W. L., Some sociological aspects of occupational choice. *American Journal of Economics and Sociology*, **18** (1959) 139–47.

SMELSER, W. T., Adolescent and adult occupational choices as a function of family socioeconomic history. *Sociometry*, **26** (1963) 393–409.

SUPER. D. E., A theory of vocational development. *American Psychologist*, **8** (1953) 185–90.

TIMPERLEY, S. R. AND GREGORY, A. M., Some factors affecting the career choice and career perceptions of Sixth Form school leavers. *Sociological Review*, **19** (1971) 95–114.

TURNER, R. H., Some family determinants of ambition. *Sociology and Social Research*, **46** (1962) 397–411.

VENESS, T., *School Leavers: their Aspirations and Expectations*. London, Methuen, 1962.

WEINBERG, I., The occupational aspirations of British public schoolboys. *School Review*, **74** (1966) 265–82.

WERTS, C. E., Career choice patterns. *Sociology of Education*, **40** (1967) 348–58.

WERTS, C. E., Paternal influence on career choice. *Journal of Counselling Psychology*, **15** (1968) 48–52.

WHITE, S., The process of occupational choice. *British Journal of Industrial Relations*, **6** (1968) 166–84.

WILSON, M. D., Vocational preferences of secondary school-children. *British Journal of Educational Psychology*, **23** (1953) 97–113.

(c) Manpower studies

BLAU, P. M., The flow of occupational supply and recruitment. *American Sociological Review*, **30** (1965) 475–90.

HARRIS, A. I. AND CLAUSEN, R., *Labour Mobility in Great Britain, 1953–63*. London, H.M.S.O., 1966.

MINISTRY OF LABOUR, *Manpower Studies No. 6: Occupational Changes, 1951–61*. London, H.M.S.O., 1967.

MINISTRY OF LABOUR, *Manpower Studies No. 1: The Pattern of the Future*. London, H.M.S.O., 1964.

ROUTH, G., *Occupation and Pay in Great Britain, 1906–60*. Cambridge, University Press, 1965.

(d) Highly educated and professional manpower

ABBOTT, J., *Employment of Sociology and Anthropology Graduates, 1966–7*. London, British Sociological Association, 1969.

BECKER, G. S., *Human Capital*. New York, Columbia University Press, 1964.

BEN-DAVID, J., Professions in the class system of present-day societies. *Current Sociology*, **12** (1963–4) 247–330.

BLAUG, M., *et al.*, *The Utilisation of Educated Manpower: a Preliminary Report*. Edinburgh, Oliver and Boyd, 1967.

CARR-SAUNDERS, A. M. AND WILSON, P. A., *The Professions*. Oxford, Clarendon Press, 1933.

CHILD, D. AND MUSGROVE, F., Career orientations of some university freshmen. *Educational Review*, **21** (1969) 209–17.

CIVIL SERVICE COMMISSION, *Annual Report, 1969*. London, H.M.S.O., 1970.

COLLIN, A., *et al.*, *The Arts Graduate in Industry*. London, Acton Society Trust, 1962.

CRAIG, C., *The Employment of Cambridge Graduates*. Cambridge, University Press, 1963.

DAVIS, J. A., The campus as a frog pond: an application of the theory of relative deprivation to career decisions of college men. *American Journal of Sociology*, **72** (1966) 17–31.

DAVIS, J. A., *Great Aspirations*. Chicago, Aldine Publishing Co., 1964.

DAVIS, J. A., *Undergraduate Career Decisions*. Chicago, Aldine Publishing Co., 1964.

DYER, D. T., The relation between vocational interests of men in college and their subsequent occupational histories for ten years. *Journal of Applied Psychology*, **23** (1939) 280–8.

ECKLAND, B., Academic ability, higher education and occupational identity. *American Sociological Review*, **30** (1965) 735–46.

GERSTL, J. E., Social origins of engineers. *New Society*, 6 June 1963, 19–20.

GERSTL, J. E. AND PERRUCCI, R., Educational channels and elite mobility: a comparative analysis. *Sociology of Education*, **38** (1964–5) 224–32.

GINZBERG, E., *et al.*, *Talent and Performance*. New York, Columbia University Press, 1964.

HIND, R. R. AND WIRTH, T. E., The effect of university experience on occupational choice among undergraduates. *Sociology of Education*, **42** (1969) 50–70.

JACKSON, J. A. (ed.), *Professions and Professionalization*. Cambridge, University Press, 1970.

KELSALL, R. K., *Higher Civil Servants in Britain from 1870 to the Present Day*. London, Routledge, 1955.

KELSALL, R. K., *et al.*, Still a low status profession. *Times Educational Supplement*, 4 December 1970, 4.

MCDONAGH, E. C., *et al.*, Relative professional status as perceived by American and Swedish university students. *Social Forces*, **38** (1959–60) 65–9.

MILLERSON, G., *The Qualifying Association: a Study in Professionalization*. London, Routledge, 1964.

MILLS, C. W., *White Collar*. London, Oxford University Press, 1951.

MORSE, N. C., *Satisfaction in the White Collar Job*. Ann Arbor, University of Michigan Press, 1953.

MORTON-WILLIAMS, R., *et al.*, *Undergraduates' Attitudes to School Teaching as a Career*. London, H.M.S.O., 1966.

NOTTINGHAM UNIVERSITY CAREERS AND APPOINTMENTS BOARD, *Graduate Employment Survey*. Nottingham University, Careers and Appointments Board, 1962.

POLITICAL AND ECONOMIC PLANNING, *Graduate Employment: a Sample Survey*. London, P.E.P., 1956.

PYM, D., The education and employment opportunities of engineers. *British Journal of Industrial Relations*, **7** (1969) 42–51.

RAYNOR, J. R., *The Middle Class*. London, Longmans, 1969.

REISS, A. J., Occupational mobility of professional workers. *American Sociological Review*, **20** (1955) 693–700.

SHARP, L. M., *Education and Employment*. Baltimore, Johns Hopkins Press, 1970.

SPAETH, J. L., Occupational prestige expectations among male college graduates. *American Journal of Sociology*, **73** (1968) 548–58.

UNIVERSITY GRANTS COMMITTEE, *First Employment of University Graduates*. London, H.M.S.O., annually from 1963.
VOLLMER, H. M. AND MILLS, D. L. (eds.), *Professionalization*. Englewood Cliffs, Prentice-Hall, 1966.
WERTS, C. E., Social class and initial career choice of college freshmen. *Sociology of Education*, **39** (1966) 74–85.

(e) Career development

BENDIX, R., *et al.*, Social origins and occupational career patterns. *Industrial and Labour Relations Review*, **7** (1952) 246–61.
FORM, W. H. AND MILLER, D. C., Occupational career patterns as a sociological instrument. *American Journal of Sociology*, **54** (1949) 317–29.
LIPSET, S. M. AND MALM, F. T., First jobs and career patterns. *American Journal of Economics and Sociology*, **14** (1955) 247–61.
PERRUCCI, C. C. AND PERRUCCI, R., Social origins, educational contexts, and career mobility. *American Sociological Review*, **35** (1970) 451–63.
STEBBINS, R. A., Career: the subjective approach. *Sociological Quarterly*, **11** (1970) 32–49.
TIEDEMAN, D. V. AND O'HARA, R. P., *Career Development, Choice and Adjustment: Differentiation and Integration in Career Development*. New York, College Entrance Examination Board, 1963.
WILENSKY, H. L., Orderly careers and social participation: the impact of work history on social integration in the middle mass. *American Sociological Review*, **26** (1961) 521–39.

VII. Women

(a) General

BEBEL, A., *Woman in the Past, Present and Future*. London, Modern Press, 1885.
BIRD, C., *Born Female: the High Cost of Keeping Women Down*. New York, McKay Co. Inc., 1968.
BRITTAIN, V., *Lady into Woman: a History of Women from Victoria to Elizabeth II*. London, Andrew Dakers, 1953.

CASSARA, B. B. (ed.), *American Women: the Changing Image.* Boston, Beacon Press, 1962.

CENTRAL OFFICE OF INFORMATION, *Women in Britain.* London, H.M.S.O., 1964.

EVANS-PRITCHARD, E. E., *The Position of Women in Primitive Societies and Other Essays in Social Anthropology.* London, Faber, 1965.

GAVRON, H., *The Captive Wife.* London, Routledge, 1966.

HACKER, H. M., Women as a minority group. *Social Forces,* **30** (1951–2) 60–9.

KLEIN, V., *The Feminine Character.* London, Routledge, 1946.

KNUDSEN, D. D., The declining status of women: popular myths and the failure of functionalist thought. *Social Forces,* **48** (1969) 183–93.

KOYAMA, T., *The Changing Social Position of Women in Japan.* Paris, UNESCO, 1961.

LUNDBERG, F. AND FARNHAM, M. F., *Modern Woman.* New York, Grosset and Dunlap, 1947.

NOTTINGHAM, E. K., Toward an analysis of the effects of two world wars on the role and status of middle-class women in the English-speaking world. *American Sociological Review,* **12** (1948) 666–75.

OPLER, M. K., Woman's social status and the forms of marriage. *American Journal of Sociology,* **49** (1943) 125–47.

SEWARD, G. H., *Sex and the Social Order.* New York, McGraw-Hill, 1946.

SEWARD, G. H., Sex roles in postwar planning. *Journal of Social Psychology Bulletin,* **19** (1944) 163–85.

STOLTE-HEISKANEN, V. AND HAAVIO-MANNILA, E., The position of women in society: formal ideology versus everyday ethic. *Social Science Information,* **6** (1967) 169–88.

(b) Education and socialization

ANGRIST, S. J., Role conceptions as a predictor of adult female roles. *Sociology and Social Research,* **50** (1965) 448–59.

ARNOTT, C. AND BENGTSON, V. L., 'Only a homemaker': distributive justice and role choice among married women. *Sociology and Social Research*, **54** (1970) 495–507.

BARUCH, R., The achievement motive in women: implications for career development. *Journal of Personality and Social Psychology*, **5** (1967) 260–7.

DAVID, O. P. (ed.), *The Education of Women*. Washington, American Council on Education, 1959.

EMPEY, L. T., Role expectations of young women regarding marriage and a career. *Marriage and Family Living*, **20** (1958) 152–5.

HOLLINGWORTH, L. S., Social devices for impelling women to bear and rear children. *American Journal of Sociology*, **22** (1916–17) 19–29.

KAMM, J., *Hope Deferred: Girls' Education in English History*. London, Methuen, 1965.

KAMMAYER, K., Sibling position and the feminine role. *Journal of Marriage and the Family*, **29** (1967) 494–9.

KITAY, P. M., A comparison of the sexes in their attitudes and beliefs about women: a study of prestige groups. *Sociometry*, **3** (1940) 399–407.

MATTHEWS, E. AND TIEDEMAN, D. V., Attitudes towards career and marriage and the development of life style of young women. *Journal of Counselling Psychology*, **11** (1964) 375–84.

NEIMAN, L., Peer groups and attitudes toward the feminine role. *Social Problems*, **2** (1954) 104–11.

OLLERENSHAW, K., *Education for Girls*. London, Faber, 1961.

OWEN, C. A., Feminine roles and social mobility in women's weekly magazines. *Sociological Review*, **10** (1962) 283–96.

ROSE, A. M., The adequacy of women's expectations for adult roles. *Social Forces*, **36** (1951–2) 69–77.

SEWARD, G. H., Cultural conflict and the feminine role: an experimental study. *Journal of Social Psychology*, **22** (1945) 177–94.

TURNER, R. H., Some aspects of women's ambition. *American Journal of Sociology*, **70** (1964) 271–85.

(c) Women and work

BAUDLER, L. AND PATTERSON, D. G., Social status of women's occupations. *Occupations*, **26** (1947–8) 421–4.

BLOOD, R. O. AND HAMBLIN, R. L., The effect of the wife's employment on the family power structure. *Social Forces*, **36** (1958) 347–52.

DODGE, N. T., *Women in the Soviet Economy*. Baltimore, Johns Hopkins Press, 1966.

GINZBERG, E., Paycheck and apron: revolution in woman-power. *Industrial Relations*, **7** (1968) 193–203.

GORDON, M. S., Women in the labour force. *Industrial Relations*, **7** (1968) 187–92.

HEER, D. M., Dominance and the working wife. *Social Forces*, **36** (1958) 341–7.

HUNT, A., *A Survey of Women's Employment*. London, H.M.S.O., 1968.

INTERNATIONAL LABOUR OFFICE, *The Law and Women's Work*. Geneva, International Labour Office, 1939.

KLEIN, V., *Britain's Married Women Workers*. London, Routledge, 1965.

KLEIN, V., Europe's working wives. *New Society*, 29 November 1962, 16–17.

MACCARTHY, F., *Work for Married Women*. London, Conservative Political Centre, 1966.

MCNALLY, G. B., Patterns of female labour force activity. *Industrial Relations*, **7** (1968) 204–18.

MAHONEY, T. A., Factors determining the labour force participation of married women. *Industrial and Labour Relations Review*, **14** (1961) 563–77.

MERCER, E. O., Some occupational attitudes of girls. *Journal of Occupational Psychology* **14** (1940) 14–25.

MYRDAL, A. AND KLEIN, V., *Women's Two Roles*, 2nd ed. London, Routledge, 1968.

NEFF, W. F., *Victorian Working Women*. London, Cass, 1966.

NYE, F. I. AND HOFFMAN, L. W., *The Employed Mother in America*. Chicago, Rand McNally, 1963.

OPPENHEIMER, V. K., The sex labelling of jobs. *Industrial Relations*, **7** (1968) 219–34.

ORDEN, S. K. AND BRADBURN, N. A., Working wives and marriage happiness. *American Journal of Sociology*, **74** (1969) 392–407.

PSATHAS, G., Toward a theory of occupational choice for women. *Sociology and Social Research*, **52** (1968) 253–68.

RENDEL, M., Do women have trouble getting jobs? *New Society*, 27 August 1964, 17–18.

SEEAR, N., *et al.*, *A Career for Women in Industry*. Edinburgh, Oliver and Boyd, 1964.

SMUTS, R. W., *Women and Work in America*. New York, Columbia University Press, 1959.

STEWARD, C. M., Future trends in the employment of married women. *British Journal of Sociology*, **12** (1961) 1–11.

THOMPSON, B. AND FINLAYSON, A., Married women who work in early motherhood. *British Journal of Sociology*, **14** (1963) 150–68.

WEIL, M. W., An analysis of the factors influencing married women's actual and planned work participations. *American Sociological Review*, **26** (1961) 91–102.

WILENSKY, H. L., Woman's work: economic growth, ideology, structure. *Industrial Relations*, **7** (1968) 235–48.

WILLIAMS, P., *Working Wonders*. London, Hodder and Stoughton, 1969.

ZWEIG, F., *Women's Life and Labour*. London, Gollancz, 1952.

(d) Highly educated and professional women

ALMQUIST, E. M. AND ANGRIST, S. M., Career salience and atypicality of occupational choice among college women. *Journal of Marriage and the Family*, **32** (1970) 242–9.

ARREGGER, C. E. (ed.), *Graduate Women at Work*. London, British Federation of University Women, 1966.

BERNARD, J., *Academic Women*. Pennsylvania, State University Press, 1964.

CANNON, C., *Married Women Graduates and the Teaching Profession*. London, Association of Headmistresses, 1962.

CHRISTENSEN, H., Postgraduate role preference of senior women in college. *Marriage and Family Living*, **18** (1956) 52–7.

COXHEAD, E., *Women in the Professions*. London, Longmans, 1961.

DAVIS, F. AND OLESON, V. L., The career outlook of professionally educated women. *Psychiatry*, **28** (1965) 334–45.

DAVIS, F. AND OLESON, V. L., Initiation into a woman's profession: identity problems in the status transition of coed to student nurse. *Sociometry*, **26** (1963) 89–101.

DAWSON, M., *Graduate and Married*. Sydney, University of Sydney Department of Adult Education, 1965.

DOLAN, E. F., Higher education for women. *Higher Education*, **20** (1963) 5–13.

FALK, L. L., Occupational satisfaction of female college graduates. *Journal of Marriage and the Family*, **28** (1966) 177–85.

FAUNCE, P. S., Personality characteristics and vocational interests related to the college persistence of academically gifted women. *Journal of Counselling Psychology*, **15** (1968) 31–40.

FAVA, S. F., The status of women in professional sociology. *American Sociological Review*, **25** (1960) 271–6.

FOGARTY, M. P., *et al.*, *Women in Top Jobs*. London, Allen and Unwin, 1971.

GINZBERG, E., *et al.*, *Life Styles of Educated Women*. New York, Columbia University Press, 1966.

GREENHALL, S., *Women and Higher Education*. London, National Union of Students, 1966.

HUBBACK, J., *Wives who went to College*. London, Heinemann, 1957.

INTERNATIONAL FEDERATION OF UNIVERSITY WOMEN, *The Position of the Woman Graduate Today: a Survey, 1956–1965*. London, I.F.U.W., [1966?].

KAMMEYER, K., Birth order and feminine sex role among college women. *American Sociological Review*, **31** (1966) 508–15.

KELSALL, R. K., *Women and Teaching*. London, H.M.S.O., 1963.

KIELL, N. AND FRIEDMAN, B., Culture lag and housewifemanship: the role of the married female college graduate. *Journal of Educational Sociology*, **31** (1957) 87–95.

KLEIN, V., The demand for professional womanpower. *British Journal of Sociology*, **17** (1966) 183–97.

LAYZELL-WARD, P., *Women in Librarianship*. London, Library Association, 1966.

PARKER, A. W., Career and marriage orientation in the vocational development of college women. *Journal of Applied Psychology*, **50** (1966) 232–5.

POLITICAL AND ECONOMIC PLANNING, *Women and Top Jobs*. London, P.E.P., 1969.

ROSSI, A. S., Women in science: why so few? *Science*, **148** (1965) 1196–1202.

SIMON, R. J., *et al.*, The woman Ph.D.: a recent profile. *Social Problems*, **15** (1967) 221–236.

STERNMANN, A., *et al.*, Self concept of college women compared with their concept of ideal woman and men's ideal woman. *Journal of Counselling Psychology*, **11** (1964) 370–4.

UNITED STATES DEPARTMENT OF LABOR, *College Women Seven Years After Graduation: Resurvey of Women Graduates – Class of 1957*. Washington, U.S. Government Printing Office, 1966.

VON MERING, F. H., Professional and non-professional women as mothers. *Journal of Social Psychology*, **42** (1955) 21–34.

(e) Feminism

BANKS, J. A. AND BANKS, O., *Feminism and Family Planning in Victorian England*. Liverpool, University Press, 1964.

CAMPBELL, O. W. (ed.), *The Feminine Point of View*. London, Williams and Northgate, 1952.

CONSERVATIVE POLITICAL CENTRE, *Fair Share for the Fair Sex*. London, Conservative Political Centre, 1969.

DENNING, LORD, *The Equality of Women*. Liverpool, University Press, 1960.

EPSTEIN, C. F., *Woman's Place*. Berkeley, University of California Press, 1970.

FARBER, S. M. AND WILSON, R. H. L. (eds.), *The Challenge to Women*. New York, Basic Books, 1966.

FAWCETT SOCIETY, *Women in a Changing World*. London, Fawcett Society, [1967?].

FIGES, E., *Patriarchal Attitudes: Women in Society*. London, Faber, 1970.

FRIEDAN, B., *The Feminine Mystique*. London, Gollancz, 1964.

GREER, G., *The Female Eunuch*. London, MacGibbon and Kee, 1970.

HOBMAN, D. L., *Go Spin, you Jade: Studies in the Emancipation of Woman*. London, Watts, 1957.

HUNKINS-HALLINAN, H. (ed.). *In Her Own Right*. London, Harrap, 1968.

LOWRIE, R. H. AND HOLLINGWORTH, L. S., Science and feminism. *Scientific Monthly*, **3** (1966) 277–84.

MEAD, M., *And Keep Your Powder Dry*. New York, William Morrow, 1942.

MILL, J. S., *The Subjection of Women*. London, Longmans, 1869.

MITCHELL, J., Women: the longest revolution. *New Left Review*, **40** (1966) 11–37.

NATIONAL COUNCIL FOR CIVIL LIBERTIES, *Women*. London, N.C.C.L., 1965.

NATIONAL FEDERATION OF BUSINESS AND PROFESSIONAL WOMEN'S CLUBS, *Justice or Prejudice?* London, National Federation of Business and Professional Women's Clubs, 1965.

RAMELSON, M., *The Petticoat Rebellion*. London, Lawrence and Wishart, 1967.

RENDEL, M., et al., *Equality for Women*. London, Fabian Society, 1968.

ROSSI, A. S., Equality between the sexes: an immodest proposal. *Daedalus*, **93** (1964) 607–52.

SEEAR, N., Womanpower needs a policy. *New Society*, 29 November 1962, 14–16.

WOOLF, V., *A Room of One's Own*. London, Hogarth Press, 1929.

S

INDEX